ISBN 978-1-331-16075-5
PIBN 10152279

1 MONTH OF
FREE
READING

at
www.ForgottenBooks.com

By purchasing this book you are eligible for one month membership to ForgottenBooks.com, giving you unlimited access to our entire collection of over 1,000,000 titles via our web site and mobile apps.

To claim your free month visit:

www.forgottenbooks.com/free152279

English
Français
Deutsche
Italiano
Español
Português

www.forgottenbooks.com

Mythology Photography **Fiction**
Fishing Christianity **Art** Cooking
Essays Buddhism Freemasonry
Medicine **Biology** Music **Ancient**
Egypt Evolution Carpentry Physics
Dance Geology **Mathematics** Fitness
Shakespeare **Folklore** Yoga Marketing
Confidence Immortality Biographies
Poetry **Psychology** Witchcraft
Electronics Chemistry History **Law**
Accounting **Philosophy** Anthropology
Alchemy Drama Quantum Mechanics
Atheism Sexual Health **Ancient History**
Entrepreneurship Languages Sport
Paleontology Needlework Islam
Metaphysics Investment Archaeology
Parenting Statistics Criminology
Motivational

MISS NIGHTINGALE.

(From a photograph by S G Payne & Son.)

THE LIFE

OF

FLORENCE NIGHTINGALE

BY

SARAH A. TOOLEY

AUTHOR OF "PERSONAL LIFE OF QUEEN VICTORIA," "LIFE OF QUEEN
ALEXANDRA," "ROYAL PALACES AND THEIR MEMORIES," "THE
HISTORY OF NURSING IN THE BRITISH EMPIRE," ETC.

MEMORIAL EDITION

CASSELL AND COMPANY, Ltd.

LONDON, NEW YORK, TORONTO AND MELBOURNE

TO

THE LADY HERBERT OF LEA

THE LIFE-LONG FRIEND OF

FLORENCE NIGHTINGALE

THIS BOOK

IS BY PERMISSION

𝔇𝔢𝔡𝔦𝔠𝔞𝔱𝔢𝔡

PREFACE

THE writing of the Life of Florence Nightingale was undertaken with the object of marking the jubilee of the illustrious heroine who left London on October 21st, 1854, with a band of thirty-eight nurses for service in the Crimean War. Her heroic labours on behalf of the sick and wounded soldiers have made her name a household word in every part of the British Empire, and it was a matter for national congratulation that Miss Nightingale lived to celebrate such a memorable anniversary.

A striking proof of the honour in which her name is held by the rising generation was given a short time ago, when the editor of *The Girl's Realm* took the votes of his readers as to the most popular heroine in modern history. Fourteen names were submitted, and of the 300,000 votes given, 120,776 were for FLORENCE NIGHTINGALE.

No trouble has been spared to make the book

as accurate and complete as possible, and when writing it I spent several months in the vicinity of Miss Nightingale's early homes, and received much kind assistance from people of all classes acquainted with her. In particular I would thank Lady Herbert of Lea for accepting the dedication of the book and for portraits of herself and Lord Herbert; Sir Edmund Verney for permission to publish the picture of the late Lady Verney and views of Claydon; Pastor Düsselhoff of Kaiserswerth for the portrait of Pastor Fliedner and some recollections of Miss Nightingale's training in that institution; the late Sister Mary Aloysius, of the Convent of Sisters of Mercy, Kinvara, co. Galway, for memories of her work at Scutari Hospital; and Mr. Crowther, Librarian of the Public Library, Derby, for facilities for studying the collection of material relating to Miss Nightingale presented to the Library by the late Duke of Devonshire.

In the preparation of the revised edition I am indebted to Lady Verney, the late Hon. Frederick Strutt, and Mrs. Dacre Craven for valuable suggestions.

SARAH A. TOOLEY

Kensington,

CONTENTS

CHAPTER I

BIRTH AND ANCESTRY

CHAPTER II

EARLIEST ASSOCIATIONS

CHAPTER III

LEA HURST

CHAPTER IV

THE DAYS OF CHILDHOOD

CONTENTS

CHAPTER V

THE SQUIRE'S DAUGHTER

CHAPTER VI

FLORENCE NIGHTINGALE'S ALMA MATER AND ITS FOUNDER

CHAPTER VII

ENTERS KAISERSWERTH: A PLEA FOR DEACONESSES

CHAPTER VIII

A PERIOD OF WAITING

CHAPTER IX

SIDNEY, LORD HERBERT OF LEA

CHAPTER X

THE CRIMEAN WAR AND CALL TO SERVICE

CHAPTER XI

PREPARATION AND DEPARTURE FOR SCUTARI

CHAPTER XII

THE LADY-IN-CHIEF

CHAPTER XIII

AT WORK IN THE BARRACK HOSPITAL

CHAPTER XIV

GRAPPLING WITH CHOLERA AND FEVER

CHAPTER XV

TIMELY HELP

CHAPTER XVI

THE ANGEL OF DEATH

CHAPTER XVII

SAILS FOR THE CRIMEA AND GOES UNDER FIRE

CHAPTER XVIII

STRICKEN BY FEVER

CHAPTER XIX

CLOSE OF THE WAR

CHAPTER XX

THE RETURN OF THE HEROINE

CONTENTS

CHAPTER XXI

THE SOLDIER'S FRIEND AT HOME

CHAPTER XXII

WISDOM FROM THE QUEEN OF NURSES

CHAPTER XXIII

THE NURSING OF THE SICK POOR

CHAPTER XXIV

LATER YEARS

LIST OF ILLUSTRATIONS

THE LIFE OF
FLORENCE NIGHTINGALE

CHAPTER I

BIRTH AND ANCESTRY

Birth at Florence—Shore Ancestry—Peter Nightingale of Lea—
Florence Nightingale's Parents.

> We are born into life—it is sweet, it is strange,
> We lie still on the knee of a mild mystery
> > Which smiles with a change;
> But we doubt not of changes, we know not of spaces,
> The heavens seem as near as our own mother's face is,
> And we think we could touch all the stars that we see.
> > ELIZABETH BARRETT BROWNING.

Thought and deed, not pedigree, are the passports to enduring
fame.—GENERAL SKOBELEFF.

A T a dinner given to the military and naval
officers who had served in the Crimean
War, it was suggested that each guest should
write on a slip of paper the name of the person
whose services during the late campaign would

be longest remembered by posterity. When the papers were examined, each bore the same name —" Florence Nightingale."

The prophecy is fulfilled to-day, for though little more than fifty years have passed since the joy-bells throughout the land proclaimed the fall of Sebastopol, the majority of people would hesitate if asked to name the generals of the Allied Armies, while no one would be at a loss to tell who was the heroine of the Crimea. Her deeds of love and sacrifice sank deep into the nation's heart, for they were above the strife of party and the clash of arms. While Death has struck name after name from the nation's roll of the great and famous, our heroine lives in venerated age to shed the lustre of her name upon a new century.

Florence Nightingale was born on May 12th, 1820, at the Villa Colombaia near Florence, where her parents, Mr. and Mrs. William Shore Nightingale, of Lea, Derbyshire, were staying.

"What name should be given to the baby girl born so far away from her English home?" queried her parents, and with mutual consent they decided to call her " Florence," after that fair city of flowers on the banks of the Arno where she first saw the light. Little did Mr. and Mrs. Nightingale then think that the name thus chosen was destined to become one of the most popular throughout the

British Empire. Every " Florence " practically owes her name to the circumstances of Miss Nightingale's birth.

It seemed as though the fates were determined to give an attractive designation to our heroine. While " Florence " suggested the goddess of flowers, "Nightingale " spoke of sweet melody. What could be more beautiful and euphonious than a name suggesting a song-bird from the land of flowers? The combination proved a special joy to Mr. *Punch* and his fellow-humorists when the bearer of the name rose to fame.

However, Miss Nightingale's real family name was Shore. Her father was William Edward Shore, the only son of William Shore of Tapton, Derbyshire, and he assumed the name of Nightingale, by the sign manual of the Prince Regent, when he succeeded in 1815 to the estates of his mother's uncle, Peter Nightingale of Lea. This change took place three years before his marriage, and five before the birth of his illustrious daughter.

Through her Shore ancestry Miss Nightingale is connected with the family of Baron Teignmouth. Sir John Shore, Governor-General of India, was created a baron in 1797 and took the title of Teignmouth. Another John Shore was an eminent physician at Derby in the reign of Charles II., and a Samuel Shore married the heiress of the Offleys, a Sheffield family.

It is through her paternal grandmother, Mary, daughter of John Evans of Cromford, the niece and sole heir of Peter Nightingale, that Florence Nightingale is connected with the family whose name she bears. Her great-great-uncle, Peter Nightingale, was a typical Derbyshire squire who more than a century ago lived in good style at the fine old mansion of Lea Hall. Those were rough and roystering days in such isolated villages as Lea, and "old Peter" had his share of the vices then deemed gentlemanly. He could swear with the best, and his drinking feats might have served Burns for a similar theme to *The Whistle*. His excesses gained for him the nickname of "Madman Nightingale," and accounts of his doings still form the subject of local gossip. When in his cups, he would raid the kitchen, take the puddings from the pots and fling them on the dust-heap, and cause the maids to fly in terror. Nevertheless, "old Peter" was not unpopular; he was good-natured and easy-going with his people, and if he drank hard, well, so did his neighbours. He was no better and little worse than the average country squire, and parson too, of the "good old times." His landed possessions extended from Lea straight away to the old market town of Cromford, and beyond towards Matlock. It is of special interest to note that he sold a portion of his Cromford property to Sir Richard Arkwright, who erected there his famous cotton mills. The beautiful mansion of Willersley Castle, which the ingenious cotton-spinner built, and where he ended his days as the great Sir Richard, stands on a part of the original Nightingale property. When "old Peter" of jovial memory passed to his account, his estates and name descended to his grand-nephew, William Edward Shore.

The new squire, Florence Nightingale's father, was a marked contrast to his predecessor. He is described by those who remember him as a tall, slim, gentlemanly man of irreproachable character. He had been educated at Edinburgh and Trinity College, Cambridge, and had broadened his mind by foreign travel at a time when the average English squire, still mindful of the once terrifying name of "Boney," looked- upon all foreigners as his natural enemies, and entrenched himself on his ancestral acres with a supreme contempt for lands beyond the Channel. Mr. Nightingale was far in advance of the county gentry of his time in matters of education and culture. Sport had no special attraction for him, but he was a student, a lover of books and a connoisseur in art. He was not without a good deal of pride of birth, for the Shores were a very ancient family.

As a landlord he had a sincere desire to benefit

the people on his estates, although not perhaps in the way they most appreciated. "Well, you see, I was not born generous," is still remembered as Mr. Nightingale's answer when solicited for various local charities. However, he never begrudged money for the support of rural education, and, to quote the saying of one of his old tenants, "Many poor people in Lea would not be able to read and write to-day, if it had not been for 'Miss Florence's' father." He was the chief supporter of what was then called the "cheap school," where the boys and girls, if they did not go through the higher standards of the present-day schools, at least learned the three R's for the sum of twopence a week. There was, of course, no compulsory education then, but the displeasure of the squire with people who neglected to send their children to school was a useful incentive to parents. Mr. Nightingale was a zealous Churchman, and did much to further Christian work in his district.

Florence Nightingale's mother was Miss Frances Smith, daughter of William Smith, Esq., of Parndon in Essex, who for fifty years was M.P. for Norwich. He was a pronounced Abolitionist, took wide and liberal views on the questions of the time, and was noted for his interest in various branches of philanthropy. Mrs. Nightingale was imbued with her father's spirit, and is remembered for her great kindness and benevolence to the poor. She was a stately and beautiful woman in her prime and one of the fast-dying-out race of gentlewomen who were at once notable house-keepers and charming and cultured ladies. Her name is still mentioned with gratitude and affection by the old people of her husband's estates.

It was from her mother, whom she greatly resembles, that Florence Nightingale inherited the spirit of wide philanthropy and the desire to break away, in some measure, from the bonds of caste which warped the county gentry in her early days and devote herself to humanitarian work. She was also fortunate in having a father who believed that a girl's head could carry something more than elegant accomplishments and a knowledge of cross-stitch. While our heroine's mother trained her in deeds of benevolence, her father inspired her with a love for knowledge and guided her studies on lines much in advance of the usual education given to young ladies at that period.

Mr. and Mrs. Nightingale had only two children—Frances Parthenope, afterwards Lady Verney, and Florence, about a year younger. Both sisters were named after the Italian towns where they were born, the elder receiving the name of Parthenope, the classic form of Naples, and was always known as " Parthe," while our heroine was Florence.

CHAPTER II

Lea Hall first English Home—Neighbourhood of Babington Plot—
Dethick Church.

. . . Those first affections,
Those shadowy recollections,
Which be they what they may,
Are yet the fountain light of all our day,
Are yet a master light of all our seeing.
WORDSWORTH.

WHEN Mr. and Mrs. Nightingale returned from abroad with their two little daughters, they lived for a time at the old family seat of Lea Hall, which therefore has the distinction of being the first English home of Florence Nightingale, an honour generally attributed to her parents' subsequent residence of Lea Hurst.

Lea Hall is beautifully situated high up amongst the hills above the valley of the Derwent. I visited it in early summer when the meadows around were golden with buttercups and scented with clover, and the long grass stood ready for the scythe. Wild roses decked the hedgerows, and the elder-bushes, which grow to a great size in this part of Derbyshire, made a fine show with their white blossoms. Seen then, the old grey Hall seemed a pleasant country residence ; but when the north wind blows and snow covers the hillsides, it must be a bleak and lonely abode. It is plainly and solidly built of grey limestone from the Derbyshire quarries, and is of good proportions. From its elevated position it has an imposing look, and forms a landmark in the open country. Leading from it, the funny old village street of Lea, with its low stone houses, some of them very ancient, curls round the hillside downwards to the valley. The butcher proudly displays a ledger with entries for the Nightingale family since 1835.

The Hall stands on the ancient Manor of Lea, which includes the villages of Lea, Dethick, and Holloway, and which passed through several families before it became the property of the Nightingales. The De Alveleys owned the manor in the reign of John and erected a chapel there. One portion of the manor passed through the families of Ferrar, Dethwick, and Babington, and another portion through the families of De la Lea, Frecheville, Rollestone, Pershall, and Spateman to that of the Nightingales.

The house stands a little back from the Lea road in its own grounds, and is approached by a gate from the front garden. Stone steps lead up to the front door, which opens into an old-fashioned flag-paved hall. Facing the door is an oak staircase of exceptional beauty. It gives distinction to the house and proclaims its ancient dignity. The balustrade has finely turned spiral rails, the steps are of solid oak, and the sides of the staircase panelled in oak. One may imagine the little Florence making her first efforts at climbing up this handsome old staircase.

In a room to the left the date 1799 has been scratched upon one of the window-panes, but the erection of the Hall must have been long before that time. For the rest, it is a rambling old house with thick walls and deep window embrasures. The ceilings are moderately high. There is an old-fashioned garden at the back, with fruit and shady trees and a particularly handsome copper beech.

The Hall has long been used as a farmhouse, and scarcely one out of the hundreds of visitors to the Matlock district who go on pilgrimages to Lea Hurst knows of its interesting association. The old lady who occupied it at the time of my visit was not a little proud of the fact that for forty-four years she had lived in the first English home of Florence Nightingale.

✢ The casual visitor might think the district amid which our heroine's early years were spent was a pleasant Derbyshire wild and nothing more, but it has also much historic interest. Across the meadows from Lea Hall are the remains of the stately mansion of Dethick, where dwelt young Anthony Babington when he conspired to release Mary Queen of Scots from her imprisonment at Wingfield Manor, a few miles away. Over these same meadows and winding lanes Queen Elizabeth's officers searched for the conspirators and apprehended one at Dethick. The mansion where the plot was hatched has been largely destroyed, and what remains is used for farm purposes. Part of the old wall which enclosed the original handsome building still stands, and beside it is an underground cellar which according to tradition leads into a secret passage to Wingfield Manor. The farm bailiff who stores his potatoes in the cellar has not been able to find the entrance to the secret passage, though at one side of the wall there is a suspicious hollow sound when it is hammered.

The original kitchen of the mansion remains intact in the bailiff's farmhouse. There is the heavy oak-beamed ceiling, black with age, the ponderous oak doors, the great open fireplace, desecrated by a modern cooking range in the centre, but which still retains in the overhanging beam the ancient roasting jack which possibly cooked venison for Master Anthony and the other gallant young gentlemen who had sworn to liberate the

captive Queen.   In the roof of the ceiling is an in-
nocent-looking little trap-door which, when opened,
reveals a secret chamber of some size.   This delightful
old kitchen, with its mysterious memories, was a place
of great fascination to Florence Nightingale and
her sister in their childhood, and many stories did
they weave about the scenes which transpired long
ago in the old mansion, so near their own home.
It was a source of peculiar interest to have the
scenes of a real Queen Mary romance close at
hand, and gave zest to the subject when the
sisters read about the Babington plot in their history books.

Dethick Church, where our heroine attended her
first public service, and continued to frequently
worship so long as she lived in Derbyshire, formed
a part of the Babingtons' domain.   It was originally
the private chapel of the mansion, but gradually
was converted to the uses of a parish church.   Its
tall tower forms a picturesque object from the
windows of Lea Hall.   The church must be one
of the smallest in the kingdom.   Fifty persons
would prove an overflowing congregation even
now that modern seating has utilised space, but in
Florence Nightingale's girlhood, when the quality
sat in their high-backed pews and the rustics on
benches at the farther end of the church, the sitting
room was still more limited.   The interior of the

church is still plain and rustic, with bare stone walls, and the bell ropes hanging in view of the congregation. The service was quaint in Miss Nightingale's youth, when the old clerk made the responses to the parson, and the preaching sometimes took an original turn. The story is still repeated in the district that the old parson, preaching one Sunday on the subject of lying, made the consoling remark that "a lie is sometimes a very useful thing in trade." The saying was often repeated by the farmers of Lea and Dethick in the market square of Derby.

Owing to the fact that Dethick Church was originally a private chapel, there is no graveyard. It stands in a pretty green enclosure on the top of a hill. An old yew-tree shades the door, and near by are two enormous elder-bushes, which have twined their great branches together until they fall down to the ground like a drooping ash, forming an absolutely secluded bower, very popular with lovers and truants from church.

The palmy days of old Dethick Church are past. No longer do the people from the surrounding villages and hamlets climb its steep hillside, Sunday by Sunday, for, farther down in the vale, a new church has recently been built at Holloway, which, if less picturesque, is certainly more convenient for the population. On the first Sunday in each month, however, a service is still held in the old church where, in days long ago, Florence Nightingale sat in the squire's pew, looking in her Leghorn hat and sandal shoes a very bonny little maiden indeed.

CHAPTER III

LEA HURST

Removal to Lea Hurst—Description of the House—Florence
Nightingale's Crimean Carriage preserved there.

L o ! in the midst of Nature's choicest scenes,
E mbosomed 'mid tall trees, and towering hills,
A gem, in Nature's setting, rests Lea Hurst.

H ome of the good, the pure at heart and beautiful,
U ndying is the fame which, like a halo's light,
R ound thee is cast by the bright presence of the holy Florence.
S aint-like and heavenly. Thou hast indeed a glorious fame
T ime cannot change, but which will be eternal.

LLEWELLYN JEWETT.

WHEN Florence Nightingale was between
five and six years old, the family removed
from Lea Hall to Lea Hurst, a house which
Mr. Nightingale had been rebuilding on a site
about a mile distant, and immediately above the
hamlet of Lea Mills. This delightful new home
is the one most widely associated with the life of
our heroine. To quote the words of the old lady
at the lodge, " It was from Lea Hurst as Miss
Florence set out for the Crimea, and it was to Lea
Hurst as Miss Florence returned from the Crimea."

For many years after the war it was a place of pilgrimage, and is mentioned in almost every guide-book as one of the attractions of the Matlock district. It has never been in any sense a show house, and the park is private, but in days gone by thousands of people came to the vicinity, happy if they could see its picturesque gables from the hillside, and always with the hope that a glimpse might be caught of the famous lady who lived within its walls. Miss Nightingale remains tenderly attached to Lea Hurst, although it is eighteen years since she last stayed there. After the death of her parents it passed to the next male heir, Mr. Shore Smith, who later assumed the name of Nightingale.

Lea Hurst is only fourteen miles from Derby, but the following incident would lead one to suppose that the house is not as familiar in the county town as might be expected. Not long ago a lady asked at a fancy stationer's shop for a photograph of Lea Hurst.

"Lea Hurst?" pondered the young saleswoman, and turning to her companion behind the counter, she inquired, "Have we a photograph of Lea Hurst?"

"Yes, I think so," was the reply.

"Who is Lea Hurst?" asked the first girl.

"Why, an actor of course," replied the second

LEA HURST, DERBYSHIRE.

(*Photo by Keene, Derby.*)

[*To face p.* 16.]

There was an amusing tableau when the truth was made known.

Miss Nightingale's father displayed a fine discrimination when he selected the position for his new house. One might search even the romantic Peak country in vain for a more ideal site than Lea Hurst. It stands on a broad plateau looking across to the sharp, bold promontory of limestone rock known as Crich Stand. Soft green hills and wooded heights stud the landscape, while deep down in the green valley the silvery Derwent—or "Darent," as the natives call it—makes music as it dashes over its rocky bed. The outlook is one of perfect repose and beauty away to Dove's romantic dale, and the aspect is balmy and sunny, forming in this respect a contrast to the exposed and bleak situation of Lea Hall.

The house is in the style of an old Elizabethan mansion, and now that time has mellowed the stone and clothed the walls with greenery, one might imagine that it really dated from the Tudor period. Mr. Nightingale was a man of artistic tastes, and every detail of the house was carefully planned for picturesque effect. The mansion is built in the form of a cross with jutting wings, and presents a picture of clustering chimneys, pointed gables, stone mullioned windows and latticed panes. The fine oriel window of the drawing-room forms a projecting

2

wing at one end of the house. The rounded
balcony above the window has become historic. It
is pointed out to visitors as the place where "Miss
Florence used to come out and speak to the people."
Miss Nightingale's room opened on to this balcony,
and after her return from the Crimea, when she
was confined to the house with delicate health, she
would occasionally step from her room on to the
balcony to speak to the people, who had come as
deputations, while they stood in the park below.
Facing the oriel balcony is a gateway, shadowed
by yew-trees, which forms one of the entrances
from the park to the garden.

In front of the house is a circular lawn with
gravel path and flower-beds, and above the hall
door is inscribed N. and the date 1825, the year
in which Lea Hurst was completed. The principal
rooms open on to the garden or south front, and
have a delightfully sunny aspect and a commanding
view over the vale. From the library a flight
of stone steps leads down to the lawn. The old
schoolroom and nursery where our heroine passed
her early years are in the upper part of the house
and have lovely views over the hills.

In the centre of the garden front of the mansion
is a curious little projecting building which goes
by the name of "the chapel." It is evidently an
ancient building effectively incorporated into Lea

Hurst. There are several such little oratories of Norman date about the district, and the old lady at Lea Hurst lodge shows a stone window in the side of her cottage which is said to be seven hundred years old. A stone cross surmounts the roof of the chapel, and outside on the end wall is an inscription in curious characters. This ancient little building has, however, a special interest for our narrative, as Miss Nightingale used it for many years as the meeting place for the Sunday afternoon Bible-class which she held for the girls of the district. In those days there was a large bed of one of Miss Nightingale's favourite flowers, the fuchsia, outside the chapel, but that has been replaced by a fountain and basin, and the historic building itself, with its thick stone walls, now makes an excellent larder.

The gardens at Lea Hurst slope down from the back of the house in a series of grassy terraces connected by stone steps, and are still preserved in all their old-fashioned charm and beauty. There in spring and early summer one sees wallflowers, peonies, pansies, forget-me-nots, and many-coloured primulas in delightful profusion, while the apple trellises which skirt the terraces make a pretty show with their pink blossoms, and the long border of lavender-bushes is bursting into bloom. In a secluded corner of the garden is an old summer-house with pointed roof of thatch which must have been a delightful playhouse for little Florence and her sister.

The park slopes down on either side the plateau on which the house stands. The entrance to the drive is in the pleasant country road which leads to the village of Whatstandwell and on to Derby. This very modest park entrance, consisting of an ordinary wooden gate supported by stone pillars with globes on the top, has been described by an enthusiastic chronicler as a "stately gateway" with "an air of mediæval grandeur." There is certainly no grandeur about Lea Hurst, either mediæval or modern. It is just one of those pleasant and picturesque country mansions which are characteristic of rural England, and no grandeur is needed to give distinction to a house which the name of Florence Nightingale has hallowed.

Beyond the park the Lea woods cover the hillside for some distance, and in spring are thickly carpeted with bluebells. A long winding avenue, from which magnificent views are obtained over the hills and woodland glades for many miles, skirts the top of the woods, and is still remembered as "Miss Florence's favourite walk."

The chief relic preserved at Lea Hurst is the curious old carriage used by Miss Nightingale

in the Crimea. What memories does it not suggest of her journeys from one hospital to another
over the heights of Balaclava, when its utmost
carrying capacity was filled with comforts for the
sick and wounded! The body of the carriage
is of basket-work, and it has special springs made
to suit the rough Crimean roads. There is a
hood which can be half or fully drawn over the
entire vehicle. The carriage was driven by a
mounted man acting as postilion.

It seems as though such a unique object ought
to have a permanent place in one of our public
museums, for its interest is national. A native
of the district, who a short time ago chanced to
see the carriage, caught the national idea and
returned home lamenting that he could not put
the old carriage on wheels and take it from
town to town. "There's a fortune in the old
thing," said he, "for most folks would pay
a shilling or a sixpence to see the very identical
carriage in which Miss Florence took the wounded
about in those Crimean times. It's astonishing
what little things please people in the way of a
show. Why, that carriage would earn money
enough to build a hospital!"

CHAPTER IV

THE DAYS OF CHILDHOOD

Romantic Journeys from Lea Hurst to Embley Park—George Eliot
Associations—First Patient—Love of Animals and Flowers—
Early Education.

> The childhood shows the man,
> As morning shows the day.
>   MILTON.

> There is a lesson in each flower;
> A story in each stream and bower;
> On every herb o'er which you tread
> Are written words which, rightly read,
> Will lead you from earth's fragrant sod,
> To hope and holiness and God.
>   ALLAN CUNNINGHAM.

THE childhood of Florence Nightingale, begun, as we have seen, in the sunny land of Italy, was subsequently passed in the beautiful surroundings of her Derbyshire home, and at Embley Park, Hampshire, a fine old Elizabethan mansion, which Mr. Nightingale purchased when Florence was about six years old.

The custom was for the family to pass the summer at Lea Hurst, going in the autumn to Embley for the winter and early spring. And what an exciting

and delightful time Florerce and her sister Parthe
had on the occasions of these alternative " flittings "
between Derbyshire and Hampshire in the days
before railroads had destroyed the romance of
travelling ! Then the now quiet little town of
Cromford, two miles from Lea Hurst, was a busy
coaching centre, and the stage coaches also stopped
for passengers at the village inn of Whatstandwell, just below Lea Hurst Park. In those times
the Derby road was alive with the pleasurable
excitements of the prancing of horses, the crack
of the coach-driver's whip, the shouts of the post-
boys, and the sound of the horn—certainly more
inspiring and romantic sights and sounds than the
present toot-toot of the motor-car, and the billows
of dust-clouds which follow in its rear.

Sometimes the journey from Lea Hurst was
made by coach, but more frequently Mr. and Mrs.
Nightingale with their two little girls drove in their
own carriage, proceeding by easy stages and putting
up at inns *en route*, while the servants went before
with the luggage to prepare Embley for the reception
of the family.

How glorious it was in those bright October
days to drive through the country, just assuming
its dress of red and gold, or again in the return
journey in the spring, when the hills and dales of
Derbyshire were bursting into fresh green beauty.

The passionate love for nature and the sights and sounds of rural life which has always characterised Miss Nightingale was implanted in these happy days of childhood. And so, too, were the homely wit and piquant sayings which distinguish her writings and mark her more intimate conversation. She acquired them unconsciously, as she encountered the country people.

In her Derbyshire home she lived in touch with the life which at the same period was weaving its spell about Marian Evans, when she visited her kinspeople, and was destined to be immortalised in *Adam Bede* and *The Mill on the Floss*. Amongst her father's tenants Florence Nightingale knew farmers' wives who had a touch of Mrs. Poyser's caustic wit, and was familiar with the " Yea " and " Nay " and other quaint forms of Derbyshire speech, such as Mr. Tulliver used when he talked to " the little wench " in the house-place of the ill-fated Mill on the Floss. She met, too, many of " the people called Methodists," who in her girlhood were establishing their preaching-places in the country around Lea Hurst, and she heard of the fame of the woman preacher, then exercising her marvellous gifts in the Derby district, who was to become immortal as Dinah Morris. In Florence Nightingale's early womanhood, Adam Bede lived in his thatched cottage by Wirksworth

Tape Mills, a few miles from Lea Hurst, and the Poysers' farm stood across the meadows.

The childhood of our heroine was passed amid' surroundings which proved a singularly interesting environment. Steam power had not then revolutionised rural England: the counties retained their distinctive speech and customs, the young people remained on the soil where they were born, and the rich and the poor were thrown more intimately together. The effect of the greater personal intercourse then existing between the squire's family and his people had an important influence on the character of Florence Nightingale in her Derbyshire and Hampshire homes. She learned sympathy with the poor and afflicted, and gained an understanding of the workings and prejudices of the uneducated mind, which enabled her in after years to be a real friend to those poor fellows fresh from the battlefields of the Crimea, many of whom had enlisted from the class of rural homes which she knew so well.

When quite a child, Florence Nightingale showed characteristics which pointed to her vocation in life. Her dolls were always in a delicate state of health and required the utmost care. Florence would undress and put them to bed with many cautions to her sister not to disturb them. She soothed their pillows, tempted them with imaginary delicacies from toy cups and plates, and nursed them to convalescence, only to consign them to a sick bed the next day. Happily, Parthe did not exhibit the same tender consideration for her waxen favourites, who frequently suffered the loss of a limb or got burnt at the nursery fire. Then of course Florence's superior skill was needed, and she neatly bandaged poor dolly and " set " her arms and legs with a facility which might be the envy of the modern miraculous bone-setter.

The first " real live patient " of the future Queen of Nurses was Cap, the dog of an old Scotch shepherd, and although the story has been many times repeated since Florence Nightingale's name became a household word, no account of her childhood would be complete without it. One day Florence was having a delightful ride over the Hampshire downs near Embley along with the vicar, for whom she had a warm affection. He took great interest in the little girl's fondness for anything which had to do with the relief of the sick or injured, and as his own tastes lay in that direction, he was able to give her much useful instruction. However, on this particular day, as they rode along the downs, they noticed the sheep scattered in all directions and old Roger, the shepherd, vainly trying to collect them together.

" Where is your dog ? " asked the vicar as he drew up his horse and watched the old man's futile efforts.

" The boys have been throwing stones at him, sir, " was the reply, " and they have broken his leg, poor beast. He will never be any good for anything again and I am thinking of putting an end to his misery."

" Poor Cap's leg broken ? " said a girlish voice at the clergyman's side. " Oh, cannot we do something for him, Roger ? It is cruel to leave him alone in his pain. Where is he ? "

" You can't do any good, missy," said the old shepherd sorrowfully. " I'll just take a cord to him to-night—that will be the best way to ease his pain. I left him lying in the shed over yonder."

" Oh, can't we do something for poor Cap ? " pleaded Florence to her friend ; and the vicar, seeing the look of pity in her young face, turned his horse's head towards the distant shed where the dog lay. But Florence put her pony to the gallop and reached the shed first. Kneeling down on the mud floor, she caressed the suffering dog with her little hand, and spoke soothing words to it until the faithful brown eyes seemed to have less of pain in them and were lifted to her face in pathetic gratitude.

That look of the shepherd's dog, which touched

her girlish heart on the lonely hillside, Florence Nightingale was destined to see repeated in the eyes of suffering men as she bent over them in the hospital at Scutari.

The vicar soon joined his young companion, and finding that the dog's leg was only injured, not broken, he decided that a little careful nursing would put him all right again.

"What shall I do first?" asked Florence, all eagerness to begin nursing in real earnest.

"Well," said her friend, "I should advise a hot compress on Cap's leg."

Florence looked puzzled, for though she had poulticed and bandaged her dolls, she had never heard about a compress. However, finding that in plain language it meant cloths wrung out of boiling water, and laid upon the affected part, she set nimbly to work under the vicar's directions. Boiling water was the first requisite, and calling in the services of the shepherd's boy, she lighted a fire of sticks in the cottage near by, and soon had the kettle boiling.

Next thing, she looked round for cloths to make the compress. The shepherd's clean smock hung behind the door, and Florence seized it with delight, for it was the very thing.

"If I tear it up, mamma will give Roger another," she reasoned, and, at an approving nod from the vicar, tore the smock into suitable lengths for fomentation. Then going back to the place where the dog lay, accompanied by the boy carrying the kettle and a basin, Florence Nightingale set to work to give "first aid to the wounded." Cap offered no resistance—he had a wise confidence in his nurse—and as she applied the fomentations the swelling began to go down, and the pain grew less.

Florence was resolved to do her work thoroughly, and a messenger having been despatched to allay her parents' anxiety at her prolonged absence, she remained for several hours in attendance on her patient.

In the evening old Roger came slowly and sorrowfully towards the shed, carrying the fatal rope, but no sooner did he put his head in at the door than Cap greeted him with a whine of pleasure and tried to come towards him.

"Deary me, missy," said the old shepherd in astonishment, "why, you have been doing wonders. I never thought to see the poor dog greet me again."

"Yes, doesn't he look better?" said the youthful nurse with pardonable pride. "You can throw away that rope now, and help me to make compresses."

"That I will, missy," said Roger, and stooping down beside Florence and Cap, he was initiated into the mysteries.

"Yes," said the vicar, "Miss Florence is quite right, Roger—your dog will soon be able to walk again if you give it a little rest and care."

"I am sure I can't thank your reverence and the young lady enough," replied the shepherd, quite overcome at the sight of his faithful dog's look of content and the thought that he would not lose him after all ; "and you may be sure, sir, I will carry out the instructions."

"But I shall come again to-morrow, Roger," interposed Florence, who had no idea of giving up her patient yet. "I know mamma will let me when I tell her about poor Cap." After a parting caress to the dog, and many last injunctions to Roger, Florence mounted her pony and rode away with the vicar, her young heart very full of joy. She had really helped to lessen pain, if only for a dumb creature, and the grateful eyes of the suffering dog stirred a new feeling in her opening mind. She longed to be always doing something for somebody, and the poor people on her father's estates soon learned what a kind friend they had in Miss Florence. They grew also to have unbounded faith in her skill, and whenever a pet animal was sick or injured, the owner would contrive to let "Miss Florence" know.

She and her sister were encouraged by Mr. and Mrs. Nightingale in a love of animals, and were allowed to have many pets. It was characteristic of Florence that her heart went out to the less favoured ones, those which owing to old age or infirmity were taken little notice of by the servants and farm-men. She was particularly attached to Peggy, an old grey pony long since past work, who spent her days in the paddock at Lea Hurst. Florence never missed a morning, if she could help it, without going to talk to Peggy, who knew her footstep, and would come trotting up to the gate ready to meet her young mistress. Then would follow some good-natured sport.

"Would you like an apple, poor old Peggy?" Florence would say as she fondled the pony's neck; "then look for it."

At this invitation Peggy would put her nose to the dress pocket of her little visitor and discover the delicacy. Or it might be a carrot, held well out of sight, which Peggy was invited to play hide-and-seek for. If the stable cat had kittens, it was Florence who gave them a welcome and fondled and played with the little creatures before any one else noticed them. She had, too, a quick eye for a hedge-sparrow's nest, and would jealously guard the brooding mother's secret until the fledgelings were hatched and ready to fly. Some of the bitterest tears of her childhood were shed over the broken-up homes of some of her feathered friends.   The young animals in the fields were quickly won by her kind nature, and would come bounding towards her.   Out in those beautiful Lea Hurst woods she made companions of the squirrels, who came fearlessly after her as she walked, to pick up the nuts mysteriously dropped in their path.   Then, when master squirrel least expected it, Florence turned sharp round and away raced the little brown creature up the tall beech, only to come down again with a quizzical look in his keen little eye at nuts held too temptingly for any squirrel of ordinary appetite to resist. With what delight she watched their funny antics, for she had the gift to make these timid creatures trust her.

Then in spring-time there was sure to be a pet lamb to be fed, and Florence and her sister were indeed happy at this acquisition to the home pets.   The pony which she rode and the dog which was ever at her side were of course her particular dumb friends.   I am not sure, however, that she thought them dumb, for she and they understood one another perfectly.   The love of animals, which was so marked a characteristic in Florence Nightingale as a child, remained with her throughout life and made her very sympathetic to invalids who craved for the company of some favourite animal.   Many nurses and doctors dis-

EMBLEY PARK, HAMPSHIRE.

(From a drawing by the late Lady Verney.)

[To face p. 32.

approve of their patients having pets about them, but, to quote the Queen of Nurses' own words, " A small pet animal is often an excellent companion for the sick, for long chronic cases especially. An invalid, in giving an account of his nursing by a nurse and a dog, infinitely preferred that of the dog. 'Above all,' he said, 'it did not talk.'"

It was a great source of pleasure to Florence in her early years to be allowed to act as almoner for her mother. Mrs. Nightingale was very kind and benevolent to the people around Lea Hurst and Embley, and supplied the sick with delicacies from her own table. Indeed, she made her homes centres of beneficence for several miles around, and, according to the best traditions of those times, was ready with remedies for simple ailments when the doctor was not at hand. Owing to the fact that Florence had never had measles and whooping cough, her parents had to exercise great caution in permitting her to visit the cottage people ; however, she could call at the doors on her pony and leave jelly and puddings from the basket at her saddle-bow without incurring special risk. And she could gather flowers from the garden to brighten a sick-room, or in the lovely spring days load her basket with primroses and bluebells and so carry the scent of the woods to some delicate girl who, like Tennyson's May Queen, was pining for the f field and hedgerow and the flowers which grew but a little distance from her cottage door.

Such attentions to the fancies of the sick were little thought of in those times, before flower missions had come into vogue, or the necessity for cheering the patients by pleasing the eye, as well as tending the body, was recognised, but in that, as in much else, our heroine was in advance of her time. Her love of flowers, like fondness for animals, was a part of her nature : it came too as a fitting heritage from the city of flowers under whose sunny sky she had been born.

Both at Embley and Lea Hurst, Florence and her sister had their own little gardens, in which they digged and sowed and planted to their hearts' delight, and in summer they ran about with their miniature watering cans, bestowing, doubtless, an almost equal supply on their own tiny feet as on the parched ground. In after years this early love of flowers had its pathetic sequel. When, after months of exhausting work amongst the suffering soldiers, Florence Nightingale lay in a hut on the heights of Balaclava, prostrate with Crimean fever, she relates that she first began to rally after receiving a bunch of flowers from a friend, and that the sight of them beside her sick couch helped her to throw off the languor which had nearly proved fatal. She dated her recovery from that hour.

In every respect the circumstances of Florence Nightingale's childhood were calculated to fit her for the destiny which lay in the future. Not only was she reared among scenes of exceptional beauty in both her Derbyshire and her Hampshire homes and taught the privilege of ministering to the poor and sick, but she was mentally trained in advance of the custom of the day. Without that equipment she could not have held the commanding position which she attained in the work of army nursing and organisation.

She and her sister Parthe, being so near in age, did their lessons together. Their education was conducted entirely at home under a private governess, and was assiduously supervised by their father. Mr. Nightingale was a man of broad sympathies, artistic and intellectual tastes, and much general cultivation, and, having no sons, he made a hobby of giving a classical education to his girls, and found a fertile soil in the quick brain of his daughter Florence. He was a strict disciplinarian, and none of the desultory ways which characterised the home education of young ladies in the early Victorian days was allowed in the schoolrooms at Embley and Lea Hurst. Rules were rigidly fixed for lessons and play, and careless work was never

passed unpunished. It was in the days of childhood that the future heroine of the Crimea laid
the foundation of an orderly mind and a habit of
method which served her so admirably when suddenly called to organise the ill-regulated hospital at
Scutari.

As a child Florence excelled in the more intellectual branches of education and showed a great
aptitude for foreign languages. She attained creditable proficiency in music and was clever at drawing,
but in these artistic branches her elder sister Parthe
excelled most. From her father Florence learned
elementary science, Greek, Latin, and mathematics,
and under his guidance, seated in the dear old
library at Lea Hurst, made the acquaintance of
standard authors and poets. But doubtless the
sisters got an occasional romance not included in
the paternal list and read it with glowing cheeks
and sparkling eyes in a secluded nook in the
garden.

If study was made a serious business, the sisters
enjoyed to the full the healthy advantages of country
life. They scampered about the park with their
dogs, rode their ponies over hill and dale, spent
long days in the woods amongst the bluebells
and primroses, and in summer tumbled about in
the sweet-scented hay. During the summer at
Lea Hurst, lessons were a little relaxed in favour

of outdoor life, but on the return to Embley for the winter, schoolroom routine was again enforced on very strict lines.

Mrs. Nightingale supervised the domestic side of her little girls' education, and before Florence was twelve years old she could hemstitch and seam, embroider bookmarkers, and had worked several creditable samplers. Her mother trained her too in matters of deportment, and nothing was omitted in her early years which would tend to mould her into a graceful and accomplished girl.

CHAPTER V

THE SQUIRE'S DAUGHTER

An Accomplished Girl—An Angel in the Homes of the Poor—
Children's "Feast Day" at Lea Hurst—Her Bible-Class for
Girls—Interests at Embley—Society Life—Longing for a
Vocation—Meets Elizabeth Fry—Studies Hospital Nursing—
Decides to go to Kaiserswerth.

> God made her so,
> And deeds of week-day holiness
> Fall from her gentle as the snow;
> Nor hath she ever chanced to know
> That aught were easier than to bless.
> LOWELL.

WHEN Florence Nightingale reached her
seventeenth year she began to take her
place as the squire's daughter, mingling in the
county society of Derbyshire and Hampshire and
interesting herself in the people and schools of
her father's estates. She soon acquired the reputa-
tion of being a very lovable young lady as well
as a very talented one. She had travelled abroad,
could speak French, German, and Italian, sang
very sweetly, and was clever at sketching, and when

38

the taking of photographs became a fashionable pastime, "Miss Florence" became an enthusiast for the art. There were no hand-cameras in those days and no clean and easy methods for developing, and young lady amateur photographers were obliged to dress for their work. Nothing daunted "Miss Florence," and she photographed groups on the lawn and her pet animals to the admiration of her family and friends, if sometimes to the discoloration of her dainty fingers.

She was also a skilful needlewoman, and worked cushions and slippers, mastered the finest and most complicated crochet patterns, sewed delicate embroideries, and achieved almost invisible hems on muslin frills. At Christmas-time her work-basket was full of warm comforts for the poor. She was invaluable at bazaars, then a newly introduced method of raising money for religious purposes, and was particularly happy at organising treats for the old people and children.

The local clergy, both at Embley and Lea, found the squire's younger daughter a great help in the parish. The traits of character which had shown themselves in the little girl who tended the shepherd's injured dog, and was so ready with her sympathy for all who suffered or were in trouble, became strengthened in the budding woman and made Florence Nightingale regarded as an angel in the homes of the poor. Her visits to the cottages were eagerly looked for, and she showed even in her teens a genius for district visiting. The people regarded her not as the " visiting lady," whom they were to impress with feigned woes or a pretence of abject poverty, but as a real friend who came to bring pleasure to their homes and to enter into their family joys and sorrows. She had a bright and witty way of talking which made the poor folks look forward to her visits quite apart from the favours she might bring.

If there was sickness or sorrow in any cottage home, the presence of " Miss Florence " was eagerly sought, for even at this period she had made some study of sick nursing and " seemed," as the people said, " to have a way with her " which eased pain and brought comfort and repose to those who were suffering. She had, too, such a clear, sweet voice and sympathetic intonation that the sick derived great pleasure when she read to them.

As quite a young girl the bent of her mind was in the direction of leading a useful and beneficent life. She was in no danger of suffering from the *ennui* which beset so many girls of the leisured classes in those times, when there was so little in the way of outdoor sport and amusements or independent interests to fill up time. In whatsoever circumstances of life Florence Nightingale had been placed, her nature would have prompted her to discover useful occupation.

The "old squire," as Mr. Nightingale is still called at Lea, took a great interest in the village school, and Florence became his right hand in looking after the amusements of the children. There were many little treats devised for them from time to time, but the great event of the year was the children's "feast day," when the scholars assembled at the school-house and walked in procession to Lea Hurst, carrying "posies" in their hands and sticks wreathed with garlands of flowers. A band provided by the squire headed the procession. Arrived at Lea Hurst, the company were served with tea in the field below the garden, Mrs. Nightingale and her daughters assisting the servants to wait upon their guests. After tea, the band struck up lively airs and the lads and lasses danced in a style which recalled the olden times in Merrie England, while the squire and his family beamed approval.

Then there were games for the little ones devised by "Miss Florence," who took upon herself their special entertainment ; and so the summer evening passed away in delightful mirth and recreation until the crimson clouds began to glow over the beautiful Derwent valley, and the children re-formed in line and marched up the garden to the top terrace of the lawn. Meantime "Miss Florence" and

" Miss Parthe " had mysteriously disappeared, and now they were seen standing on the terrace behind a long table laden with presents. As the procession filed past, each child received a gift from one or other of the young ladies, and there were kindly words from the squire and gracious smiles from Mrs. Nightingale and much bobbing of curtseys by the delighted children, and so the " feast day " ended in mutual joy and pleasure.

The scene was described to me by an old lady who had many times as a ¡child attended this pretty entertainment at Lea Hurst, and still treasures the little gifts—fancy boxes, books, thimble cases and the like—which she had received from the hands of the then beloved and now deeply reverenced " Miss Florence." She recalls what a sweet young lady she was, with her glossy brown hair smoothed down each side of her face, and often a rose placed at the side, amongst the neat plaits or coils. Her appearance at this period can be judged from the pencil sketch by her sister, afterwards Lady Verney, in which, despite the quaint attire, one recognises a tall, graceful girl of charm and intelligence.

In Derbyshire, Florence Nightingale's interest in Church work was divided between the historic little church of Dethick, described in a former chapter, and the beautiful church which Sir Richard Arkwright had built at Cromford on the opposite

side of the river from his castle of Willersley.
To-day, Cromford Church is thickly covered with
ivy and embowered in trees, and, standing on the
river bank with greystone rocks towering on one
side and the wooded heights of Willersley on
the other, presents a mellowed and picturesque
appearance. In our heroine's girlhood it was
comparatively new and regarded as the wonder of
the district for the architectural taste and decoration
which Sir Richard had lavished upon it. The great
cotton-spinner himself had been laid beneath its
chancel in 1792, but an Arkwright reigned at
Willersley Castle in Miss Nightingale's youth—as
indeed there does to-day—and carried on the
beneficent schemes of the founder for the people
of the district. Then the Arkwright Mills—long
since disused—gave employment to hundreds of
people, and the now sleepy little town of Cromford
was alive with an industrial population. It was
something of a model village, as the neat rows
of low stone houses which flank Cromford hill
testify, and there were schools, reading-rooms, and
other means devised for the betterment of the
people. Many schemes originated with the vicar
and patron of Cromford Church, and the young
ladies from Lea Hurst sometimes assisted at
entertainments.

We may imagine " Miss Florence " when she

drove with her parents down to Cromford Church making a very pretty picture indeed, dressed in her summer muslin, with a silk spencer crossed over her maiden breast and her sweet, placid face beaming from out the recesses of a Leghorn bonnet, wreathed with roses.

It was, however, in connection with the church of Dethick and the adjoining parishes of Lea and Holloway that Florence Nightingale did most of her philanthropic work. This district was peculiarly her father's domain, and also embraced the church and village of Crich. Like Cromford, it was the seat of a village industry. Immediately below Lea Hurst were Smedley's hosiery mills, which employed hundreds of women and girls, many of whom lived on the Nightingale estate, and Miss Florence took great interest in their welfare. As she grew into womanhood, she started a Bible-class for the young women of the district, holding it in the old building at Lea Hurst known as the "chapel." The class was unsectarian, for "Smedley's people," following the example of their master, "Dr." John Smedley, were chiefly Methodists. However, religious differences were not bitter in the neighbourhood, and Miss Nightingale welcomed to her class all young girls who were disposed to come, whether their parents belonged to "chapel" or "church."

The memory of those Sunday afternoons, as they sat in the tiny stone "chapel" overlooking the sunny lawns and gardens of Lea Hurst, listening to the beautiful expositions of Scripture which fell from their beloved "Miss Florence," or following her sweet voice in sacred song, is green in the hearts of a few elderly people in the neighbourhood. A softness comes into their voice, and a smile of pleasure lights up their wrinkled faces, as they tell you how "beautifully Miss Florence used to talk." In years long after, when she returned for holiday visits to Lea Hurst, nothing gave Miss Nightingale greater pleasure than for the young girls of the district, some of them daughters of her former scholars, to come on summer Sunday afternoons and sing on the lawn at Lea Hurst as she sat in her room above. Infirmity prevented her from mingling with them, but the girls were pleased if they could only catch a sight of her face smiling down from the window.

During the winter months spent in her Hampshire home, Florence Nightingale was also active amongst the sick poor and the young people. Embley Park is near the town of Romsey, in the parish of East Willow, and Mr. Nightingale and his family attended that church. "Miss Florence" had many friends amongst the cottagers, and a few of the old people still recall seeing the "young

ladies" riding about on their ponies, and stopping
with kind inquiries at some of the house doors.
Although the sisters were such close companions,
it is always "Miss Florence" who is remembered
as the chief benefactress. She had the happy gift
for gaining the love of the people, and the instinct
for giving the right sort of help, though "Miss
Parthe" was no less kind-hearted.

At Christmas, Embley Park was a centre from
which radiated much good cheer. "Florence"
was gay indeed, as, in ermine tippet and muff and
beaver hat, she helped to distribute the parcels of
tea and the warm petticoats to the old women.
She devised Christmas entertainments for the children
and assisted in treats for the workhouse poor. Local
carol-singers received a warm welcome at Embley,
especially from Miss Florence, who would come into
the hall to see the mince-pies and coin distributed
as she chatted with the humble performers. Training
the boys and girls to sing was to her a matter of
special interest, and she did much in those far-
away days to promote a love of music amongst
the villagers both at Lea Hurst and Embley. It
would afford her pleasure to-day could she listen
to the well-trained band formed by the mill-workers
at Lea, which one hears discoursing sweet music
outside the mills on a summer's evening.

Embley overlooked the hills of the Wiltshire

border, and the cathedral city of Salisbury, only some thirteen miles distant, afforded Miss Nightingale a wider field of philanthropic interest. She was always willing to take part in beneficent work in the neighbourhood, and the children's hospital and other schemes founded and conducted by her friends Mr. and Mrs. Sidney Herbert, afterwards Lord and Lady Herbert of Lea, formed a special interest for her in the years immediately preceding the outbreak of the Crimean War.

It must not, however, be supposed that in the early years of her womanhood Miss Nightingale gave herself up entirely to religious and philanthropic work, though it formed a serious background to her social life. Mr. Nightingale, as a man of wealth and influence, liked to see his wife and daughters taking part in county society. During the winter he entertained a good deal at Embley, which was a much larger and handsomer residence than Lea Hurst. Mr. and Mrs. Nightingale had a large circle of friends, and their house was noted as a place of genial hospitality, while their charming and accomplished daughters attracted many admirers.

The family did not confine themselves only to county society. They sometimes came to London for the season, and Florence and her sister made their curtsey to Queen Victoria when in the heyday of her early married life, and entered into the gaieties of the time.

However, as the years passed by Florence Nightingale cared less and less for the excitement and pleasures of society. Her nature had begun to crave for some definite work and a more extended field of activity than she found in private life. Two severe illnesses among members of her family had developed her nursing faculty, and when they no longer required her attention, she turned to a systematic study of nursing.

To-day it seems almost impossible to realise how novel was the idea of a woman of birth and education becoming a nurse. Miss Nightingale was a pioneer of the pioneers. She herself had not then any clear course before her for the future, but she realised the important point that she could not hope to accomplish anything without training. The faculty was necessary and the desire to be helpful to the sick and suffering, but a trained knowledge was the important thing. In a letter which Miss Nightingale wrote in after years to young women on the subject of " Work and Duty " she remarked : " I would say to all young ladies who are called to any particular vocation, qualify yourselves for it as a man does for his work. Don't think you can undertake it otherwise. Submit yourselves to the rules of business as men do, by

MISS NIGHTINGALE.
(From a Drawing.)

[To face p. 48.

which alone you can make God's business succeed.;
for He has never said that he will give His success
and his blessing to sketchy and unfinished work."
And on another occasion she wrote : " Three-fourths
of the whole mischief in women's lives arises from
their excepting themselves from the rules of training
considered needful for men."

This was the spirit in which Miss Nightingale
entered upon her chosen work, for she was the
last person to "preach and not practise." The
advice which she gave to other women, when she
had herself risen to the head of her profession, had
been the guiding influence of her own probation.

The beneficent work which distinguished her as
the squire's daughter had given her useful experience, and had opened her eyes to the need of
trained nurses for the sick poor. What is now
called " district nursing" at this period exercised the
mind of Florence Nightingale, and her attention
to military nursing was called forth later by a
national emergency.

It was at this critical period of her life, when
her mind was shaping itself to such high purpose,
that Florence Nightingale met Elizabeth Fry. The
first grasping of hands of these two pioneer women
would serve as subject for a painter. We picture
the stately and beautiful old Quakeress in the characteristic garb of the Friends extending a sisterly

welcome to the young and earnest woman who came to learn at her feet. The one was fast drawing to the close of her great work for the women prisoners, and the other stood on the threshold of a philanthropic career to be equally distinguished. We have no detailed record of what words were spoken at this meeting, but we know that the memory of the heavenly personality of Elizabeth Fry was an ever-present inspiration with Florence Nightingale in the years which followed.

It was a meeting of kindred spirits, but of distinct individualities. We do not find Miss Nightingale making any attempt to take up the mantle fast falling from the experienced philanthropist : she had her own line of pioneer work forming in her capable brain, but was eager to glean something from the wide experience through which her revered friend had passed. Mrs. Fry had during the past few years been visiting prisons and institutions on the Continent, and had established a small training home for nurses in London. She was a friend of Pastor Fliedner, the founder of Kaiserswerth, and had visited that institution. The account of his work, and of the order of Protestant deaconesses which he had founded for tending the sick poor, given by Mrs. Fry, made a profound impression on Florence Nightingale, and resulted a few years later in her enrolment as a voluntary nurse at that novel institution

In the meantime she studied the hospital system at home, spending some months in the leading London hospitals and visiting those in Edinburgh and Dublin. Then she undertook a lengthened tour abroad and saw the different working of institutions for the sick in France, Germany, and Italy. The comparison was not favourable to this country. The nursing in our hospitals was largely in the hands of the coarsest type of women, not only untrained, but callous in feeling and often grossly immoral. There was little to counteract their baneful influence, and the atmosphere of institutions which, as the abodes of the sick and dying, had special need of spiritual and elevating influences, was of a degrading character. The occasional visits of a chaplain could not do very much to counteract the behaviour of the un-principled nurse ever at the bedside. The habitual drunkenness of these women was then proverbial, while the dirt and disorder rampant in the wards was calculated to breed disease. The " profession," if the nursing of that day can claim a title so dignified, had such a stigma attaching to it that no decent woman cared to enter it, and if she did, it was more than likely that she would lose her character.

In contrast to this repulsive class of women, whom Miss Nightingale had encountered to her horror in the hospitals of London, Edinburgh, and Dublin, and to the "Sairey Gamps" who were the only "professional" nurses available for the middle classes in their own homes, she found on the Continent the sweet-faced Sister of Charity —pious, educated, trained.

For centuries the Roman Catholic community had trained and set apart holy women for ministering to the sick poor in their own homes, and had established hospitals supplied with the same type of nurse. A large number of these women were ladies of birth and breeding who worked for the good of their souls and the welfare of their Church, while all received proper education and training, and had abjured the world for a religious life. An excellent example of the work done by the nun-nurses is seen in the quaint old-world hospital of St. John, with which visitors to Bruges are familiar. It was one of the institutions visited by Miss Nightingale, and, religious differences apart, she viewed with profound admiration the beneficent work of the sisters.

After pursuing her investigations from city to city, Miss Nightingale decided to take a course of instruction at the recently founded institution for deaconesses at Kaiserswerth on the Rhine. There a Protestant sisterhood were working on similar lines to Sisters of Charity, and had already done much to mitigate the poverty, sickness, and misery in their own district, and were beginning to extend their influence to other German towns. At Kaiserswerth the ideal system of trained sick nursing which Miss Nightingale had been forming in her own mind was an accomplished fact.

CHAPTER VI

FLORENCE NIGHTINGALE'S ALMA MATER AND ITS FOUNDER

Enrolled a Deaconess at Kaiserswerth—Paster Fliedner—His Early Life—Becomes Pastor at Kaiserswerth—Interest in Prison Reform—Starts a Small Penitentiary for Discharged Female Prisoners—Founds a School and the Deaconess Hospital—Rules for Deaconesses—Marvellous Extension of his Work—His Death —Miss Nightingale's Tribute.

> Just precepts thus from great examples given,
> She drew from them what they derived from Heaven.
> POPE.

THE year 1849 proved a memorable one in the career of Florence Nightingale, for it was then that she enrolled herself as a voluntary nurse in the Deaconess Institution at Kaiserswerth on the Rhine, which may be described as her Alma Mater. It was the first training school for sick nurses established in modern times, and it seems a happy conjunction of circumstances that she who was destined to hold the blue riband of the nursing sisterhood of the world should have studied within its walls.

Although she had already gained valuable insight into hospital work and management during her visits to various hospitals at home and abroad, it

PASTOR FLIEDNER, FOUNDER OF KAISERSWERTH.

was not until she came to Kaiserswerth that she found her ideals realised. Here was a Protestant institution which had all the good points of the

Roman Catholic sisterhoods without their restrictions. It further commended itself as being under the guidance of Pastor Fliedner, a man of simple and devoted piety and a born philanthropist.

He had had the perspicacity to see that the world needed the services of trained women to grapple with the evils of vice and disease, and to this end he revived the office of deaconess which had been instituted by the early Christian Church. The idea of training women to minister to the sick and the poor seems natural enough to-day, but in Miss Nightingale's young womanhood it was entirely novel. The district nurse had not then been invented. The Kaiserswerth institution combined hospital routine and instruction with beneficent work among the poor and the outcast.

Pastor Fliedner, the founder, was indeed a kindred spirit, and it seems fitting to give a little account of the man who exercised such a remarkable influence over our heroine in the days of her probation. Theodore Fliedner was just twenty years her senior, having been born in 1800 at Eppstein, a small village near the Rhine. He was "a son of the manse," both his father and grandfather having been Lutheran clergymen. At an early age he showed a desire to become a power for good in the world, and his sensitive feelings were much hurt when a child, by his father playfully calling him "the little beer-brewer" on account of his plump round figure. The jest caused little Theodore much heart-searching and made him feel that his nature must be very carnal and in need of great discipline. In these days he would probably have resorted to Sandow's exercises or a bicycle.

Of course Theodore was poor and had to work his way from school to college. He studied at the Universities of Giessen and Göttingen, giving instruction in return for food and lodging, and was not above doing manual labour also. He sawed wood, blacked boots, and did other odd jobs. He also mended his own clothes, but in a somewhat primitive fashion, for in a letter to his mother he says that he sewed up the holes in his trousers with white thread which he afterwards inked over. His vacations were spent in tramping long distances and subsisting on the barest necessaries of life, in order to gain an acquaintance with the world. He studied foreign languages, read widely, and as a college student showed the after bent of his mind by collecting songs and games for children which later were used in his own kindergarten, and have spread throughout the world. He also learned the use of herbs and acquired much homely knowledge on the treatment of disease.

After leaving college he became tutor in a private family at Cologne, and the mother of his pupils took his deportment in hand.   Possibly this lady had physical culture views about the rotundity of his figure.   However, Theodore in speaking of the benefit derived from lessons in deportment quaintly confesses that " gentle ways and polite manners help greatly to further the kingdom of God."   While at Cologne he assisted a clergyman of the place in parish work, and occasionally preached in the prison, thus gaining an insight into the unhappy condition of discharged prisoners which inspired his later beneficent work on their behalf.

When he had reached the age of twenty-two, Theodore Fliedner received a call to become the pastor of a struggling Protestant community at the little town of Kaiserswerth on the Rhine, near Düsseldorf, which he accepted.   At Eppstein, his native village, he was ordained, surrounded by a delighted family circle.   It is characteristic that the young pastor set out on foot for Kaiserswerth, and arrived before he was expected in order to save his parishioners the expense of giving him a reception.

His position was humbler even than Goldsmith's Vicar, for he received the modest yearly stipend of 180 thaler (£27), and had to share the parsonage with the mother of his predecessor, while in order to relieve his own widowed mother he took two younger brothers and a sister to live with him. Hardly was his modest household arranged, than a velvet-factory upon which the Protestant population of Kaiserswerth depended failed, and the young pastor found himself with a destitute flock. He received two other calls, but his heart was fixed at Kaiserswerth, and he determined to set forth staff in hand like the Apostles, and tramp through the Protestant countries seeking aid for his people. He visited Germany, Holland, and England, and received help and encouragement.

The most important friendship which the young Lutheran pastor made in London was with Elizabeth Fry. The work of this noble philanthropist amongst the prisoners of Newgate was a revelation to him, and he returned to his parish of Kaiserswerth burning with zeal to do something for the prisoners of his own land. He began work in the neighbouring prison of Düsseldorf, where he became a regular visitor and started services. On June 26th, 1826, he was instrumental in founding at Düsseldorf the first German society for improving prison discipline.

The great problem which confronted him was how to protect the discharged female prisoners from the life of evil to which their unhappy circumstances drove them when the term of their imprisonment ended. They had as a rule neither

home nor protector, and were cast upon the
world with the prisoner's brand upon them. He
determined to devote himself to the rescue and
protection of these unfortunate women.

In September of 1833 he began his experiment
by preparing with his own hands an old summer-
house, some twelve feet square, which stood in a
retired part of his garden as a refuge for discharged
female prisoners. He protected it from wind and
rain, made it clean and habitable, and placing there
a bed, a table, and a chair, prayed that God would
direct some outcast wanderer to its shelter. One
night a poor forlorn woman presented herself, and
the pastor and his good wife led her to the room
prepared. This destitute creature housed in the
old summer-house was practically the inauguration
of the now famous Kaiserswerth institution. In the
course of the winter nine other women voluntarily
sought the refuge, and the work went forward until
a new separate building was erected near the pastor's
house, having its own garden and field and affording accommodation for twenty women. Madame
Fliedner, the founder's wife, and Mademoiselle
Göbel, a voluntary helper, had charge of the
penitentiary.

Some of the women had children, and Pastor
Fliedner's next step was to start an infant school
on very much the same lines as a modern kinder-

MISS NIGHTINGALE.

(From the bust at Claydon)

This bust was presented to Miss Nightingale by the soldiers after the
Crimean War, and was executed by the late Sir John Steele

[*To face p* 61.

garten. Now it was that the children's games and songs which it had been his hobby to collect during his tramps abroad when a college student became of use. Teachers were needed for the increasing school, and in course of time a Normal school for the training of infant-school mistresses was started.

However, the idea which most actively dominated the pastor's mind was the training of women in hospital work and to tend the poor. In his parish of Kaiserswerth there was much poverty and incompetence amongst the people and no provision for dealing with disease. Three years after he had founded the penitentiary for discharged female prisoners, as already described, he started his more important venture of founding a hospital for the reception of poor patients and for the training of nurses or deaconesses.

On October 13th, 1836, the " Deaconess Hospital, Kaiserswerth," was opened, practically without patients and without deaconesses. For his hospital the pastor had secured a part of the deserted factory, the stopping of which had plunged his people into destitution in the first year of his pastorate—a singular example of the realisation of poetic justice. He fitted the " wards " with mended furniture, cracked earthenware, and such utensils as he could beg. His stock of linen embraced only six sheets.

But cleanliness cost nothing, and the hospital certainly had that. On the Sunday morning after the opening the first patient, a poor suffering servant girl, knocked at the door for admittance. Four other sick persons came during the month, and in the course of a year sixty patients had been received in the primitive hospital, and funds were coming in for the support of the work.

Almost simultaneously with the patients came the nurses. First a solitary candidate presented herself for training as a deaconess and several probationers followed. In the course of a year seven nurses had entered the institution. There was nothing haphazard about their admission, for the pastor, when he instituted his order of Protestant deaconesses, made a simple code of rules. No deaconess was to be under twenty-five years of age, and although she was engaged for a term of five years, she was free to leave at any moment. The candidates were solemnly received into the community and consecrated to their work by the laying on of hands by the pastor, who invoked a final blessing in the words: " May God the Father, the Son, and the Holy Ghost, three Persons in one God, bless you ; may He stablish you in the Truth until death, and give you hereafter the Crown of Life. Amen."

The dress of the deaconesses is very quaint and simple, but not unbecoming. It consists of a plain blue cotton gown, a white apron, large white turned-down collar, and a white muslin cap surrounding the face in the old style and tied under the chin with a large bow. The young girl probationers look very sweet and attractive in the cap, which has a tendency to heighten the beauty of a fresh young face while it seems singularly appropriate to the elderly women who have passed from active service to the Home of Rest, later provided.

Unlike their Roman Catholic sisters, the Kaiserswerth deaconesses were not fettered by a vow. Their vocation was to be the servants of Christ and the servants of the sick and poor. They could at any time return to their families if their services were needed, and were at liberty to marry, but not to remain in the hospital afterwards, as it was considered that the new ties would interfere with entire devotion to their work.

Pastor Fliedner was a man of social instincts and had himself married twice. His first wife lived only a short time, and the story of his second wooing is quaintly told in his journal. He went to Hamburg to ask Amalia Sieveking to take charge of a deaconess home. She was unable to comply with the request, but recommended in her place a young friend and pupil, Caroline Bertheau, who had been nursing in the Hamburg Hospital.

The pastor was so pleased with the substitute that he offered her the choice of either taking charge of a deaconess home or becoming his wife. Caroline demurely elected to do both. They were married at once, and spent their honeymoon in Berlin for the purpose of establishing the first five deaconesses in the Charité Hospital, returning in due course to Kaiserswerth, where the young wife became the Deaconess Mother of the institution and the devoted helpmeet of her husband in all his after-work.

But to return to the training of the deaconesses. After the institution had become established in all its branches, a candidate decided on entering whether she wished to train as a teacher or as a nurse, and was enrolled in the *Krankenschwestern* or *Lehrschwestern* according to her choice. Each probationer goes through a course of practical housework. She learns to cook, sew, iron, and scrub by taking a share in the menial work of the hospital, and this fits her to be of real help when she comes to enter the homes of the poor. The probationer also has instruction in simple book-keeping, letter-writing, and reading aloud. After she has gone through the general course, she goes into particular training according to her choice. If she desires to become a nurse, she enters the surgical and medical wards of the

hospital ; and if a teacher, she trains in the kindergarten and the other schools.

The Kaiserswerth deaconesses receive no salaries,
the primary idea being that they should give themselves to the work. They have free board and are
supplied each year with two blue cotton gowrs
and two aprons, and every five years with a new
blue woollen gown and a black alpaca apron for
best wear. They receive at intervals new outdoor
dress, which consists of long black cloaks and
black bonnets which fit closely over the white cap.
If a deaconess has private property, she retains
the full control of it, and on her death it reverts
to her nearest of kin unless she has otherwise
disposed of it by will. Each deaconess is allowed
a small sum for pocket money.

During the first ten years of the founding of
Kaiserswerth Pastor Fliedner spread his system of
deaconesses until he had established sixty nurses
in twenty-five different centres, and calls were
coming from all sides. In 1849 he resigned his
pastorate in order to journey about establishing
branch houses in different parts of the world.
His first long journey was to the United States,
to conduct deaconesses to Dr. Passavant's German
parish at Pittsburg ; and the second was to Jerusalem,
where he founded a " mother house " with four
deaconesses on Mount Zion in a building given

by the King of Prussia. This branch undertakes to nurse all sick persons irrespective of creed, and forms a training school for nurses in the East.

From Jerusalem he proceeded to Constantinople, established a branch there, and then proceeded to Alexandria, Beyrout, Smyrna, Bucharest, and other places. He had already started a deaconess home in London. The institutions spread rapidly through Germany, and to-day there is scarcely a town of any size in the Fatherland which has not its deaconess home which sends nurses to the poor without charge and supplies middle-class families at moderate fees. The last years of the pastor's life were passed in bodily suffering, but he still kept his hand on the helm. His last work was to found at Kaiserswerth a Home of Rest for retired deaconesses. The good man was much cheered not only by the marvellous extension of his work—he left behind him a hundred houses attended by four hundred and thirty deaconesses—but at the fruit which seeds of his sowing had produced in the heart of the English lady who became the heroine of the Crimean War. It was with peculiar interest that he followed the work of Florence Nightingale in that campaign, for her deeds shed a reflected lustre on her Alma Mater.

On October 4th, 1864, Pastor Fliedner, to use Miss Nightingale's words, " passed to his *glorious* rest." Almost his last words were: "As I look back upon my life, I appreciate how full it has been of blessings ; every heart-beat should have been gratitude and every breath praise."

Commenting upon his work, Miss Nightingale made this characteristic summary: "Pastor Fliedner began his work with two beds under a roof, not with a castle in the air, and Kaiserswerth is now diffusing its blessings and its deaconesses over almost every Protestant land."

CHAPTER VII

ENTERS KAISERSWERTH: A PLEA FOR DEACONESSES

An Interesting Letter—Description of Miss Nightingale when she entered Kaiserswerth—Testimonies to her Popularity—Impressive Farewell to Pastor Fliedner.

The travelled mind is the catholic mind educated from exclusiveness and egotism.—A. BRONSON ALCOTT.

WHEN Florence Nightingale entered the Deaconess Hospital at Kaiserswerth, the institution, if we count the first primitive penitentiary, had been in existence sixteen years. It already consisted of a hospital and training home for deaconesses, a seminary for infant-school teachers, a kindergarten, an orphan asylum, and a penitentiary, but was small compared with the extensive settlement of to-day. It was managed on very simple and primitive lines, and the nurses came almost entirely from the peasant class. The fashion of "lady" nurses was practically unknown. Deaconess Reichardt, the first sister enrolled in the institution, was still there at the time of Miss Nightingale's sojourn.

An interesting bit of autobiography regarding her Kaiserswerth days is given by Miss Nightingale in a letter preserved by the authorities of the British Museum. The letter was sent in reply to their request for a copy of the little history of Kaiserswerth which Miss Nightingale published after her return from the institution, and was hastily written in pencil. It is dated September 24th, 1897, from her house 10, South Street, Park Lane, and runs as follows :—

" MESSRS. DUBAU,—

" A gentleman called here yesterday from you, asking for a copy of my *Kaiserswerth* for, I believe, the British Museum.

" Since yesterday, a search has been instituted— but only two copies have been found, and one of those is torn and dirty. I send you the least bad-looking. You will see the date is 1851, and after the copies then printed were given away, I don't think I have ever thought of it.

" I was twice in training there myself. Of course, since then hospital and district nursing have made great strides. Indeed, district nursing has been invented.

" But never have I met with a higher love,

a purer devotion than there. There was no neglect.

"It was the more remarkable because many of the deaconesses had been only peasants—(none were gentlewomen when I was there).

"The food was poor—no coffee but bean coffee—no luxury but cleanliness.

"FLORENCE NIGHTINGALE."

One can imagine the flutter of excitement amongst the good simple deaconesses as they flitted about in their blue cotton gowns, white aprons, and prim muslin caps when it was known that an English lady of wealth and position had come to study amongst them. That such a woman should voluntarily undertake the duties of a hospital nurse, tending the sick poor with her own delicate hands, was at that time almost unprecedented. But the " Fraulein Nightingale " was quickly at home amongst her fellow-nurses and eager to learn all that the more experienced could teach her. She took both day and night nursing and entered into all branches of work. Garbed in the simple nurse's dress she moved through the wards of the hospital carrying the charm of her presence from bed to bed, as she was later to do at Scutari. Was there a difficult case to attend or an operation to be performed, the English Fraulein was sure to be on the scene.

At this period Miss Nightingale was in the strength and beauty of her early womanhood. She was tall, slight, and graceful, with abundance of brown hair neatly arranged on either side her high broad forehead, and had penetrating grey-blue eyes and a mouth which though firm indicated a sense of humour. The deaconesses, with whom she could talk in their own language, found her a diverting companion, for she had a sharp incisive wit, a certain homely shrewdness of expression, and a knowledge acquired not only from a superior education, but from a good experience of foreign travel. Above everything else she was distinguished by the power of adapting herself to circumstances, and she settled down to the humble fare and simple routine of life at Kaiserswerth as easily as though she had never known the refined luxuries of her father's house. It is small wonder that the sweet old faces of the retired deaconesses, living out the last spell of life in the Kaiserswerth Home of Rest, light up with smiles to-day at the mention of the "Fraulein Nightingale." Some can recall her gracious kindly presence amongst them, and all feel a community of satisfaction that her honoured name is enrolled among the sisterhood.

Sister Agnes Jones, the devoted and famous nurse of Liverpool, was at Kaiserswerth in 1860, and records the impression which Miss Nightingale's personality had left on the deaconesses. She wrote in a letter to a friend : " Their love for Miss Nightingale is so great ; she was only a few months there, but they so long to see her again. I was asking much about her ; such a loving and lovely womanly character hers must be, and so religious. Sister S. told me many of the sick remembered much of her teaching, and some died happily, blessing her for having led them to Jesus."

Although training in hospital work was Miss Nightingale's primary object in going to Kaiserswerth, she was deeply interested in all Pastor Fliedner's schemes for helping the poor in his parish, and did a good deal of what in these days would be termed " district visiting," along with Frau Fliedner. She also took a keen interest in the school and the teachers' seminary, and formed a warm friendship with Henrietta Frickenhaus, the first schoolmistress at Kaiserswerth, who was still in charge of the seminary, and had at that time trained four hundred candidates.

Pastor Fliedner had given up parish work to travel abroad and found deaconess institutions in various towns at the time when Miss Nightingale first came to Kaiserswerth, but they occasionally met, and during the latter part of her residence he was at home and took, as may be readily imagined, a deep interest in the training of so brilliant and dis-

tinguished a pupil. Mr. Sidney Herbert visited
Kaiserswerth during Miss Nightingale's probation,
and had therefore an opportunity of seeing the
efficient training of the lady who was later to be
his honoured coadjutor in hospital and nursing
reforms.

A very impressive scene took place when
Florence Nightingale left Kaiserswerth. The
present head of the institution, Pastor Düsselhoff,
tells me that his mother, the eldest daughter of
Pastor Fliedner, vividly recalls the scene to-day.
After bidding good-bye to the deaconesses, Miss
Nightingale bent her head to the pastor and asked
for his blessing. With hands resting on her head,
and face upturned to heaven, he prayed that her
sojourn at Kaiserswerth might bear precious fruit
and her great powers be dedicated to the service of
humanity. Then, repeating his usual formula—
" May God the Father, the Son, and the Holy
Ghost, three Persons in one God, bless you ; may
He stablish you in the Truth until death, and give
you hereafter the Crown of Life. Amen "—he sent
her forth dedicated to the service of the sick and
suffering. Little did he think what the magnitude
of that service was to be. Teacher and pupil were
not destined to meet again, but the good pastor
lived to hear the name of Florence Nightingale
resound through the world.

After Miss Nightingale's return home from her second sojourn at Kaiserswerth, she published in 1851 a booklet on the institution, and in the introduction gives some excellent advice to the girls of the time. Her remarks may seem a little out of date to-day, but are interesting as showing the desire for useful work which was beginning to actuate women of the leisured classes and which needed to be directed into fitting channels. There was then the great cry of the untrained. Women were longing for occupation, but few had received definite courses of training.

Miss Nightingale was at this period a pioneer of her sex and a decidedly " advanced " woman, but the desire for freedom of action was tempered by a naturally well-balanced nature. She put forward the plea on women's behalf that they should be encouraged to seek occupation and properly trained for their work. In *Kaiserswerth* she deals more particularly with the vocation of a nurse or deaconess, but as a prelude to the little work she refers to the position of women in her own century. There is " an old legend," she writes, " that the nineteenth century is to be the century of women," but she thinks that up to the present (1851) it has not been theirs. She magnanimously exempts man from blame. The fault has not been his, for " in no country has woman been given such freedom to cultivate her powers" as in England. "She [woman] is no longer called pedantic if her powers appear in conversation. The authoress is courted not shunned." Women, she thinks, have made extraordinary intellectual development, but as human beings cannot move two feet at once, except they jump, so while the intellectual foot of woman has made a step in advance, the practical foot has remained behind. "Woman," says Miss Nightingale, "stands askew. Her education for action has not kept pace with her education for acquirement. The woman of the eighteenth century was perhaps happier, when practice and theory were on a par, than her more cultivated sister of the nineteenth century. The latter wishes, but does not know how to do many things! The former, what she wished at least *that* she could do."

It appears that when Miss Nightingale was a young woman, the fashion for extolling the single girl as against her sister who had entered the bonds of matrimony was coming into vogue, but on this point our heroine was racily sincere. "It has become of late the fashion," she says, "to cry up 'old maids,' to inveigh against regarding marriage as the vocation of all women, to declare that a single life is as happy as a married one, if people would but think so. So is the air as good an element for fish as the water, if they did but know how to live in it.

Show us *how* to be single and we will agree.   But hitherto we have not found that young English-women have been convinced.   And we must confess that, *in the present state of things,* their horror of being 'old maids' seems justified . . . a life without love, and an activity without an aim, is horrible in idea and wearisome in reality."

Miss Nightingale does not touch on the point that the disparity between the numbers of the sexes makes singleness not a choice but a necessity to many women, and that in the interests of those who must remain unwed, training for a definite calling in life should be given to girls as well as to boys.

She goes on to speak of the longing of women for work and the *ennui* which results from the lack of it, and draws the picture of five or six daughters living in well-to-do houses with no other occupation than taking a class in a Sunday-school and of the middle-class girls who become burdensome to fathers and brothers.

She expends some characteristic witticisms on the young ladies who try to drive away *ennui* by a little parish visiting, and because of their want of know-ledge only succeed in demoralising the poor.   In evidence of this, Miss Nightingale tells the story that one day on entering a cottage which was usually neat and tidy she found everything upside down.

"La! now! why, miss," said the cottage woman

at her visitor's look of astonishment, "when the district-visiting ladies comes, if we didn't put everything topsy-turvy they would not give us anything."

"To be able to visit *well*," says Miss Nightingale, commenting upon the foregoing incident, "is one of the rarest accomplishments. But when attained, what a blessing to both visitors and visited!"

These remarks in regard to the work of women were by way of preliminary to introducing the subject of deaconesses. Miss Nightingale had returned from Kaiserswerth full of enthusiasm for the vocation of trained nurse and visitor to the poor, and was endeavouring to introduce the then highly novel subject to her young countrywomen as a way of getting rid of listlessness and *ennui*. That she felt the ground to be dangerous is shown by the detailed account of the connection of the office of a deaconess with the early Christian Church, which she deemed it necessary to give in order to allay the Protestant fear that a deaconess was a nun in disguise.

In these days, when women are actively employed in Church work and philanthropy, and when their assistance is welcomed by the clergy in parishes all over the land, it seems strange to find how cautiously Miss Nightingale recommended the office of deaconess. She labours through scholastic argu-

ments and cites the Fathers. St. Chrysostom
speaks of forty deaconesses at work in Constantinople in the fourth century. Holy women
of the order worked amongst the Waldensian,
Bohemian and Moravian Brotherhoods.   Luther
complained of the lack of deaconesses in his neighbourhood, adding, " Women have especial graces to
alleviate woe, and the words of women move the
human being more than those of men." Under
Queen Elizabeth, deaconesses were instituted into the
Protestant Church during public service. The Pilgrim
Fathers when first driven to Amsterdam and Leyden
carried their deaconesses with them, and Miss
Nightingale cites the improving example of the
Amsterdam deaconess who sat in her place at
church with a little birchen rod in her hand to
correct the children, and relates how she called
upon the young maidens for their services, when
they were sick, and she was " obeyed like a mother
in Israel."

She considers it clearly proved that before the
establishment of the order of sisters of mercy by
St. Vincent de Paul in 1633, the office of deaconess
had been recognised by all divisions of Christians,
and was therefore not borrowed from the Roman
Catholic Church. The reason why such sisterhoods
had not flourished among Protestants was owing
to the lack of preparatory schools and training

homes. This want had been supplied at the Kaiserswerth institution, and she proceeds to give a history of its foundation and growth. There she had found her ideal, and for the next few years her life was devoted to philanthropic and religious work. Military nursing had not as yet dawned upon her horizon.

CHAPTER VIII

A PERIOD OF WAITING

Visits the Sisters of St. Vincent de Paul in Paris—Illness—
Resumes Old Life at Lea Hurst and Embley—Interest in John
Smedley's System of Hydropathy—Mr. and Mrs. Sidney
Herbert's Philanthropies—Work at Harley Street Home for
Sick Governesses—Illness and Return Home.

They also serve who only stand and wait.—MILTON.

THREE years had yet to transpire before
Florence Nightingale was called to her great
life work. After leaving Kaiserswerth, she stayed
for a time on her way home with the Sisters of St.
Vincent de Paul in Paris. She was without religious
bigotry in the pursuit of knowledge, and sincerely
admired the devoted and unselfish work of this
Roman Catholic sisterhood. They were indeed sisters
of mercy, and the hospitals and schools of their
community had obtained world-wide renown. Their
institutions had the advantage over Kaiserswerth,
at that period, of being in long-established working
order. In Paris, too, Miss Nightingale found
opportunity for studying surgery in the hospitals.

The skill of the Paris surgeons stood remarkably high, and she could scarcely have had a better ground for observation than the French capital. With her good friends the sisters, too, Miss Nightingale visited the homes of the poor and made a minute inspection of their methods of organised charity.

While pursuing this interesting work, Miss Nightingale was taken ill. She had now a personal experience of the skill and tender care of the sisters, who nursed her back to convalesence.

As soon as she was able to travel, she returned to her family and completed her restoration to health in the beautiful surroundings of her well-loved homes of Embley Park and Lea Hurst. There she spent the ensuing months in her old work of quiet benevolence amongst the poor and infirm in the parishes, where her name was even then a household word. Added to her kindness of heart, which the people had long known, " Miss Florence " had now returned from " furren parts " with a knowledge of sick nursing which astounded the rustic mind. It was rumoured that she could set a broken leg better than the doctor, and had remedies for " rheumatiz " and lumbago which made old men feel young again, and as for her lotions for the eyes, " Why, they was enough to ruin the spectacle folk."

At this period the immediate vicinity of Miss

6

Nightingale's Derbyshire home was the scene of the labours of " Dr." John Smedley, the Father of Hydropathy and the founder of the now famous " Smedley's Hydropathic" at Matlock Bank. Although Miss Nightingale did not, I believe, specially ally herself with hydropathy, she has always been an advocate for the simple rules of health and diet as against the drug treatment. She could not fail to have been deeply interested in the experiments which good John Smedley and his mother were conducting practically at her own door, and they form a part of the environment which was shaping her mind at this period.

The old stone house in which John Smedley lived while he was experimenting still stands near the bottom of the steep road leading to Lea Hurst. It has been divided into three small dwellings, but the outside railings over which Mrs. Smedley used to hand her son's simple remedies to the villagers, and to the employees at Smedley's Mills, on the opposite side of the road, are still pointed out by old inhabitants. The hamlet was particularly good for pioneer work of this kind, because of the hundreds of workers, chiefly women and girls, from the surrounding countryside who obtained employment at Lea Mills. The Derbyshire quarries and smelting works in the vicinity also yielded further patients for treatment. In course of time John

Smedley started two free hospitals near his house, one for men and one for women, and the patients were subjected to the hydropathic regimen with such beneficial results that he started the hydropathic establishment known by his name at Matlock.

When at Embley, Miss Nightingale was much interested in the benevolent schemes of Mr. Sidney Herbert, afterwards Lord Herbert of Lea, and his accomplished and beautiful wife, who were friends and neighbours. The Herberts' residence, Wilton House, was a few miles from Embley on the Wiltshire border, and at this period they were engaged in the founding of a children's hospital, schools, and other philanthropic ventures, and were actively interested in schemes for the emigration of poor women. We shall, however, deal later with the very congenial friendship existing between Miss Nightingale and Lord and Lady Herbert of Lea.

As soon as Miss Nightingale had recovered her health she left the quiet surroundings of her country homes for a life of philanthropic activity in London. She was greatly interested in the Ragged School work of the Earl of Shaftesbury, and devoted the proceeds of her recently published booklet on Kaiserswerth, which had been printed by the inmates of the London Ragged Colonial Training School, to charitable objects.

In choosing a line of benevolent activity, Miss Nightingale was at this period actuated by a desire to help poor ladies, so many of whom were suffering silently and unheeded, and largely through their lack of proper training for remunerative callings. Reference has already been made to her common-sense plea that women should receive training to fit them for work, in her advocacy of a revival of the order of deaconesses. But while she sought to influence the girls of the future, Miss Nightingale made it a present duty to soothe and brighten the lives of poor ladies who had fallen helpless in the race of life. With this end in view she took in charge the Harley Street Home for Sick Governesses,* which was in a very unsatisfactory condition.

Much has been written on the underpaid and badly treated private governess in days gone by. Her woes, and sometimes her machinations, were the stock-in-trade of romancers. When a pretty young creature in cheap mourning appeared at the Grange as governess to the younger children, you might predict a proud, harsh mistress, troublesome and insulting pupils, and a broken heart by reason of the squire's son, almost to a certainty. But the novelist rarely followed the governess beyond the interesting age of youth and beauty ; if he had, there would have been sad tales to tell of friendless

* Now known as the Hospital for Invalid Gentlewomen.

old age, penury, and want. The Harley Street Home had been founded to help such, more particularly those who were in bad health. In this institution Miss Nightingale found a work which brought into active use the knowledge of sick nursing which she had been acquiring, gave a vent for her womanly benevolence, afforded a field for the exercise of her organising abilities, and proved a valuable preparation for what lay in the future.

The Home had been languishing through mismanagement and lack of funds, and its new superintendent set to work with characteristic method. She got donations from her friends, inspired old subscribers with a new confidence, and managed to get the institution on its feet again, but not without a serious strain of overwork.

A lady who visited her at this time speaks of the untiring labour which Miss Nightingale gave to the institution. "She was to be found," she writes, "in the midst of the various duties of a hospital—for the Home was largely a sanatorium —organising the nurses, attending to the correspondence, prescriptions, and accounts; in short, performing all the duties of a hard-working matron as well as largely financing the institution."

Miss Nightingale shut herself off entirely from outside society and only occasionally received her most intimate friends. Her assiduity bore fruit in the improved state of the Home, not only on its comfort which she brought to it. The task of dealing with sick and querulous women, embittered and rendered sensitive and exacting by the unfortunate circumstances of their lives, was not an easy one, but Miss Nightingale had a calm and cheerful spirit which could bear with the infirmities of the weak. And so she laboured on in the dull house in Harley Street summer and winter, bringing order and comfort out of a wretched chaos and proving a real friend and helper to the sick and sorrow-laden women. At length the strain proved too much for her delicate body, and she was compelled most reluctantly to resign her task.

Again she returned to Embley Park and Lea Hurst to recruit her health. When a few months later the supreme call of her life came and she was summoned to the work for which a special Providence seemed to have been preparing her from childhood, she was found ready.

CHAPTER IX

SIDNEY, LORD HERBERT OF LEA.

Gladstone on Lord Herbert—Early Life of Lord Herbert—His Mother—College Career—Enters Public Life—As Secretary for War—Benevolent Work at Salisbury—Lady Herbert—Friendship with Florence Nightingale—Again Secretary for War.

> Formed on the good old plan,
> A true and brave and downright honest man.
> WHITTIER.

> None knew thee but to love thee,
> None named thee but to praise,
> HALLECK.

" I WISH," wrote Gladstone to Richard Monckton-Milnes (afterwards Lord Houghton) in October, 1855, "that some one of the thousand who in prose justly celebrate Miss Nightingale would say a single word for the man of 'routine' who devised and projected her going—Sidney Herbert."

Acting on such distinguished advice I propose to attempt a slight account of the career and personality of this singularly attractive man, who was at the head of the War Office when Florence Nightingale and her staff of nurses were sent to the aid of the soldiers wounded in the Crimea. No *Life* of Lord Herbert of Lea has at the time of writing been published, although one is, I understand, in course of preparation. The name of Sidney Herbert is distinguished as that of the War Minister who, in defiance of official tradition, enlisted the devotion and organising power of women on behalf of our soldiery perishing in the pestilential hospitals of the East.

Sidney Herbert was born at Richmond in Surrey on September 16, 1810, and was the second son of George Augustus, eleventh Earl of Pembroke, by his second wife, Countess Catherine, only daughter of Count Woronzoff, Russian Ambassador to the British Court. His maternal uncle, Prince Michael Woronzoff, was a companion in arms of Wellington, and the founder of the prosperous era in the Crimea. Sidney Herbert's mother, though of Russian birth, was chiefly brought up and educated in this country, and owing to her father's official position, moved as a girl in the atmosphere of the Court. He owed much to her example and training. She is described as having been a woman of quick intelligence and sound judgment, of large generosity and noble bearing. Her husband, Lord Pembroke, died when their son Sidney was about seventeen, and her influence moulded his early manhood.

He was educated at Harrow under Dr. Butler, and

matriculated at Oriel College, Oxford, in 1828, where he was counted an elegant scholar and noted as a speaker at the Union Debating Society, when he matched his strength beside Gladstone, Roundell Palmer, and other distinguished young orators. Upon his entrance into public life, as M.P. for South Wiltshire in the first Reformed Parliament of 1832, Sidney Herbert was considered a graceful and accomplished young Tory.

Sir Robert Peel on taking office in 1834 offered Sidney Herbert a post in the Government, and it was characteristic of him that he refused the Lordship of the Treasury because the duties were slight, and accepted the laborious post of Secretary to the Board of Control, which he held during Peel's Administration. He returned to office with his old leader in 1841 as Secretary to the Admiralty. While holding that position Sidney Herbert set to work to reform the Naval School at Greenwich, which then contained some eight hundred boys and was the nursing-ground for the navy. While thus engaged he exhibited that administrative faculty which was later so conspicuously shown in his efforts on behalf of the sister service.

In 1845 he was transferred to the office of Secretary of War, with a seat in the Cabinet. He gave special attention to the regimental schools and introduced very necessary reforms in their management, and also instituted an inquiry into the state of the Royal Military Asylum at Chelsea. On the resignation of Sir Robert Peel's Ministry, Sidney Herbert left office, and his work of military reform remained in abeyance.

He remained out of office for six years, and during that period devoted himself largely to private philanthropy in the vicinity of his home, Wilton House, near Salisbury. He had married in 1846 Elizabeth, the daughter of General Aske A'Court and the niece of Lord Heytesbury, a young lady of singular beauty and charm, who entered most sympathetically into his many philanthropic enterprises, and herself instituted several benevolent schemes. She became the authoress of several books dealing with biography and travel.

Florence Nightingale was a frequent visitor at Wilton House and Mr. and Mrs. Sidney Herbert were amongst her dearest and most sympathetic friends. She took a great interest in the home for scrofulous children which they had founded and maintained at Mudiford in Hampshire, and was able to give much practical help in its management. Having heard from Miss Nightingale of a particular bath which she had seen employed with good effect at Kaiserswerth, Mr. Herbert procured the ingredients from that distant institution for use in the Mudiford home. One can readily imagine how useful her technical knowledge was to her friends in their various undertakings, and how congenial interests drew them more and more together.

Humanity in every form appealed to Mr. and Mrs. Sidney Herbert. They erected at Wilton a model lodging-house for agricultural labourers, and formulated schemes for the emigration of poor women. So actively interested were they in the latter that they frequently accompanied parties of emigrants on to the vessel to speed them on their way. Some of their later schemes were for the establishment of day-rooms and institutes in the rural districts around their county town of Salisbury.

Like Miss Nightingale, Sidney Herbert was a devoted worker in connection with the Established Church, and proved a generous benefactor to his diocese. He built at his own cost of £30,000 the magnificent church at Wilton, and presented a new rectory and grounds. He also built the new church at Bemerton in memory of his saintly kinsman, George Herbert, and gave liberally to the restoration of churches in the Salisbury diocese. He was a great supporter of missionary bishops. It has well been said of him that the " bede-role of his private charities would weary the patience of any reader." He was the founder of hospitals, the builder of churches, the maintainer of schools, and his right hand knew not what his left hand gave.

In social life Sidney Herbert was a fascinating personality, and might be described as a modern hero of chivalry. He was strikingly handsome, with a commanding figure and courtly manners. He appeared to possess every social advantage—high birth, a great estate, a beautiful wife and children, one of the happiest homes in England, many accomplishments, a ready address, a silvery voice, irresistible manners, and a rare power for making friends. It was said that men would give up to Sidney Herbert what they would grant to no one else. In his younger days Sidney Herbert was sneered at by Disraeli as a maker of " pretty speeches," but he later proved that there was grit behind the polished exterior of his personality.

He was also, as Gladstone described him, a " man of routine." His labours were unceasing ; he never spared himself, and gave up life and luxury for toil and trouble. His industry and power of organisation were remarkable. " Great as were the works of Lord Herbert," said Mr. Gladstone in referring to the army reforms which he executed after the Crimea, " there was something if possible still greater, and that was the character of Lord Herbert. . . . His gentleness combined with a modesty such as I, for one, never knew equalled in any station of life."

Such, then, was the perfect knight, the gallant

gentleman, under the stimulus of whose private friendship and official supervision and support Florence Nightingale entered upon the great work of her life.

In 1852 Sidney Herbert, after six years' retirement, again took office and became Secretary of War in Lord Aberdeen's Government. Immediately on his return to the War Office he began his schemes for army reform. He instituted classes for army school-masters, established industrial and infant schools in regiments, and also matured a plan for forming a board of examiners who should conduct all examinations for commissions by direct appointment or for promotion within the ranks of regimental officers. His plans were interrupted by the outbreak of the Crimean War.

CHAPTER X

THE CRIMEAN WAR AND CALL TO SERVICE

Tribute to Florence Nightingale by the Countess of Lovelace—
Outbreak of the Crimean War—Distressing Condition of the
Sick and Wounded—Mr. W. H. Russell's Letters to *The Times*
—Call for Women Nurses—Mr. Sidney Herbert's Letter to
Miss Nightingale—She offers her Services.

> The bullet comes—and either
> A desolate hearth may see;
> And God alone to-night knows where
> The vacant place may be.
>
> ADELAIDE PROCTER.

> Then, then a woman's low soft sympathy
> Comes like an angel's voice to teach us how to die.
>
> EDWIN ARNOLD.

BEFORE the more heroic elements in Florence Nightingale's character had been evoked by the events of the Crimean War, her intimate friends had begun to regard her as a woman for whom the future held some great destiny. This was strikingly shown in a poem by Ada, Countess of Lovelace, the daughter of Byron, who described the future heroine of the Crimea in a poem entitled *A Portrait from Life*. She draws the picture of her slender form, her "grave but large and lucid eye," her " peaceful, placid loveliness," refers to her love of books, her " soft, silvery voice " and delight in singing sacred songs—

> She walks as if on heaven's brink,
> Unscathed through life's entangled maze—

and in a concluding verse Lady Lovelace makes the following remarkable prophecy :—

> In future years in distant climes
>   Should war's dread strife its victims claim,
> Should pestilence, unchecked betimes,
>   Strike more than sword, than cannon maim,
> He who then reads these truthful rhymes
>   Will trace her progress to undying fame.

The " war's dread strife " which, in fulfilment of the poet's intuition, was to lift Florence Nightingale into " undying fame," began in the early spring of 1854. An outbreak of hostilities between Great Britain and Russia had been impending for some months. Russia made no reply to the ultimatum sent by Great Britain, and on March 27th, 1854, the Queen's Message to Parliament announced that the negotiations were broken off with Russia and she felt bound to give aid to the Sultan of Turkey. The following day, March 28th, Her Majesty's formal declaration of war was read amid scenes of excitement and enthusiasm from the steps of the Royal Exchange.

France was England's ally for the protection of

Turkey against Russian aggression, and vigorous preparations for the campaign proceeded on either side of the Channel.

A few days after the declaration of war, the English fleet, under the command of the gallant Sir Charles Napier, sailed for the Baltic, speeded on its way by thousands of cheering spectators and by the Queen and Prince Consort, who came in their yacht, the *Fairy*, to take leave of the officers and men. The eyes of elderly people still beam and brighten if one mentions this memorable sailing of the fleet for the Baltic. It was then forty years since Wellington had returned victorious from Waterloo, and the blood of the nation was up for another fight. Time had deadened the memory of the horrors and suffering which war entails : only a thirst for glory and conquest remained. The whole nation echoed the words of Napier to his men : "Lads, war is declared. We are to meet a bold and numerous enemy. Should they offer us battle, you know how to dispose of them. Should they remain in port, we must try to get at them. Success depends upon the quickness and decision of your fire. Lads, sharpen your cutlasses, and the day is ours."

In due time tidings came of the victory of Alma. But alas for the brave "lads," for the news came too of the wounded lying uncared for, the sick

SIDNEY, LORD HERBERT OF LEA.

[*To face p.* 96.

untended, the dying unconsoled. In the midst of the nation's rejoicings at victory a cry of indignation arose on behalf of her soldiers.

There had been gross neglect in the war administration, and the commissariat had broken down. Food, clothing, and comforts had been stowed in the hold of vessels beneath ammunition and could not be got at when required, while other stores rotted on the shores of the Bosphorus while awaiting delivery. Not only were food and clothing lamentably scarce, but the surgeons were often without even lint and bandages, to say nothing of other requisites for ambulance and hospital work. " The commonest accessories of a hospital are wanting," wrote *The Times* war correspondent, William Howard Russell, " there is not the least attention paid to decency or cleanliness, the stench is appalling ; . . . and for all I can observe, the men die without the least effort to save them. There they lie just as they were let gently down on the ground by the poor fellows, the comrades, who brought them on their backs from the camp with the greatest tenderness, but who are not allowed to remain with them."

The staff of army doctors was insufficient to deal with the wounded, which after the battles of Alma and Inkerman accumulated in appalling numbers, and there were no nurses except the untrained

7

male orderlies, many of whom were only a little less sick than those whom they were supposed to tend.   There was no woman's hand to soothe the fevered brow, administer nourishment, perform the various little offices for the sick, and console the dying.

The untended and uncared-for state of our own soldiers was rendered more conspicuous by the humane system which prevailed amongst our French allies   In camp and hospital sisters of mercy glided from stretcher to stretcher, and from bed to bed, administering food and help to the wounded.   In their convent homes all over France they had been trained in the work of sick nursing, and their holy vocations did not prevent them from going forth to the scene of battle.

Soon came the appeal which roused Englishwomen and their country to a sense of duty, and the honour of uttering it belongs to Mr. (later Sir) William Howard Russell, the veteran war correspondent, then representing *The Times* at the seat of war.   After describing the suffering which he had witnessed amongst the sick and wounded soldiers, he raised the clarion note :—

"Are there no devoted women amongst us, able and willing to go forth to minister to the sick and suffering soldiers of the East in the hospitals at Scutari ?   Are none of the daughters of England, at this extreme hour of need, ready for such a work of mercy? . . . France has sent forth her sisters of mercy unsparingly, and they are even now by the bedsides of the wounded and the dying, giving what woman's hand alone can give of comfort and relief. . . . Must we fall so far below the French in self-sacrifice and devotedness, in a work which Christ so signally blesses as done unto Himself? 'I was sick and ye visited Me.'"

The wives of officers at the seat of war sent home harrowing accounts of the distress amongst the wounded and the futility of their own efforts to cope with it. "Could you see the scenes that we are daily witnessing," wrote one lady to her friends, "you would indeed be distressed. I am still in barracks, but the sick are now lying in the passages, within a few yards of my room. Every corner is filled up with the sick and wounded. However, I am enabled to do some little good, and I hope I shall not be obliged to leave just yet. My time is occupied in cooking for the wounded. Three doors from me there is an officer's wife who devotes herself to cooking for the sick. There are no female nurses here, which decidedly there ought to be. The French have sent fifty sisters of mercy, who, we need hardly say, are devoted to the work. We are glad to hear that some efforts are being made at home."

The reason why female nurses had not been sent out at the beginning of the war was explained by the Duke of Newcastle, Secretary of State for War, when he gave evidence before Mr. Roebuck's Commission, which sat in 1855 to inquire into the conduct of the campaign, and it is of interest to quote the evidence as it so exactly explains the train of circumstances which led to Miss Nightingale's appointment. Asked " When did you first determine on sending nurses to Scutari ? " the Duke replied :—

"The employment of nurses in the hospital at Scutari was mooted in this country, at an early stage before the army left this country, but it was not liked by the military authorities. It had been tried on former occasions. The class of women employed as nurses had been very much addicted to drinking, and they were found even more callous to the sufferings of soldiers in hospitals than men would have been. Subsequently, in consequence of letters in the public press, and of recommendations made by gentlemen who had returned to this country from Scutari, we began to consider the subject of employing nurses. The difficulty was to get a lady to take in hand the charge of superintending and directing a body of nurses. After having seen one or two I almost despaired of the practicability of the matter until Mr. Sidney Herbert suggested Miss Nightingale, with whom he had been previously acquainted, for the work, and that lady eventually undertook it."

Here we have the difficulty of the situation revealed. The nurses hitherto employed in military hospitals had been of a coarse, low character. They had neither education, training, nor sympathy for their work. To compare them to "Sairey Gamp" would be an insult to that immortal lady's memory, for she had her good points and a certain professional knowledge and respectability to maintain, while the average soldiers' nurse was little more than a mere camp follower. On the other hand were the good, kindly ladies who felt that they had a vocation for nursing, but, alas! were absolutely devoid of training and incapable of organising and controlling subordinates. Between these two impossible classes the war authorities had come to the conclusion that the army in the Crimea would be better without female nurses.

The rousing appeal to the women of the country from Mr. Russell, *The Times* correspondent, already quoted, had the effect of inundating the authorities with applications from women of all classes who, moved by the harrowing accounts of the suffering soldiers, were anxious to go out as nurses. The offers of help were bewilderingly numerous, but there was no organisation and no leader.

Mr. Sidney Herbert was at the head of the War
Department, and, in the midst of the excitement
and general futility of things, his thoughts naturally
turned to his honoured friend, Florence Nightingale.
In his opinion she was the " one woman " in England
who was fitted by position, knowledge, training, and
character to organise a nursing staff and take them
out to the aid of the suffering soldiers. He had,
as we have already seen, an intimate personal
knowledge of Miss Nightingale, was aware of the
thorough and systematic study which she had for
some years been giving to hospital nursing at home
and abroad, and he knew also of the organising skill
which she had been recently displaying in the
management of the Harley Street Home for Sick
Governesses. Mrs. Herbert, a lady of great insight
and knowledge, felt with her husband that if Miss
Nightingale could be induced to undertake the
hazardous task of organising a band of military
nurses, the success of the scheme would be ensured.

But Mr. and Mrs. Herbert had a natural
hesitation in making such a suggestion. It was
tantamount to asking their dear friend to go out
with her life in her hands, as well as to brave the
adverse criticism of a large number of short-sighted
but well-meaning people, who would lift up their
hands in protest at the idea of a lady of birth and
breeding going out to nurse the common soldier.

Poor " Tommy " had a worse character then than now.

It was clear to Mr. Herbert that if Miss Nightingale were to be asked to undertake this work, she must be placed in an undisputed position of authority and supported by the Government. Everything depended on having a recognised head. To allow bands of lady nurses to start for the seat of war, each carrying out their pet and immature notions on hospital work, would have been futile and useless. To send them to Scutari and place them under the control of the authorities then in charge of the hospital, would have defeated the chief object of the plan, which was to reform and amend the existing order of nursing prevailing at the hospital. Neither was it likely that so shrewd and capable a woman as Miss Nightingale would consent to organise a new nursing system—for it practically amounted to that—unless she was guaranteed a position of undisputed authority. How necessary that was to the success of the enterprise after events fully proved.

Fortunately, Sidney Herbert was a statesman in a position to influence his colleagues in the Government, and his recommendation of Miss Nightingale as a lady fully qualified to perform the task of Superintendent of Nurses for the Crimea was received with approval, and indeed with a sense of

relief. Here was the woman whom distraught
Ministers had been vainly looking for amidst the
motley throng of the unfit. When things were so
far arranged, Sidney Herbert addressed the following
letter to his friend :—

"*October 15th, 1854.*

"Dear Miss Nightingale,—

"You will have seen in the papers that
there is a great deficiency of nurses at the hospital
of Scutari. The other alleged deficiencies—namely,
of medical men, lint, sheets, etc.—must, if they ever
existed, have been remedied ere this, as the number
of medical officers with the army amounted to one
to every ninety-five men in the whole force, being
nearly double what we have ever had before; and
thirty more surgeons went out there three weeks
ago, and must by this time, therefore, be at Constantinople. A further supply went on Monday,
and a fresh batch sail next week. As to medical
stores, they have been sent out in profusion, by
the ton weight—fifteen thousand pairs of sheets,
medicine, wine, arrowroot in the same proportion;
and the only way of accounting for the deficiency at
Scutari, if it exists, is that the mass of the stores
went to Varna, and had not been sent back when
the army left for the Crimea, but four days would
have remedied that.

" In the meanwhile, stores are arriving, but the deficiency of female nurses is undoubted ; none but male nurses have ever been admitted to military hospitals. It would be impossible to carry about a large staff of female nurses with an army in the field. But at Scutari, having now a fixed hospital, no military reason exists against the introduction, and I am confident they might be introduced with great benefit, for hospital orderlies must be very rough hands, and most of them, on such an occasion as this, very inexperienced ones. I receive numbers of offers from ladies to go out, but they are ladies who have no conception of what a hospital is, nor of the nature of its duties ; and they would, when the time came, either recoil from the work or be entirely useless, and consequently, what is worse, entirely in the way ; nor would those ladies probably even understand the necessity, especially in a military hospital, of strict obedience to rule. . . ."

Mr. Sidney Herbert then proceeds to name certain people who were anxious to organise and send out nurses, but about whose capability for the work he is in doubt. The letter then continues :—

" There is but one person in England that I know of who would be capable of organising and superintending such a scheme, and I have been several times on the point of asking you hypothetically if, supposing the attempt were made,

you would undertake to direct it. The selection
of the rank and file of nurses would be difficult—
no one knows that better than yourself. The
difficulty of finding women equal to a task after
all full of horror, and requiring, besides knowledge
and goodwill, great knowledge and great courage,
will be great ; the task of ruling them and introducing system among them great, and not the
least will be the difficulty of making the whole
work smoothly with the medical and military
authorities out there. This it is which makes
it so important that the experiment should be
carried out by one with administrative capacity and
experience.

" A number of sentimental enthusiastic ladies
turned loose in the hospital at Scutari would probably, after a few days, be *mises à la porte* by
those whose business they would interrupt, and
whose authority they would dispute. My question
simply is, Would you listen to the request to go
out and supervise the whole thing ? You would,
of course, have plenary authority over all the nurses,
and I think I could secure you the fullest assistance
and co-operation from the medical staff, and you
would also have an unlimited power of drawing
on the Government for whatever you think requisite
for the success of your mission. . . .

" I do not say one word to press you," continues

Mr. Sidney Herbert, and then proceeds to pay a tribute to Miss Nightingale's capabilities for filling a public post at an hour of crisis such as no responsible Minister of a Government had ever paid to a woman before, or indeed since.

"I must not conceal from you," he continues, "that upon your decision will depend the ultimate success or failure of the plan. Your own personal qualities, your knowledge, and your power of administration, and, among greater things, your rank and position in society, give you advantages in such a work which no other person possesses. If this succeeds, an enormous amount of good will be done now, and to persons deserving everything at our hands ; and which will multiply the good to all time.

"I hardly like to be sanguine as to your answer. If it were yes, I am certain the Bracebridges would go with you, and give you all the comforts you would require, and which her [Mrs. Bracebridge's] society and sympathy only could give you. I have written very long, for the subject is very near my heart. Liz [Mrs. Sidney Herbert] is writing to our mutual friend Mrs. Bracebridge, to tell her what I am doing. I go back to town to-morrow morning. Shall I come to you between three and five? Will you let me have a line at the War Office, to let me know?

"There is one point which I have hardly a right to touch upon, but I trust you will pardon me. If you were inclined to undertake the great work, would Mr. and Mrs. Nightingale consent? The work would be so national, and the request made to you proceeding from the Government, your position would ensure the respect and consideration of every one, especially in a service where official rank carries so much weight. This would secure you any attention or comfort on your way out there, together with a complete submission to your orders. I know these things are a matter of indifference to you, except as far as they may further the great object you may have in view, but they are of importance in themselves, and of every importance to those who have a right to take an interest in your personal position and comfort. I know you will come to a right and wise decision. God grant it may be one in accordance with my hopes.

　　　　"Believe me, dear Miss Nightingale,
　　　　　　"Ever yours,
　　　　　　　　"SIDNEY HERBERT."

Meantime the "one woman in all England" deemed worthy of this high trust was in the quietude of her country home pondering over the stirring words of Mr. Russell, *The Times* correspondent : " Are there no devoted women amongst us, able and willing to go forth to minister to the sick and suffering soldiers in the hospitals of Scutari ? " Each morning the newspapers revealed fresh sufferings and privations amongst the stricken soldiers, and the cries for help grew more importunate. Florence Nightingale was not the woman to listen in vain, and ere the sun had faded away behind the beech-trees on that memorable 15th of October, she had written to Mr. Sidney Herbert offering her services in the hospitals at Scutari.

Her letter crossed that of Mr. Herbert, of which she was in complete ignorance. The unique circumstance gives a rounded completeness to the call of Florence Nightingale which came as the voice of God speaking through her tender woman's heart.

CHAPTER XI

PREPARATION AND DEPARTURE FOR SCUTARI.

Public Curiosity Aroused—Description of Miss Nightingale in the Press—Criticism—She Selects Thirty-Eight Nurses—Departure of the "Angel Band"—Enthusiasm of Boulogne Fisherwomen—Arrival at Scutari.

> Lo, what gentillesse these women have,
> If we coude know it for our rudenesse !
> How busie they be us to keepe and save,
> Both in hele, and also in sickenesse !
> And always right sorrie for our distresse,
> In every manner; thus shew thy routhe,
> That in hem is al goodnesse and trouthe.
>
> CHAUCER.

IT is characteristic of Miss Nightingale's method and dispatch that only a week elapsed from the day on which she made her great resolve to go to the help of the wounded soldiers until she had her first contingent of nurses in marching order. She was a "general" who had no parleying by the way, but worked straight for her ultimate object, and she possessed also the rare faculty of inspiring others to follow her lead. Her attention was now concentrated on procuring the right kind of nurses to accompany her to the hospital at Scutari.

Her mission was duly proclaimed from the War Office in an official intimation that "Miss Nightingale, a lady with greater practical experience of hospital administration and treatment than any other lady in this country," had undertaken the noble and arduous work of organising and taking out nurses for the soldiers. *The Times* also notified that "Miss Nightingale had been appointed by Government to the office of Superintendent of Nurses at Scutari," and subscriptions for the relief of the soldiers were solicited.

Lady Canning, writing on October 17th, 1854, immediately after Miss Nightingale's appointment was made known, gave the following interesting description of her quiet demeanour in the midst of the general excitement : " You will be glad to hear that Government sends out a band of nurses to Scutari, and Miss Nightingale is to lead them. Her family have consented, and no one is so well fitted as she is to do such work—she has such nerve and skill, and is so gentle and wise and quiet. Even now she is in no bustle or hurry, though so much is on her hands, and such numbers of people volunteer services."

The public naturally asked the question, " Who is Miss Nightingale ? " and were answered by a descriptive and biographic account in *The Examiner*, which was repeated by *The Times*. One feels that the account must have appeared startling in days before attention had been given to the Higher Education of women, and when Girton and Newnham were not even dreams of the future. It ran that Miss Nightingale was " a young lady of singular endowments both natural and acquired. In a knowledge of the ancient languages and of the higher branches of mathematics, in general art, science, and literature, her attainments are extraordinary. There is scarcely a modern language which she does not understand, and she speaks French, German, and Italian as fluently as her native English. She has visited and studied all the various nations of Europe, and has ascended the Nile to its remotest cataract. Young (about the age of our Queen), graceful, feminine, rich, popular, she holds a singularly gentle and persuasive influence over all with whom she comes in contact. Her friends and acquaintances are of all classes and persuasions, but her happiest place is at home, in the centre of a very large band of accomplished relatives, and in simplest obedience to her admiring parents."

The last clause would satisfy apprehensive people that a young lady of such unusual attainments was not a " revolting daughter."

Another and more intimate description of Miss

Nightingale at this period reveals to us the true and tender womanhood which learning had left untouched. " Miss Nightingale is one of those whom God forms for great ends. You cannot hear her sav a few sentences—no, not even look at her,

MR. *PUNCH S* CARTOON OF THE " LADY-BIRDS."

without feeling that she is an extraordinary being. Simple, intellectual, sweet, full of love and benevolence, she is a fascinating and perfect woman. She is tall and pale. Her face is exceedingly lovely ; but better than all is the soul's glory that shines through every feature so exultingly. Nothing can

8

be sweeter than her smile. It is like a sunny day in summer."

The euphonious name of the lady nurse who had thus suddenly risen into fame was quickly caught by the populace, and the nurses selected to accompany her were dubbed the "nightingales," and there was much pleasantry about their singing. Mr. *Punch* slyly surmised that some of the "dear nightingales" going to nurse the sick soldiers would "in due time become ringdoves." A cartoon showed a hospital ward with the male inmates beaming with content as the lady-birds hovered about them. Another illustration depicted a bird, with the head of a nurse, flying through the air carrying by one claw a jug labelled "Fomentation, Embrocation, Gruel." It was entitled "The Jug of the Nightingale."

Punch's poet contributed "The Nightingale's Song to the Sick Soldier," which became a popular refrain, and is worthy of quotation :—

Listen, soldier, to the tale of the tender nightingale,
    'Tis a charm that soon will ease your wounds so cruel,
Singing medicine for your pain, in a sympathetic strain,
    With a jug, jug, jug of lemonade or gruel.

Singing bandages and lint; salve and cerate without stint,
    Singing plenty both of liniment and lotion,
And your mixtures pushed about, and the pills for you served out,
    With alacrity and promptitude of motion.

Singing light and gentle hands, and a nurse who under-
   stands
   How to manage every sort of application,
From a poultice to a leech; whom you haven't got to
   teach
   The way to make a poppy fomentation.

Singing pillow for you, smoothed; smart and ache and
   anguish smoothed,
   By the readiness of feminine invention;
Singing fever's thirst allayed, and the bed you've tumbled
   made,
   With a cheerful and considerate attention.

Singing succour to the brave, and a rescue from the
   grave,
   Hear the nightingale that's come to the Crimea,
'Tis a nightingale as strong in her heart as in her song,
   To carry out so gallant an idea.

While there was a large majority to wish God-
speed to the enterprise, there were also many people
who considered it an improper thing for women to
nurse in a military hospital, while others thought it
nonsense for young ladies to attempt "to nurse
soldiers when they did not even yet know what it
was to nurse a baby." Others predicted that no
woman could stand the strain of work in an Eastern
hospital, that the scheme would prove futile, and all
the nurses be invalided home after a month's
experience.

The undertaking was so new, and so much at
variance with English custom and tradition, that

criticism was to be expected.   But Florence Nightingale was one of those lofty souls who listen to the voice within, and take little heed of the voices without.   It was for her to break down the "Chinese wall" of prejudices, religious, social, and professional, and establish a precedent for all time.

In the midst of the pleasantries, satire, and condemnation she placidly pursued the work of organising her band, having indefatigable assistants in Mr. and Mrs. Sidney Herbert.   Applications were made for volunteer nurses to the few nursing institutions which existed, and advertisements were put in *The Record* and *The Guardian*.   A bewildering number of fair applicants besieged the War Office, and Sidney Herbert was driven to make a little proclamation to the effect that "many ladies whose generous enthusiasm prompts them to offer services as nurses are little aware of the hardships they would have to encounter, and the horrors they would have to witness.   Were all accepted who offer," he added with a touch of grim humour, "I fear we should have not only many indifferent nurses, but many hysterical patients."

This astute Minister was very cautious about the admission of society ladies in the guise of amateur nurses into the military hospital.   He managed things with a stricter hand than did the authorities during the South African War, as illustrated by the story of a soldier in the Capetown Hospital who, when a visiting lady asked if he would like her to wash his face, replied, " Excuse me, miss, but I've already promised fourteen ladies as they shall wash my face!"

The first appeal for nurses did not bring satisfactory applicants. Kind, generous, and sympathetic women volunteered by the score, but Miss Nightingale and her friends felt that they were dealing with a crisis of urgency. There was no time to start ambulance classes and train candidates. It was an imperative necessity that the nurses should start without delay, and therefore they must have been already trained for the work. In the emergency Miss Nightingale applied to both Protestant and Roman Catholic institutions for volunteers. This caused a good deal of adverse criticism. The " No Popery " cry was raised, and zealous clerics inveighed against Miss Nightingale as a Puseyite who was bent on perverting the British soldier to papacy. She certainly was at the time more engaged with the bodily than with the spiritual needs of the soldiers. Nurses were required, not religious instructors.

With some of the Protestant institutions a difficulty arose in respect to the rule of strict obedience to Miss Nightingale as the Superintendent appointed by the Government. These institutions were unwilling that their members should be separated from home control. Miss Nightingale and her advisers remained firm on this point. Strict obedience was the pivot upon which the organisation would have to work, if it was to be successful. The military nurse, like the military man, must render obedience to her superior officer. The St. John's House, one of the most important of the Protestant sisterhood, stood out for a day or two, but finally yielded the point.

The Roman Catholic bishop at once agreed to the regulations laid down, and signed a paper agreeing that the sisters of mercy joining the expedition should give entire obedience to Miss Nightingale, and that they should not enter into religious discussion except with the soldiers of their own faith. Mutual arrangement was made that the Roman Catholic sisters should attend on the soldiers of their own faith, and the Protestant sisters on those of their faith.

The position was later defined by Mr. Sidney Herbert to allay the agitation which prevailed after the band had set forth. He said : " The Roman Catholic bishop has voluntarily, and in writing, released the benevolent persons who were previously under his control from all subjection to himself. Englishmen may have the pleasure of feeling that a number of kind-hearted British women, differing in faith, but wishing to do practical good, are gone in one ship, as one corps, with one aim, without any compromise of our national Protestantism. . . . Thirty-eight nurses on their way to Scutari are truer successors of the Apostles shipwrecked at Melita than an equal number of cardinals. May the war teach men many such lessons."

The thirty-eight nurses selected to accompany Miss Nightingale as the first contingent were made up of fourteen Church of England sisters, taken from St. John's House and Miss Sellon's Home ; ten Roman Catholic sisters of mercy ; three nurses selected by Lady Maria Forrester, who had first formed a plan for sending nurses to Scutari ; and eleven selected from among miscellaneous applicants. Miss Nightingale's friends, Mr. and Mrs. Bracebridge of Atherstone Hall, and a clergyman and courier accompanied the expedition. It started from London on the evening of October 21st, 1854.

Our heroine has ever been one of those who shunned the glare of publicity, and it was characteristic of her that she set forth with her devoted band under cover of night. Only a few relations and friends stood on the platform of the terminus on that October evening when Florence Nightingale bade farewell to home and kindred and started on her great mission, the magnitude and difficulty of which she had yet to discover. Quietly dressed

in black, plain as a Quakeress, she was yet a striking
figure.   As the last hand-shake was given and the
last farewells said her beautiful face retained its
calm demeanour and was illumined by a sweet smile.
Ever thoughtful for others, her chief wish was to
spare her nearest and dearest, who had yielded a
hesitating consent to her undertaking, from anxiety.
None knew better than herself the perils which lay
in those far-off Eastern hospitals.

Early next morning the " Angel Band," as Kinglake so beautifully termed Miss Nightingale and
her nurses, landed at Boulogne, where a reception
awaited them which was in marked contrast to the
quiet and almost secret departure from London the
night before.   France was our ally ; her sons had
fallen in the recent battle of the Alma beside our own,
and here was a band of English sisters, Protestant
and Roman Catholic, united in a common errand
of mercy passing through her land to the relief of
the sick and wounded.   It was a circumstance to
arouse French enthusiasm, and when Miss Nightingale
and her nurses stepped ashore they were met by
a stalwart company of Boulogne fishwives, a merry
and picturesque band in snowy caps and gay
petticoats, who seized trunks and bags and almost
fought for the privilege of carrying the luggage
of *les sœurs* to the railway station.   They would
accept no pay, not *a sou,* and they bustled along

with their brawny arms swinging to straps and
handles, or with boxes hoisted on their broad backs,
chattering of "Pierre" or of "Jacques" out at
the war, and praying the *bon Dieu* that if he
suffered the sisters might tend him. The tears
streamed down many of the old and weather-beaten
cheeks when they said adieu. They claimed but
one reward, a shake of the hand, and then as the
train steamed out of the station they waved their
hands and cried *Vive les sœurs !*

They proceeded to Paris and made a passing stay
at the mother-house of the sisters of St. Vincent
de Paul, where Miss Nightingale was no stranger.
The good sisters were overwhelmed with joy to
receive her, and delighted to have the opportunity
of entertaining the company. Before leaving Paris
Miss Nightingale called on her friend Lady Canning,
who, in a letter, October 24th, 1854, says : "To-day
we are appointed to go to St. Cloud, and I have
had to rush about after bonnets, etc. It is horrid
to be given to frivolities just now, when one is
hearing all the horrors from the Crimea, and in the
expectation of more. . . . Miss Nightingale came to
see me—very happy and stout-hearted, and with an
ample stock of nurses." When, after a short rest
in Paris, Miss Nightingale and her band set out
for Marseilles, the port of embarkation, they met
with the utmost attention as they travelled. Porters

declined to be tipped and hotel proprietors would make no charges. It was an honour to serve *les bon^nes sœurs*.

At Marseilles they embarked for Constantinople in the *Vectis*, a steamer of the Peninsular line. Alas! the elements showed no more favour to the "Angel Band" than they did to St. Paul in the same seas. The passage was a terrible one. A hurricane blew straight against the *Vectis* in the Mediterranean, and for a time the ship was in danger. The company reached Malta on October 31st, and after a brief stay set sail for Scutari. Miss Nightingale arrived at the scene of her labours on November 4th, the day before the battle of Inkerman. What that victory meant in the tale of suffering and wounded men even the hospital authorities then formed no adequate conjecture. Never surely did a band of women arriving in an unknown land meet such a gigantic task.

The sufferers already in hospital had heard of the coming of the sisters, but the news seemed too good to be true, and when Miss Nightingale went her first round of the wards, accompanied by members of her devoted band, "Tommy's" heart was full. One poor fellow burst into tears as he cried, "I can't help it, I can't indeed, when I see them. Only think of English women coming out here to nurse us! It seems so homelike and comfortable."

CHAPTER XII

THE LADY-IN-CHIEF.

The Barrack Hospital—Overwhelming Numbers of Sick and Wounded—General Disorder—Florence Nightingale's "Commanding Genius"—The Lady with the Brain—The Nurses' Tower—Influence over Men in Authority.

> A perfect woman, nobly planned,
> To warn, to comfort and command ;
> And yet a spirit still and bright,
> With something of an angel light.
>
> WORDSWORTH.

THE official position which the Government had accorded Miss Nightingale was Superintendent of the Nursing Staff in the East, and the title by which she eventually became known was that of Lady-in-Chief.

Her control extended over the nursing staffs of all the hospitals, some eight in number, in which our wounded soldiers were placed on the Bosphorus and the Levantine. The first and chief scene of Miss Nightingale's personal ministrations, however, was the great Barrack Hospital at Scutari, lent to the British Government by the Turkish authorities.

It was beautifully situated on a hill overlooking the glittering waters of the Bosphorus, and commanded a view of the fair city of Constantinople, with its castellated walls, marble palaces, and domes, rising picturesquely on the horizon. No more enchanting prospect could have been desired than that which met the Lady-in-Chief when she reached Scutari, the "silver city," held in such veneration by the Turks. The town seemed placed in a perfect Garden of Eden, and the lovely blue of the Eastern sky enhanced the beauty of the scene.

The Barrack Hospital was a fine handsome building, forming an immense quadrangle with a tower at each corner. An idea of its size may be gathered from the fact that each side of the quadrangle was nearly a quarter of a mile long. It was estimated that twelve thousand men could be exercised in the central court. Galleries and corridors, rising story above story, surrounded three sides of the building, and, taken continuously, were four miles in extent. The building and position were alike good, but the interior of the hospital, as Miss Nightingale soon discovered, was a scene of filth, pestilence, misery, and disorder impossible to describe. On either side the endless corridors the wounded men lay closely packed together without the commonest decencies or necessaries of life.

After being disembarked at the ferry below the hospital from the vessels which brought them from the battlefields of the Crimea, the wounded men either walked or were dragged or carried up the hill to the hospital. Surgical, fever, and even cholera cases came along the road together in one long stream of suffering humanity.

THE BARRACK HOSPITAL AT SCUTARI.

Several days had elapsed since the men left the battlefield, and the majority had not had their wounds dressed or their fractured limbs set. The agony and misery of the poor fellows in this un-tended and often starving state can be well imagined. And how their hearts sank when they at length reached the hospital, where at least they expected food and comfort. Alas! there was little provision of any kind for the sufferers. Nolan, in his history of the campaign, says that in these early months of the war " there were no vessels for water or utensils of any kind ; no soap, towels, or cloths, no hospital clothes ; the men lying in their uniforms, stiff with gore and covered with filth to a degree and of a kind no one could write about ; their persons covered with vermin, which crawled about the floors and walls of the dreadful den of dirt, pestilence, and death to which they were consigned.

" Medical assistance would naturally be expected by the invalid as soon as he found himself in a place of shelter, but many lay waiting for their turn until death anticipated the doctor. The medical men toiled with unwearied assiduity, but their numbers were inadequate to the work." Invalids were set to take care of invalids and the dying nursed the dying.

It was a heart-breaking experience for the Lady-in-Chief when she made her first round of the wards at Scutari. The beds were reeking with infection and the " sheets," she relates, " were of canvas, and so coarse that the wounded men begged to be left in their blankets. It was indeed impossible to put men in such a state of emaciation into those sheets. There was no bedroom furniture of *any* kind, and only empty beer or wine bottles for candlesticks."

In addition to the miseries entailed by overcrowding, the men lying on the floors of the corridors were tormented by vermin and their limbs attacked by rats as they lay helpless in their pain.

The immediate surroundings of the hospital were a hotbed of pestilence ; Miss Nightingale counted six dogs lying under the windows in a state of decomposition. Add to this that in this vast caravanserai of wounded, sick, and dying men there was no proper provision for washing, no kitchens, culinary conveniences, or cooks suitable for hospital needs, and no sanitation, and some conception may be formed of the Augean stable which the Lady-in-Chief and her nurses had to cleanse, and the chaos out of which order was to be brought.

It is not altogether surprising that the doctors and hospital authorities did not immediately welcome the very unique band of sisters who had come to their assistance. These already overwrought gentlemen were disposed to think that the ladies would prove a greater hindrance than help. In those days it was regarded as unavoidable that a soldier should suffer, and humanitarian attempts to lessen the sufferings were considered sentimental and effeminate.

Possibly some of the younger medical men thought that the rats which infested the hospital would prove the needed scare to the newly arrived nurses. Of course it was held that the most strong-minded women would fly at the approach of a mouse :

what therefore would be the effect of a rat? But
this idea was dispelled when it was known that the
Lady-in-Chief had fearlessly dislodged a rat from
above the bed of one of the nurses with an umbrella.
The sheds where the sisters sorted the stores were
over-run with the pests. "Our home rats," said
one of them, "would run if you 'hushed' them;
but you might 'hush' away, and the Scutari rats
would not take the least notice."

Only twenty-four hours after the arrival of Miss
Nightingale at Scutari the wounded from the battle
of Inkerman began to arrive in appalling numbers,
and soon every inch of room in the General and
in the Barrack Hospitals was filled with sufferers.
Many of the men had indeed no other resting-place
than the muddy ground outside. The Lady-in-
Chief had had no time to initiate reform, collect
stores, or get any plans for the relief of the patients
into working order before this fearful avalanche
of wounded soldiery came upon her.

It was the testing moment of her life. Had
Florence Nightingale failed at this crisis in personal
endurance, or in power to inspire her subordinates
with a like courage, her mission would have sunk
into a benevolent futility. She and her nurses might
have run hither and thither smoothing pillows,
administering gruel, and doing other kind and
womanly service, but grateful as that would be to

BOULOGNE FISHERWOMEN CARRYING THE LUGGAGE OF MISS NIGHTINGALE AND HER NURSES.

[To face p. 128.

the poor fellows in their extreme misery, it would not have remedied the root of the evil. The Lady-in-Chief had to look beyond the present moment, though not neglectful of its demands, to the more important future, and institute a system of nursing reform which should make such scenes as she now witnessed impossible. It was her ability to do this which lifted Florence Nightingale into such a supreme position.

The attention and praises bestowed on her during the Crimean period roused a little jealousy and resentment in some quarters. Other women engaged in nursing the sick soldiers possibly thought that they had made equal personal sacrifices with Miss Nightingale—some indeed gave their life in the cause. Others again, returning to a life of seclusion after toiling through the arduous nursing of the campaign, might perhaps have felt some injustice that one name alone rang through the land, while others who also had borne the heat and burden of the day remained unhonoured and unsung. No one would wish to exempt from due praise even the humblest of that "Angel Band" who worked with Florence Nightingale and still less would she, but in every great cause there is the initiating genius who stands in solitary grandeur above the rank and file of followers.

Such was the Lady-in-Chief: she came to

Scutari as something far more even than an efficient nurse. She brought the organising and governing faculty and the brain power of which the officials in charge seemed bereft. Delicate, high-bred, and retiring in nature as Miss Nightingale was, she possessed the subtle quality which gave her command over others, that undefinable something which broke down the opposition of the most conservative obstructionist when he came under her personal influence. She was unfettered by precedent or red tape, and brought to her task a clear idea of the administrative mechanism which was needed to afford due care and provision for the prostrate soldiery.

Her woman's nature was roused to indignation at the sight of suffering which she could only regard as the result of unbending and unthinking routine, and she brought her quick intuitions and agile brain to remedy the evil. When men were dying daily by the score for the want of suitable nourishment, she declined to listen to under officials who feared to disobey regulations by opening stores without the usual order, and took the responsibility of having the packages undone. The Lady-in-Chief was herself a strict disciplinarian, or she would never have brought order out of chaos, but she had humanity enough to know when the iron rule might be relaxed in the interests of those under her care. Her common sense, her spirit of unselfish

devotion, and her strong, though gentle, persuasive-
ness gradually overcame the predjudice of the
constituted authorities against the new element
introduced into hospital work.

Mr. Sidney Herbert in his letter to the Principal
Medical Officer at Scutari (Dr. Menzies) announcing
the coming of the nurses, had enjoined him " to
receive with attention and deference the counsels
of the Lady-in-Chief." Great as was the power
which the unflinching support of this distinguished
man gave her, it was secondary to the influence
which she attained by the force of her own character.
The late Dean Stanley, who was not a man to
misuse the English language, described Miss Nightingale's faculty as " commanding genius."

We read in the thrilling accounts of the period
how the Lady-in-Chief went her rounds at night,
passing along the endless corridors and through
the hospital wards carrying a little lamp, the gleam
of which lighted her progress of mercy and love.
Dying men turned on their pillows to bless her
shadow as it passed. In far-away New England
the idea of " The Lady with the Lamp " inspired
the muse of Longfellow :—

> A Lady with a Lamp shall stand
> In the great history of the land,
> A noble type of good
> -Heroic womanhood;

and it has remained the most beautiful and popular title bestowed upon Florence Nightingale, but at the risk of appearing modern and prosaic we venture to re-christen our heroine " The Lady with the Brain."

When Miss Nightingale began her work, her energies were concentrated on the Barrack Hospital already described, and on the General Hospital at Scutari, which was a little farther removed. The other British hospitals in the East also came under her supervision, but Scutari claimed at first her undivided personal attention. Attached to her staff were the thirty-eight trained nurses who had accompanied her, the Rev. Sidney Osborne, the chaplain, and her friends, Mr. and Mrs. Bracebridge of Atherstone Hall. Mrs. Bracebridge was to act as overseer of the housekeeping department. A most valuable helper also was Mr. Stafford, a young man of family who had left the drawing-rooms of Mayfair to go to Scutari and "fag" for the Lady-in-Chief. He wrote letters, went on missions of inquiry, and did anything and everything which a handy and gallant gentleman could do to make himself useful to a lady whom he felt honoured to serve.

Taken collectively, this little group may be termed the "party of reform" who were installed at Scutari at the beginning of the winter of 1854. Lady Stratford de Redcliffe, the wife of our Ambas-

sador at Constantinople, and her " beauteous guest,"
Lady George Paget, were also most helpful in
sending little comforts for the wounded officers, but
it was said of Miss Nightingale that she " thought

THE LADY-IN-CHIEF IN HER QUARTERS AT THE BARRACK HOSPITAL.

only of the men." The common soldier was
undoubtedly her chief concern.

The Lady-in-Chief and her staff had their
quarters in a tower at one of the corners of the
hospital, and the busy life which went on there from

day to day is thus described by the Rev. Sidney Osborne. " Entering the door leading into the Sisters' Tower," he writes, " you at once find yourself a spectator of a busy and interesting scene. There is a large room with two or three doors opening from it on one side ; on the other, one door opening into an apartment in which many of the nurses and sisters slept, and had, I believe, their meals. In the centre was a large kitchen table : bustling about this might be seen the high-priestess of the room, Mrs. C——. Often as I have had occasion to pass through this room I do not recollect ever finding her absent from it or unoccupied. At this table she received the various matters from the kitchen and stores of the sisterhood, which attendant sisters or nurses were ever ready to take to the sick in any and every part of these gigantic hospitals. It was a curious scene, and a close study of it afforded a practical lesson in the working of true common-sense benevolence.

" The floor on one side of the room was loaded with packages of all kinds—stores of things for the internal and external consumption of the patients ; bales of shirts, socks, slippers, dressing-gowns, flannel, heaps of every sort of article likely to be of use in affording comfort and securing cleanliness. . . . It was one feature of a bold attempt upon the part of extraneous benevolence to supply the deficiencies of the various departments which as a matter of course should have supplied all these things.

" In an adjoining room were held those councils over which Miss Nightingale so ably presided, at which were discussed the measures necessary to meet the daily-varying exigencies of the hospital. From hence were given the orders which regulated the female staff working under this most gifted head. This, too, was the office from which were sent those many letters to the Government, to friends and supporters at home, telling such awful tales of the sufferings of the sick and wounded, their utter want of so many necessaries."

We have in this description a glimpse into the beginning of the Lady-in-Chief's organising work. In the sisters' quarters she was from the first undisputed head, and by degrees the order and method which she established there affected every other part of the hospital.

While she was battling with red-tapism in order to get access to stores which lay unpacked in the vicinity of a hospital filled with poorly fed, badly clothed, and suffering men because nobody seemed to know who had the right to dispense them, sympathetic friends were keeping the store in the Sisters' Tower replenished. But it was impossible to keep pace with the needs. The published letters sent home by the nursing staff at this period all contain requests for invalid requisites and clothing. The wounded were dying in scores for want of a little stimulant to rouse their exhausted systems when they first arrived at the hospitals, and men lying in clothing stiff with gore could not even procure a change of garment. As the cold increased, the frost-bitten patients, arriving from the trenches before Sebastopol, had not even the luxury of a warm shirt. One of the nurses writing home said : " Whenever a man opens his mouth with ' Please, ma'am, I want to speak to you,' my heart sinks within me, for I feel sure it will end in flannel shirts."

The task of the Lady-in-Chief was to bring benevolent as well as neglectful chaos into order. She had to inquire into the things most urgently needed and advise her friends in England. All this was unexpected work, for it will be remembered that Mr. Sidney Herbert, in the letter inviting Miss Nightingale to go to Scutari, had dwelt on the fact, as he believed it, that the hospitals were supplied with every necessary. " Medical stores," he had said, " had been sent out by the ton weight."

Alas ! through mismanagement, these stores had been rotting on the shore at Varna, instead of reaching Scutari, and much that had arrived was packed beneath heavy ammunition and difficult to get at. The loss of the *Prince*, laden with supplies, was a culminating disaster which occurred on November 14th, about two weeks after Miss Nightingale's arrival.

The reticence of the hospital authorities prevented the true state of affairs from reaching the British public. Indeed, the whole Service, from commandant to orderly, conspired to say " All right," when all was wrong. One of the sisters has described how this policy worked in the wards. An orderly officer took the rounds of the wards every night, to see that all was in order. He was of course expected by the orderlies, and the moment he raised the latch he received the word, " All right, your honour," and passed on. This was hospital inspection !

In excuse for the officers who were thus easily put off, it may be said that the wards were filled with pestilence, and the air so polluted by cholera and fever patients that it seemed courting death to enter.

For that reason orderlies already on the sick list were set to act as nurses, and they often drank the brandy which it was their duty to administer to the patients, in order to keep up their spirits, or " drown their grief," as they preferred to put it. Men in this condition became very callous. Those stricken with cholera had their sufferings terribly enhanced by the dread of being buried alive, and used to beseech the orderlies not to send them to the dead-house until quite sure that they had breathed their last. Utter collapse was the last stage of Asiatic cholera, and the orderlies took little pains to ascertain when the exact moment of dissolution came ; consequently numbers of still living men were hurried to the dead-house. One does not wish to hold up to blame and execration the seeming inhumanity of the orderlies. They were set to do work for which they were untrained and often physically unfit, and were also demoralised by the shocking condition of the wards. It was the system rather than individuals which was to blame.

Into these insanitary, filthy, and pestilential wards came the Lady-in-Chief, and she did not say " All right." It was useless for officialdom to " pooh-pooh " : she, fortunately, had Government authority. What her quick eye saw was communicated to the Commander-in-Chief, Lord Raglan, and to Mr. Sidney Herbert at the War Office, and brought in due course the needed instructions for reform.

Not the least quality of the Lady-in-Chief was her influence over men in authority. She was not dictatorial, she was not aggressive, but she possessed the judgment which inspired confidence and the knowledge which compelled respectful attention.

Her letters to the War Minister at home, and to Lord Raglan, the General in the field, were models of clear and concise documents, devoid of grumbling, rancour, or fidgety complaints, but they contained some appalling facts. Unerringly she laid her finger on the loose joints of the commissariat and hospital administration. By the enlightening aid of her letters from Scutari the Home Government was enabled to pierce the haze which surrounded the official accounts from the Bosphorus, and gradually the hospital management was put on a footing which harmonised with the Lady-in-Chief's recommendations.

Lord William Paulet, who succeeded Major Sillery as Military Commandant at Scutari shortly after Miss Nightingale's arrival, soon learned to place entire confidence in her judgment. " You will find her most valuable, . . . her counsels are admirable suggestions," wrote the War Minister to the new Commandant and Lord William proved the truth of the statement. Lord Raglan in one of his dispatches to the Duke of Newcastle said, " Lord William [Paulet] like Brown [Sir George Brown] speaks loudly in praise of Miss Nightingale," adding that he was confident that she had " done great good." As the weeks passed by, Lord Raglan grew to consider the Lady-in-Chief a most efficient auxiliary " general."

CHAPTER XIII

AT WORK IN THE BARRACK HOSPITAL

An Appalling Task—Stories of Florence Nightingale's interest in the Soldiers—Lack of Necessaries for the Wounded—Establishes an Invalids' Kitchen and a Laundry—Cares for the Soldiers' Wives—Religious Fanatics—Letter from Queen Victoria—Christmas at Scutari.

> Neglected, dying in despair,
>   They lay till woman came,
> To soothe them with her gentle care,
>   And feed life's flickering flame.
> When wounded sore, on fever's rack,
>   Or cast away as slain,
> She called their fluttering spirits back,
>   And gave them strength again.
>
> FRANCIS BENNOCH.

THE events of the war in the autumn of 1854 will convey some idea of the number of wounded men crowded into the hospitals on the Bosphorus when Florence Nightingale entered upon her duties at Scutari. Balaclava was fought on October 25th, four days after she left London; the battle of Inkerman followed on November 5th, the day after she landed. Before the average woman would have found time to unpack her boxes, Miss

Nightingale was face to face with a task unparalleled in its magnitude and appalling in its nature.

The wounded arrived by the shipload until every ward, both in the General and in the Barrack Hospital, was crowded to excess, and the men lay in double rows down the long corridors, forming several miles of suffering humanity. During these terrible days Florence Nightingale was known to stand for *twenty hours* at a time, on the arrivals of fresh detachments of sick, apportioning quarters, directing her nurses and attending at the most painful operations where her presence might soothe and support. She would spend hours over men dying of cholera or fever. " Indeed," wrote one who watched her work, " the more awful to every sense any particular case might be, the more certainly might be seen her slight form bending over him, administering to his ease by every means in her power and seldom quitting his side until death released him."

Her womanly heart prompted her to acts of humanity which at once made her recognised by the men as the soldier's friend. When the wounded were brought by hundreds to Scutari after Inkerman, the first duty of the surgeons was to separate the hopeful cases from the desperate. On one occasion Miss Nightingale saw five soldiers set aside in a hopeless condition. She inquired if nothing could be done for the poor fellows, and the surgeons replied that their first duty was with those whom there seemed to be more hope of saving.

" Will you give me these five men ?" said the Lady-in-Chief.

" Do as you like with them," replied the surgeons ; "we think their case is hopeless."

If life could be saved, Florence Nightingale was determined to save it, and throughout the night, assisted by one of the nurses, she sat beside the men, feeding them with a spoon until their senses awakened and their strength began to return. She washed their wounds, cheered their hearts with kind words, and in the morning had the satisfaction of finding that they were in a fit condition to be operated on.

At another time a Highland soldier was about to undergo an amputation. Miss Nightingale asked that the operation might be delayed, as she thought that careful nursing might render it unnecessary. Through her unremitting care the man's arm was saved ; and when asked what he felt towards his preserver, he said that the only mode he had of giving vent to his feelings was to kiss her shadow when it fell on his pillow as she passed through the wards on her nightly rounds.

When cholera and plague cases came in, foaming at the mouth and black in the face, none were too bad for Florence Nightingale's patient care. Her influence over the men was established from the first. She was their "good angel," and their confidence in her was unbounded.

Still, her task was a heavy one in these first days. There was official prejudice to overcome, and an overwhelming number of patients to deal with in a huge building devoid of the commonest hospital accessories and arrangements. The Barrack "Hospital," so called, had been designed only for soldiers' barracks, so that when suddenly converted into a hospital it lacked almost everything necessary for the sick, and the supplies forwarded from England had by a series of misadventures been delayed. A letter sent home by one of the nurses six days after the arrival of Miss Nightingale and her band may be quoted as giving a graphic picture of the state of affairs at this time. She writes :—

"I have come out here as one of the Government nurses, and the position in which we are placed induces me to write and ask you, at once, to send out a few dozens of wine, or in short anything which may be useful for the wounded or dying, hundreds of whom are now around us, under this roof, filling up even the passages to the very rooms we occupy. Government is liberal, and for one moment I would not complain of their desire to meet all our wants, but with such a number of the wounded coming in from

Sebastopol, it does appear absolutely impossible to meet the wants of those who are dying of dysentery and exhaustion ; out of four wards committed to my care, eleven men have died in the night, simply from exhaustion, which, humanly speaking, might have been stopped, could I have laid my hand at once on such nourishment as I knew they ought to have had.

" It is necessary to be as near the scene of war as we are, to know the horrors which we have seen and heard of. I know not which sight is most heartrending—to witness fine strong men and youths worn down by exhaustion and sinking under it, or others coming in fearfully wounded.

" The whole of yesterday was spent, first in sewing the men's mattresses together, and then in washing them, and assisting the surgeons, when we could, in dressing their ghastly wounds, and seeing the poor fellows made as easy as their circumstances would admit of, after their five days' confinement on board ship, during which space their wounds were not dressed.

" Miss Nightingale, under whom we work, is well fitted in every way to fill her arduous post, the whole object of her life having hitherto been the superintendence of hospitals abroad. Wine and bottles of chicken broth, preserved meat for soups, etc., will be most acceptable.

MISS NIGHTINGALE IN THE HOSPITAL AT SCUTARI.

" We have not seen a drop of milk, and the bread is extremely sour. The butter is most filthy—it is Irish butter in a state of decomposition ; and the meat is more like moist leather than food. Potatoes we are waiting for until they arrive from France."

Nursing in a hospital which received soldiers straight from the battlefield, their wounds aggravated by days of neglect, was a difficult task under the most favourable circumstances, but when intensified by the lack even of proper food, such as the above letter discloses, the task was indeed formidable.

There was an organising brain, however, at work n that dreadful Barrack Hospital now, and *within ten days* of her arrival, in spite of the terrible influx of patients which taxed her powers to the utmost, Miss Nightingale had fitted up an impromptu kitchen, from which eight hundred men were daily supplied with well-cooked food and other comforts. It was largely supplied with the invalid food from the private stores of the Lady-in-Chief, which fortunately she had brought out with her in the *Vectis*. Beef-tea, chicken broth, jelly, and little delicacies unheard of before were now administered to the sick by the gentle hands of women nurses. Small wonder that the poor fellows could often only express their gratitude in voices half-choked with sobs !

One Crimean veteran told the writer that when he received a basin of arrowroot on his first arrival at the hospital early in the morning, he said to himself, " Tommy, me boy, that's all you'll get into your inside this blessed day, and think yourself lucky you've got that. But two hours later, if another of them blessed angels didn't come entreating of me to have just a little chicken broth! Well, I took that, thinking maybe it was early dinner, and before I had well done wondering what would happen next, round the nurse came again with a bit o' jelly, and all day long at intervals they kept on bringing me what they called ' a little nourishment.' In the evening, Miss Nightingale she came and had a look at me, and says she, ' I hope you're feeling better.' I could have said, ' Ma'am, I feels as fit as a fightin' cock,' but I managed to git out somethin' a bit more polite."

Hitherto, not only had there been a lack of food, but the cooking had been done by the soldiers themselves in the most free and easy manner. Meat and vegetables were boiled together in the huge coppers, of which there were thirteen in the kitchen attached to the barracks. Separate portions were enclosed in nets, and all plunged together into the seething coppers, and taken up when occasion demanded. Some things were served up done to rags, while others were almost raw. This kind of cooking was bad enough for men in ordinary health, but for the sick it meant death.

The daily comforts which the nurses' kitchen afforded received ample testimony from the witnesses before Mr. Roebuck's Commission for inquiry into the conduct of the war. In one day sometimes thirteen gallons of chicken broth and forty gallons of arrowroot were distributed amongst the sick. At first nearly all the invalid food had to come from the private stores brought out by the Lady-in-Chief, which the charitable at home replenished as the true state of affairs became known, for not only was there a deficiency in the Government stores, but the things supplied officially were often not fit for food. It was the general testimony of witnesses before the Commission that Miss Nightingale's services were invaluable in the hospital as well for what she did herself as for the manner in which she kept the purveyors to their duties.

The method of distributing the Government stores was as erratic as the cooking. There appeared to be no regulations as to time. Things asked for in a morning were probably not forthcoming until evening, when the cooking fires in the barracks kitchen were all but out. Nothing could be obtained until various "service rules" had been observed. An official board must inspect and approve all stores before they could be distributed. One can think of nothing more exasperating to the Lady-in-Chief, in her responsible duty towards the sick, than to see exhausted men dying for want of the proper nourishment because the board of inspection had not completed its arrangements. On one recorded occasion she took the law into her own hands, and insisted that the stores should be given out, inspected or not. She could not ask under-officials to incur the penalty of martial law by fulfilling her behests, but she could brave the authorities herself and did so. The storehouse was opened on the responsibility of the Lady-in-Chief, and the goods procured for the languishing soldiery.

Miss Nightingale's defiance of red-tape made her some enemies, and the " groove-going men," as Kinglake calls them, " uttered touching complaints, declaring that the Lady-in-Chief did not choose to give them time, and that the moment a want declared itself, she made haste to supply it herself."

" This charge," says the same authority in an appendix note, " was so utterly without foundation as to be the opposite of truth. The Lady-in-Chief used neither to issue her stores, nor allow any others to do so, until the want of them had been evidenced by a duly signed requisition. Proof of this is complete, and has been furnished even by adversaries of the Lady-in-Chief."

After her improvised kitchen was in working

order, Miss Nightingale next set to work to establish a laundry for the hospital and institute a system for disinfecting the clothes of fever and cholera patients. Up to the time of her arrival there was practically little washing done, the "authorities" had only succeeded in getting *seven* shirts washed, and no attempt was made to separate the bed-linen and garments of infectious patients from those suffering only from wounds. Washing contracts were in existence, but availed little. At the General Hospital the work was in the hands of a corps of eight or ten Armenians. There was no fault to be found with the manner in which they did the work, only they stole so habitually that when a man sent his shirt to be washed he was never sure that he would get it back again, and in consequence the sick were unwilling to part with their garments.

At the Barrack Hospital a Levantine named Uptoni had the washing contract, but broke it so repeatedly that the sick were practically without clean linen, except when they were able to get the soldiers' wives to do a little washing for them. Such was the state of affairs in a hospital where two to three thousand men lay wounded and sick.

Miss Nightingale hired a house close to the hospital and set up an efficient laundry, partly out of her private funds, and partly out of money subscribed to *The Times* fund started for the relief of the soldiery. She had it fitted up with coppers and regulated under sanitary conditions, and there five hundred shirts and one hundred and fifty other articles were washed each week.

There was a further difficulty to meet, and that was to provide the men with a change of linen while the soiled went to the wash. Many of the wounded had been obliged to leave their knapsacks behind and had no clothing save the dirty and dilapidated garments in which they arrived. In the course of the first three months Miss Nightingale provided the men with ten thousand shirts from her own private sources.

There was the same scarcity in surgical dressings, and the nurses had to employ every minute that could be spared from the bedside of the sufferers in making lint, bandages, amputation stumps, and in sewing mattresses and making pillows.

Great confusion existed with regard to the dispensing of drugs. The apothecaries' store at Scutari, which supplied the hospitals and indeed the whole army in the Crimea, was in the same state of confusion as everything else. The orderlies left to dispense often did not know what the store contained. On one occasion Mrs. Bracebridge, Miss Nightingale's invaluable friend and helper, applied three times for chloride of lime and was told there was none. Miss Nightingale insisted on a more thorough search being made, with the result that 90 lbs. were discovered.

The defective system of orderlies was another evil which the Lady-in-Chief had to contend with. These men had been taken from the ranks, most of them were convalescents, and they did not trouble to understand the duties of an orderly because they were liable to return and serve in the ranks. The advent of the ladies had an excellent effect upon the orderlies in arousing their sense of chivalry, and they soon grew to think it an honour to serve the Lady-in-Chief. During all that dreadful period, when she had to tax the patience and devotion of the orderlies and other soldiers attending in the wards to the utmost, not one of them failed her " in obedience, thoughtful attention, and considerate delicacy." For her they toiled and endured a strain and stress of work which mere officialdom would have failed to obtain. Yet " never," Miss Nightingale says, " came from any one of them one word nor one look which a gentleman would not have used ; and while paying this humble tribute to humble courtesy, the tears come into my eyes as I think how amidst scenes of loathsome disease and death there arose above it all the innate dignity, gentleness, and chivalry of the men (for never surely was chivalry so strikingly exemplified), shining in the

midst of what must be considered as the lowest
sinks of human misery, and preventing instinctively
the use of one expression which could distress a
gentlewoman."

If such was the chivalrous devotion yielded by
the orderlies and convalescent soldiers, it can readily
be understood that the prostrate sufferers worshipped
the Lady-in-Chief. Her presence in the operating
room acted like magic. Case after case became
amenable to the surgeon under the calming influence
of her presence. It is not surprising that men
prostrate with weakness and agonised with pain
often rebelled against an operation. Anæsthetics
were not administered as freely then as they are to-
day, and many brave fellows craved death rather than
meet the surgeon's knife. But when they felt the
pitying eyes of the Lady-in-Chief fixed upon them,
saw her gentle face, heard her soothing words of
comfort and hope for the future, and were conscious
that she had set herself to bear the pain of
witnessing pain, the men would obey her silent
command, and submit and endure, strengthened by
her presence.

Those who at first were inclined to cavil at the
power which the Government had placed in the
hands of the Lady-in-Chief speedily reversed their
judgment, as day by day they witnessed her
strength of character and her amazing fortitude

and self-control in the midst of scenes which tried the strongest men.

The magnitude of Miss Nightingale's work in the hospital wards has caused historians to overlook the womanly help and sympathy which she gave to the soldiers' wives who had come out with their husbands. Even Kinglake, who is unsurpassed in his admiration for the Lady-in-Chief, does not mention this side of her work.

When Miss Nightingale arrived at Scutari she found a number of poor women, the wives or the widows (may be) of soldiers who had gone to the front, living in a distressing condition, literally in the holes and corners of the Barrack Hospital. These women, being detached from their husbands' regiments, had no claim for rations and quarters. The colonel of each regiment had power to allow a certain number of women to accompany their husbands on foreign service. Each woman belonged to her regiment, and if separated, even through no choice of her own, there was no provision for her. No organisation to deal with them existed at this period, because for forty years there had been no general depôt of an English army. The widows were by degrees sent home by order of the Commandant, but the other women, many of them wives of soldiers in the hospital or of orderlies, refused to return home without their husbands.

Miss Nightingale found these poor creatures, for the most part respectable women, without decent clothing—their clothes having worn out—going about bonnetless and shoeless and living as best they could. After many changes from one "hole" to another the women were housed by the authorities in three or four dark rooms in the damp basement of the hospital. The only privacy to be obtained was by hanging up rags of clothes on lines. There, by the light of a rushlight, the meals were taken, the sick attended, and there the babies were born and nourished. There were twenty-two babies born from November to December, and many more during the winter.

It needs no words to picture the gratitude of the women to the dear Lady-in-Chief who sought them out in their abject misery, gave them decent clothing and food from her own stores in the Nurses's Tower, and saw that the little lives ushered into the world amid the horrors and privations of war had at least tender care. At the end of January, owing to a broken drain in the basement, fever broke out, and Miss Nightingale now persuaded the Commandant to remove the women to healthier quarters. A Turkish house was procured by requisition and Miss Nightingale had it cleaned and furnished out of her funds. Throughout the winter the women were assisted with money, food and clothes, and outfits were provided for widows returning home. Miss Nightingale also organised a plan to give employment to all the soldiers' wives who were willing to work in her laundry at ten shillings to fourteen shillings a week. The upper part of the wash-house was divided into a sick ward and a laundry, and offered a refuge for the more respectable women. She obtained situations for others in families in Constantinople. A school was also started for the children. Lady Alicia Blackwood, wife of Dr. Blackwood, an army chaplain, visited the women and helped to care for them. Through Miss Nightingale's initiative about five hundred women were raised from their wretched condition at Scutari and enabled to earn honest livings. "When," wrote Miss Nightingale later, "the improvements in our system which the war must suggest are discussed, let not the wife and child of the soldier be forgotten."

While Florence Nightingale was thus heroically grappling with disease, suffering, and death, and bringing order out of chaos in the hospitals at Scutari, small-minded fanatics at home were attacking her religious opinions. Some declared that she had gone to the East for the purpose of spreading Puseyism amongst the British soldiers, others that she had become a Roman Catholic, some people were certain that she was a Unitarian, while others whispered the dreadful heresy, "Supralapsarian." A clergyman warned his flock against subscribing money for the soldiers in the East if it was to pass through Popish hands. Controversy waxed strong in *The Times* and *The Standard*, and Mr. and Mrs. Sidney Herbert warmly defended their absent friend.

"It is melancholy to think," wrote Mrs. Herbert to a lady parishioner of an attacking clergyman, "that in Christian England no one can undertake anything without these most uncharitable and sectarian attacks, and, had you not told me so, I could scarcely believe that a clergyman of the Established Church could have been the mouth-piece of such slander. Miss Nightingale is a member of the Established Church of England, and what is called rather Low Church, but ever since she went to Scutari her religious opinions and character have been assailed on all points. It is a cruel return to make towards one to whom all England owes so much."

An Irish clergyman, when asked to what sect Miss Nightingale belonged, made the effective reply : "She belongs to a sect which, unfortunately, is a very rare one—the sect of the Good Samaritan."

Queen Victoria and the Prince Consort had from the first taken a sympathetic interest in Miss Nightingale's work, and the following letter from the Queen to Mr. Sidney Herbert did much towards silencing adverse criticism, as it showed the confidence which her Majesty had in Miss Nightingale and her nurses :—

"WINDSOR CASTLE.
"*December 6th,* 1854.

"Would you tell Mrs. Herbert," wrote the Queen to Mr. Sidney Herbert, "that I beg she would let me see frequently the accounts she receives from Miss Nightingale or Mrs. Bracebridge, as *I hear no details of the wounded,* though I see so many from officers, etc., about the battlefield, and naturally the former must interest *me* more than any one.

"Let Mrs. Herbert also know that I wish Miss Nightingale and the ladies would tell these poor, noble wounded and sick men that *no one* takes a warmer interest or feels *more* for their sufferings or admires their courage and heroism *more* than their Queen. Day and night she thinks of her beloved troops. So does the Prince.

"Beg Mrs. Herbert to communicate these my words to those ladies, as I know that *our* sympathy is much valued by these noble fellows.

"VICTORIA."

This kindly letter, coming straight from the good Queen's heart, without any official verbiage to smother the personal feeling, was forwarded to Miss Nightingale, and on its receipt she placed it in the hands of one of the chaplains, who went from ward to ward reading it to the men, ending each recital of the letter with " God save the Queen," in which the poor sufferers joined with such vigour as they possessed.   Copies of the letter were afterwards posted up on the walls of the hospital.

Although the Lady-in-Chief's work and personality had already overcome much official prejudice, there is no doubt that Queen Victoria's letter greatly strengthened her position.   It was now evident that it was to Miss Nightingale that the Sovereign looked for tidings of the wounded and in her that she trusted for the amelioration of their terrible sufferings.

When Christmas Day dawned in the great Barrack Hospital in that terrible war winter of 1854, it at least found its suffering inmates lying in cleanliness, with comfortable surroundings and supplied with suitable food.   Not a man throughout the huge building but had such comforts as the willing hands and tender hearts of women could devise.   This change had been brought about in less than two months by the clear head and managing brain which ruled in the Nurses' Tower.

The " Merry Christmas " passed from **man to**

man was not a misnomer, despite the pain and suffering ; the men were at least " merry " that the "nightingales " had come. When the Queen's health was drunk, in some cases from medicine glasses, each man in his heart coupled with the loyal toast the names of the Lady-in-Chief and her devoted band.

CHAPTER XIV

GRAPPLING WITH CHOLERA AND FEVER

Florence Nightingale describes the Hardships of the Soldiers—
Arrival of Fifty More Nurses—Memories of Sister Mary
Aloysius—The Cholera Scourge.

> So in that house of misery,
> A lady with a lamp I see
> Pass through the glimmering gloom,
> And flit from room to room.
>
> LONGFELLOW.

THE New Year of 1855 brought no mitigation in Florence Nightingale's arduous task. Though there was no longer the influx of wounded from the battlefields, disease was making fearful ravages amongst the soldiers now engaged in the prolonged siege of Sebastopol. Miss Nightingale thus described the hardships endured by the men in a letter to a friend. "Fancy," she writes, "working five nights out of seven in the trenches! Fancy being thirty-six hours in them at a stretch, as they were all December, lying down, or half lying down, after forty-eight hours, with no food but raw salt pork sprinkled with sugar, rum, and biscuit ; nothing hot, because the exhausted soldier could not collect his own fuel, as he was expected to do, to cook his own rations ; and fancy through all this the army preserving their courage and patience as they have done. There is something sublime in the spectacle."

The result of this life of exposure in the trenches during the rigours of the Crimean winter was terrible suffering amongst the soldiers from frostbite and dysentery, and there was a great increase in cholera and fever, which kept the hospitals more crowded than ever.

At the beginning of the year a further staff of fifty trained nurses under Miss Stanley, the sister of the late Dean, arrived at Scutari and were distributed amongst the various hospitals in the East. Miss Nightingale had now five thousand sick and wounded under her supervision, and eleven hundred more were on their way from the Crimea. Under her immediate personal care in the Barrack Hospital were more than two thousand wounded, all severe cases. She had also now established her *régime* in the General Hospital at Scutari, and some of the new nurses were installed there under Miss Emily Anderson, while others went to Kullali Hospital on the other side of the Bosphorus and worked under Miss Stanley until she returned to England.

Sisters of mercy from some of the Irish convents

were among the new nurses, and one of the number, Sister Mary Aloysius, is still at the time of writing living in her convent home at Gort, Co. Galway. Her "Memories" of the Crimea afford a graphic picture of the state of the General Hospital at Scutari and of the arduous toil of the nurses.

The aged sister has a keen sense of humour, and in describing the departure of Miss Stanley's company from London Bridge for Scutari, evidently derived some satisfaction that her nun's garb was less extraordinary than the dresses provided by the Government for its nurses. "The ladies and the paid nurses," she relates, "wore the same uniform—grey tweed wrappers, worsted jackets, white caps and short woollen cloaks, and a frightful scarf of brown holland embroidered in red with the words 'Scutari Hospital.' The garments were contract work and all made the same sizes. In consequence the tall ladies appeared to be attired in short dresses and the short ladies in long." It was a similar evidence of official blundering to that which sent a cargo of boots for the soldiers in the Crimea all shaped for the left foot. "That ladies could be found to walk in such a costume was certainly a triumph of grace over nature," adds Sister Aloysius. The fact is interesting as showing the advance made in modern times in a nurse's official dress as exemplified in the charming though useful costumes worn by military nurses in the South African war.

However, all honour to the noble pioneers who sank personal considerations and effaced self in a desire to discharge their errand of mercy.

A powerful sidelight is thrown on the work of the Lady-in-Chief by the experiences of her subordinates. Sister Mary Aloysius writes : " Where shall I begin. or how can I ever describe my first day in the hospital at Scutari ? Vessels were arriving and orderlies carrying the poor fellows, who with their wounds and frost-bites had been tossing about on the Black Sea for two or three days and sometimes more. Where were they to go ? Not an available bed. They were laid on the floor one after another, till the beds were emptied of those dying of cholera and every other disease. Many died immediately after being brought in—their moans would pierce the heart—and the look of agony on those poor dying faces will never leave my heart. They may well be called ' the martyrs of the Crimea.'

" The cholera was of the very worst type, and the attacked men lasted only four or five hours. Oh, those dreadful cramps ! You might as well try to bend a piece of iron as to move the joints. The medical staff did their best, and daily, hourly, risked their own lives with little or no success. At last every one seemed to be getting paralysed and the orderlies indifferent as to life or death. . . . The usual remedies ordered by the doctors were stuping and poultices of mustard. They were very anxious to try chloroform, but did not trust any one with it except the sisters."

If the Lady-in-Chief and her nurses had been at first rather coldly welcomed in the surgery wards, their presence when the epidemic of cholera set in was indeed counted a blessing. These trained and devoted women could be entrusted with applying the desperate remedies needed for the disease, which the medical staff would have felt it useless to leave in the hands of orderlies. The stuping, for example, required the most careful attention to have any chance of success. The method of the sisters was to have a large tub of boiling water, blankets torn in squares, and a piece of canvas with a running at each end to hold a stick. The blankets were put into the boiling water, lifted out with tongs and put into the canvas. An orderly at each end wrung the flannel out so dry that not a drop of moisture remained. Then chloroform was sprinkled on the hot blanket, which was then applied to the patient's stomach. Rubbing with mustard and even with turpentine followed, until the iron grip which had seized the body was released or the end had come.

The nurses fought with the dread disease in the most heroic manner, but the proportion saved among the stricken was small indeed. The saddest thing was that it was generally the strong and healthy soldier who was attacked.

"One day," says Sister Aloysius, "a fine young fellow, the picture of health and strength, was carried in on a stretcher to my ward. I said to the orderlies, 'I hope we shall be able to bring him through.' I set to work with the usual remedies ; but the doctor shook his head, and said, 'I am afraid it's all no use, sister.' When the orderlies, poor fellows, were tired, I set to work myself, and kept it on till nearly the end—but you might as well rub iron ; no heat, no movement from his joints. He lived about the usual time—four or five hours."

Week after week the fearful scourge continued, until the avenues to the wards were never free from the two streams of stretchers, one bringing in the stricken, the other carrying out the dead. The spread of the infection was thought to be largely due to the graves not being deep enough, and the air surrounding the hospitals had become putrid.

Scarcely less dreadful than the cholera patients were the men suffering from frost-bite, who arrived in hundreds from the trenches before Sebastopol. Nothing enables one to realise their terrible condition like the narrative of one on the spot. Referring to her experience amongst the frost-bitten patients, Sister Aloysius says : "The men who came from the 'Front,' as they called it, had only thin linen suits—no other clothing to keep out the severe Crimean frost. When they were carried in on the stretchers, which conveyed so many to their last resting-place, their clothes had to be cut off. In most cases the flesh and clothes were frozen together ; and, as for the feet, the boots had to be cut off bit by bit—the flesh coming off with them ; many pieces of the flesh I have seen remain in the boot. Poultices were applied with some oil brushed over them. In the morning, when these were removed—can I ever forget it ?—the sinews and bones were seen to be laid bare. We had surgical instruments ; but in almost every case the doctors or staff-surgeons were at hand, and removed the diseased flesh as tenderly as they could. As for the toes, you could not recognise them as such."

One could multiply these ghastly descriptions if further evidence was needed to show the terrible sufferings endured by officers and men alike in the trenches before Sebastopol. Mention the famous siege to any of the old Crimean veterans as they sit beneath the trees in the grounds of Chelsea Hospital, and they will tell you stories of hardships endured which makes one regard their still living bodies with amazement. And they are not mere soldiers' tales : the old heroes could scarcely invent greater horrors than history has recorded. The weary weeks were passed for the most part by the men sitting or lying in holes dug in the frozen ground deep enough to shelter their heads from the flying bullets and bursting bombs. If a poor fellow decided to stretch his numbed and cramped legs, he was more than likely to have his head blown off. Lord Wolseley bears to-day the marks of his experiences as a venturesome young subaltern in the trenches at Sebastopol, when, riddled with bullets and a part of his face blown away, he was laid on one side by the surgeons as a " dead un." Fortunately he managed to prove that he was yet alive. The *Life of Captain Hedley Vicars* reveals also the privations of the time. He himself lay in the open air on a bed of stones and leaves, having given up his tent to men who were sick.

The cold was so intense that in a sudden skirmish the men were often unable to draw their triggers. A frost-bitten soldier lying ill at Balaclava, when he tried to turn in the night, found that his feet were frozen to those of another soldier lying opposite.

Hundreds of these poor men, worn out by every imaginable kind of suffering, were constantly arriving at the already crowded hospitals at Scutari. As many as sixty men were known to die in a single night, and for two months the death rate stood at 60 per cent.

Florence Nightingale seemed to be everywhere, and particularly did her deep religious feelings prompt her to speak with the dying and point their thoughts to heaven. She was a ministering angel alike for soul and body. In her ear was often murmured the last message home, and to her was entrusted the bit of money, the watch, or the cherished keepsake to be sent to wife or sweetheart. How faithfully these dying commissions were carried out, in spite of overwhelming duties to the living, is known to families all over the land who have loved ones sleeping beneath the cypress-trees on the shores of the Bosphorus.

At night, after the surgeons had gone their rounds, the figure of the Lady-in-Chief was seen in her simple black dress, white apron, and small closely fitting white cap gliding through the wards and corridors carrying a tiny lamp in her hand. By its light she saw where pain was greatest, where the Angel of Death was about to descend, and she would pause to smooth a pillow, or give the word of consolation.

Florence Nightingale's sublime courage was strikingly shown in these nocturnal rounds. Then, when silence for the most part reigned, and the sufferers were courting slumber, the ear was most likely to be startled by some heart-breaking sound. The delirious call of the poor emaciated fellow who still fancied himself in the trenches before Sebastopol, or on the blood-stained ridges of Inkerman fighting for dear life, the smothered sob at thought of home, the hacking cough, the groan of agony, the gasp of death—these were the sounds which fell on the stillness as " the lady with the lamp " moved from bed to bed. One such experience would be a memory for a lifetime, but night after night, week after week, and month after month, our heroine fulfilled this sad and tender ministry to the suffering. Longfellow paid his beautiful tribute to the lady with the lamp in verses which impel quotation, familiar as they are :—

> So in that house of misery,
> A lady with a lamp I see
>   Pass through the glimmering gloom,
>   And flit from room to room.
>
> And slowly, as in a dream of bliss,
> The speechless sufferer turns to kiss
>   Her shadow, as it falls
>   Upon the darkening walls.
>
> On England's annals, through the long
> Hereafter of her speech and song,
>   A light its rays shall cast
>   From portals of the past.
>
> A lady with a lamp shall stand
> In the great history of the land,
>   A noble type of good,
>   Heroic womanhood.

To the poet's vision, Florence Nightingale was the modern Santa Filomena, the beautiful saint pictured by Sabatelli descending from heaven with attendant angels to minister to the sick and maimed.

CHAPTER XV

TIMELY HELP

Lavish Gifts for the Soldiers—*The Times* Fund—*The Times* Commissioner Visits Scutari—His Description of Miss Nightingale—Arrival of M. Soyer, the Famous *Chef*—He Describes Miss Nightingale.

This is true philanthropy, that buries not its gold in ostentatious charity, but builds its hospital in the human heart.—G. D. HARLEY.

MISS NIGHTINGALE'S personal efforts for the sick and wounded soldiery were nobly and most generously seconded by sympathisers at home. Ladies were continually arriving at the Admiralty Office in carriages piled with huge boxes and chests labelled "Miss Nightingale," and such large cargoes reached Scutari that it was said at the time the officials might fancy that the Indian mail had been landed by mistake.

The Queen in her palace, assisted by the young princesses, in common with women of all degrees throughout the land, were making lint and bandages, sewing shirts and knitting socks, for the poor soldiers. Nothing indeed was deemed too good

for the suffering heroes. Sister Mary Aloysius relates that when she first began to sort the stores
in the sheds at Scutari, she thought that the
" English nobility must have emptied their ward-
robes and linen stores to send out bandages for
the wounded. There was the most beautiful under-
clothing, and the finest cambric sheets, with merely
a scissors run here and there through them, to
ensure their being used for no other purpose, some
from the Queen's palace, with the Royal monogram
beautifully worked." Amongst these delicate things
the rats had a fine time, and on the woollen goods
they feasted sumptuously ere the sisters could get
them sorted and distributed from their temporary
resting-place in the sheds outside the hospitals.

While private charity was sending its promiscuous
bales of goods, *The Times*, to which belonged the
honour of having first aroused public interest in
the suffering soldiery, had organised a fund for the
relief of the wounded which met with the most
generous support. The great journal undertook to
distribute the fund, and for this purpose appointed
Mr. Macdonald, a man of high character and
endowed with good sense and discrimination, to
proceed to the East and ascertain on the spot the
manner in which the money could be best applied
for the relief of the distressed army.

Before setting forth Mr. Macdonald called on the

Duke of Newcastle, Secretary of State for War, also on Dr. Andrew Smith, the Inspector-General, and was assured by both that such ample measures had been taken by Government that *The Times* fund was really scarcely needed for the relief of the sick and wounded. However, Mr. Macdonald proceeded on his way, for there was at least one man connected with the War Office—Sidney Herbert —who knew from Florence Nightingale's letters what the true state of affairs was.

When *The Times* commissioner reached the Bosphorus, he again had cold water thrown on his mission. Officialdom laughed amiably over "bringing coals to Newcastle." Mr. Macdonald found, however, that the men of the 39th Regiment on their way to the seat of war were going to face the rigours of a Crimean winter in the trenches before Sebastopol in the light and airy garments which they had been wearing at Gibraltar, and he got rid of some of his *Times* gold by going into the markets of Constantinople and purchasing suits of flannels for the men.

When Mr. Macdonald at length reached the hospitals at Scutari—those hospitals the deficient and insanitary state of which had moved the heart of the country to its core—he must have felt dumfounded when Dr. Menzies, the chief medical officer, in answer to his offer of help, told him that " nothing was wanted." It seemed that officialdom was leagued together to deny the existence of wants which the Government ought to have met. In a higher quarter still, Kinglake relates that *The Times* commissioner was met with the astounding proposal that as the fund was wholly unneeded, he might disembarrass himself of it by building an Episcopal Church at Pera !

However, there was one person to whom Mr. Macdonald had not yet offered his money-bags, and he forthwith proceeded to the Barrack Hospital and sought an interview with the Lady-in-Chief and related his experiences

"Help not needed ! the soldiers provided with all necessaries ! the proffered money thrown back on the donors ! " Florence Nightingale must have taken a long gasp when she heard that. She marshalled the excellent Mr. Macdonald and his superfluous cash away to her office in the Nurses' Tower, where he could see for himself the daily demands on her private stores made by the sick and wounded soldiers, and how impossible it was, despite the generous gifts already received from the charitable at home, to meet all requirements.

The Lady-in-Chief could tell of men arriving by hundreds without a shred of decent clothing on their backs, of the lack of hospital furniture, of beds, pillows, sheets, and sanitary appliances, even of drugs, to say nothing of materials for invalid food. Before the narration was concluded Mr. Macdonald must have come to the conclusion that there would be no church built at Pera just yet.

The Times almoner now found his days fully taken up in visits of investigation to the wards, under the guidance of the Lady-in-Chief, and many hours of each day were spent in her office in the Nurses' Tower, taking down in his notebook the things which were pressingly needed and dispatching orders to the storekeepers of Constantinople. Miss Nightingale had now found the kind of help really needed. Here was English gold to replenish her stores at discretion, and she was no longer left to depend on promiscuous charity, which sent embroidered cambric when good stout calico would have been more useful, or fancy mufflers to men who needed shirts. On the eve of his return to England Mr. Macdonald wrote of the Lady-in-Chief :—

" Wherever there is disease in its most dangerous form, and the hand of the spoiler distressingly nigh, there is this incomparable woman sure to be seen. Her benignant presence is an influence for good comfort even among the struggles of expiring nature. She is a 'ministering angel' without any exaggeration in these hospitals, and as her slender form glides quietly along each corridor, every poor fellow's face softens with gratitude at the sight of her. When all the medical officers have retired for the night, and silence and darkness have settled down upon those miles of prostrate sick, she may be observed alone, with a little lamp in her hands, making her solitary rounds.

" The popular instinct was not mistaken which, when she had set out from England on the mission of mercy, hailed her as a heroine ; I trust she may not earn her title to a higher though sadder appellation. No one who has observed her fragile figure and delicate health can avoid misgivings lest these should fail. With the heart of a true woman and the manners of a lady, accomplished and refined beyond most of her sex, she combines a surprising calmness of judgment and promptitude and decision of character.

" I have hesitated to speak of her hitherto as she deserves, because I well knew that no praise of mine could do justice to her merits, while it might have tended to embarrass the frankness with which she has always accepted the aid furnished her through the fund. As that source of supply is now nearly exhausted and my mission approaches its close, I can express myself with more freedom on this subject, and I confidently assert that but for Miss Nightingale the people of England would scarcely, with all their solicitude, have been spared the additional pang of knowing, which they must

MISS NIGHTINGALE AND THE DYING SOLDIER—A SCENE AT SCUTARI HOSPITAL WITNESSED BY M. SOYER.

[*To face p. 176.*

have done sooner or later, that their soldiers, even in the hospital, had found scanty refuge and relief from the unparelleled miseries with which this war has hitherto been attended."

After the departure of Mr. Macdonald, Miss Nightingale received another welcome and also an entertaining visitor in the person of M. Soyer, an expert in cooking and culinary matters generally, to offer his services at the hospitals. M. Soyer's " campaign " was initiated in February, 1855, by the following letter to the editor of *The Times* :—

"Sir,—

" After carefully perusing the letter of your correspondent, dated Scutari, in your impression of Wednesday last, I perceive that, although the kitchen under the superintendence of Miss Nightingale affords so much relief, the system of management at the large one in the Barrack Hospital is far from being perfect. I propose offering my services gratuitously, and proceeding direct to Scutari at my own personal expense, to regulate that important department, if the Government will honour me with their confidence, and grant me the full power of acting according to my knowledge and experience in such matters.

" I have the honour to remain, sir,
" Your obedient servant,
" A. Soyer."

12

The services of M. Soyer having been accepted, he in due course sailed for the East and arrived at Scutari in April. The gallant Frenchman was all anxiety to pay his respects to "Mademoiselle Nightingale," and was gratified to hear that she had heard of his arrival and would be much pleased to see him. As soon as he reached the Barrack Hospital he inquired for Miss Nightingale's apartment, and was immediately shown into what he terms "a sanctuary of benevolence."

Upon entering the room, M. Soyer was received by the Lady-in-Chief, to whom, after the inevitable complimentary speech, he presented parcels and letters from Mr. Stafford, who had been such an indefatigable helper to Miss Nightingale in the past winter, and other friends, among them one from Harriet, Duchess of Sutherland, who strongly commended M. Soyer to Miss Nightingale as likely to be of service in the kitchen department. The Lady-in-Chief arranged to accompany her visitor in a tour of inspection, and M. Soyer thus records his impressions :—

"On my arrival I first visited, in company with Miss Nightingale and one of the medical officers, all the store-rooms, cook-houses, kitchens, and provision departments, to glean an idea of the rules, regulations, and allowances made by the authorities. Instead of there being no appropriate kitchen, as was represented by several Government employees prior to my embarkation for the East, I found ample room and space adapted for culinary purposes even upon the most elaborate and extensive scale.

"I must especially express my gratitude to Miss Nightingale, who from her extraordinary intelligence and the good organisation of her kitchen procured me every material for making a commencement, and thus saved me at least one week's sheer loss of time, as my model kitchen did not arrive until Saturday last."

The Lady-in-Chief found a very valuable ally in M. Soyer, who was eagerly ready to carry out her suggestions for the furtherance of various schemes for the better dietary arrangements for the sick, and who introduced new stoves and fuel and many other reforms of which she had hardly dared to dream in the first months of her work. To these new arrangements Lord William Paulet, the military Commandant, and Drs. Cummings, Menzies and Macgregor the principal medical officers, gave their entire approval, and Miss Nightingale had at length the satisfaction of seeing the culinary arrangements of the Scutari hospitals arranged on a model plan.

During his stay M. Soyer obtained a glimpse into the "ministering angel" side of the lady

whose excellent business faculty had filled him
with admiration as he inspected stoves and boilers
and discussed rations and diets in their rounds of
the kitchens. He had been spending a jovial
evening in the doctors' quarters, and in making
his way at two o'clock in the morning to his own
apartment, he saw, at an angle of one of the long
corridors filled with sick and wounded, a group
revealed in silhouette by a faint light. A dying
soldier was half reclining upon his bed, at the side
of which sat Florence Nightingale pencilling down
his last wishes home. A sister stood at her back
holding a lighted candle. The group thus outlined,
like a sombre study of Rembrandt, drew M. Soyer
to the spot, and for a time unseen he observed
the dying man pass his watch and trinkets into
those tender womanly hands of the Lady-in-Chief,
and heard the laboured gasp of the man to articulate
the last message to wife and children. Then
approaching Miss Nightingale, M. Soyer inquired
as to the complaint of her patient, when she replied
in French that the poor fellow had been given up
by the doctors and was not likely to last many
hours, and she was noting down his last wishes for
his relatives. The incident enables one to realise
how manifold were Miss Nightingale's duties and
how after laborious days she gave up hours of
needed rest in order to comfort the dying.

Soon after the opening of his model kitchen, M. Soyer received a visit from General Vivian, and while the General was there Miss Nightingale entered the kitchen, and an animated conversation ensued regarding hospital treatment. At the conclusion, M. Soyer relates that the General said, " M. Soyer, Miss Nightingale's name and your own will be for ever associated in the archives of this memorable war."

One can understand the ecstasy of the volatile Frenchman at finding himself coupled in such distinguished company and forgive his little conceit, for he was an enthusiastic admirer of our heroine, and has left one of the best pen portraits of her extant. " She is rather high in stature," he writes, " fair in complexion and slim in person ; her hair is brown, and is worn quite plain ; her physiognomy is most pleasing ; her eyes, of a bluish tint, speak volumes, and are always sparkling with intelligence ; her mouth is small and well formed, while her lips act in unison, and make known the impression of her heart—one seems the reflex of the other. Her visage, as regards expression, is very remarkable, and one can almost anticipate by her countenance what she is about to say : alternately, with matters of the most grave import, a gentle smile passes radiantly over her countenance, thus proving her evenness of temper ; at other times, when wit or a pleasantry prevails, the heroine is lost in the happy, good-natured smile which pervades her face, and you recognise only the charming woman.

"Her dress is generally of a greyish or black tint; she wears a simple white cap, and often a rough apron. In a word, her whole appearance is religiously simple and unsophisticated. In conversation no member of the fair sex can be more amiable and gentle than Miss Nightingale. Removed from her arduous and cavalier-like duties, which require the nerve of a Hercules—and she possesses it when required—she is Rachel on the stage in both tragedy and comedy."

CHAPTER XVI

THE ANGEL OF DEATH

Death of Seven Surgeons at Scutari—The First of the " Angel Band "
Stricken—Deaths of Miss Smythe, Sister Winifred, and Sister
Mary Elizabeth—Touching Verses by an Orderly.

> Sleep that no pain shall wake,
> Night that no morn shall break,
> Till joy shall overtake
> Her perfect calm.
>
> CHRISTINA ROSSETTI.

It is the cause, and not the death, that makes the martyr.—NAPOLEON.

THROUGHOUT the spring of 1855 disease continued its ravages amongst the soldiers in the Crimea without abatement, and there was an increase of typhus fever in its worst form. The constitutions of the men were so undermined by the privations through which they had passed that they were unable to fight against the disease.

The " men with the spades " had no cessation from their melancholy toil at Scutari. Deaths occurred daily in the hospitals, and the stricken took the places of the dead only themselves to die before another day had dawned.

The fever also attacked the hospital staff. Eight of the surgeons were prostrated, and of these seven died. Miss Nightingale herself tended Dr. Newton and Dr. Struthers in their last moments, a matter of inexpressible comfort to their friends. For a time there was only one medical attendant in a fit state of health to wait on the sick in the Barrack Hospital, and his services were needed in twenty-four wards. Three of the nurses were also attacked by the fever. With the medical staff prostrated and fever threatening her own band, the duties and responsibilities of the Lady-in-Chief became more formidable. She bore the strain in a marvellous manner, and there is no record that throughout this terrible winter at Scutari she was once unable to discharge her duties. An inflexible will and iron nerve carried her over all difficulties, and it seemed as though Florence Nightingale led a charmed life.

Hitherto she had been spared the sorrow of seeing any of her own band stricken by death, but just when the sweet spring-time was lifting the gloom of this winter of terrible experiences the call came to one of the best beloved of her nurses, Miss Elizabeth Anne Smythe. She had accompanied Miss Nightingale to Scutari, was a personal friend, and had been trained by her. Miss Smythe's beautiful character and her capabilities as a nurse made her very valuable to her chief, who with great regret consented that she should go from Scutari to the hospital at Kullali, where help seemed more urgently needed. Miss Nightingale had hoped that they might have continued to work side by side until the end of the campaign, but the young sister felt a call to go to Kullali, where help was needed.

Shortly after her arrival she wrote to her friends in excellent spirits with every indication of being in good health, and said how glad she was to have had the courage to come. The presence of such a bright, well-qualified nurse was a great acquisition to the hospital staff, and she soon became a favourite with the patients. In a few days, however, she was stricken with the malignant fever. It was hoped against hope that her youth and good constitution would enable her to resist the attack, and for eight days she lay between life and death, anxiously watched by doctors and nurses. Then peacefully she fell asleep and passed to her martyr's crown.

She was the first of the " Angel Band " to be stricken by death, and her loss cast a gloom over those that remained, but as Miss Nightingale has herself said, " Martyrs there must be in every cause."

The funeral of the beloved young sister took place at Easter-time under bright azure skies, when Nature was decking that Eastern land in a fresh garb of loveliness. The simple coffin, covered

with a white pall, emblematic of the youthful purity
of her who slept beneath, was conveyed through
the streets of Smyrna to the English burying-ground,
a route of two miles, through crowds of sympathetic
spectators. The coffin was preceded by a detach-
ment of fifty soldiers, marching sorrowfully with
arms reversed. Immediately in front of the coffin
walked two chaplains, and on either side were sisters
and nurses. Military and medical officers followed
the *cortège*, which passed through the silent streets,
a touching and pathetic spectacle. Christian and
Moslem alike joined in paying a tribute of homage
to one whose deeds of mercy lifted her above the
strife of creeds.

> The first young Christian martyr
> Is carried to the tomb,
> And busy marts and crowded streets
> Are wrapt alike in gloom.
>
> And men who loathe the Cross and name
> Which she was proud to own,
> Yet pay their homage, meet and due,
> To her good deeds alone.

Before many weeks had passed by, Miss Nightingale was again called to mourn the loss of another
of her helpers. The next claimed by death was
Sister Winifred, a Sister of Charity, who, with other
nuns from Ireland, was tending the Irish soldiers
in the hospital at Balaclava, to which they had

recently come from Scutari and Kullali. Only a few days after her arrival Sister Winifred was attacked by cholera, which had broken out afresh at Balaclava.

Very touching is the account which Sister Mary Aloysius gives of the death of her comrade : " Our third day in Balaclava was a very sad one for us. One of our dear band, Sister Winifred, got very ill during the night with cholera. She was a most angelic sister, and we were all deeply grieved. She was attacked at about three o'clock in the morning with the symptoms which were now so well known to us; every remedy was applied ; our beloved Rev. Mother never left her. She was attended by Father Unsworth, from whom she received the last rites of our holy religion ; and she calmly breathed her last on the evening of the same day. A hut was arranged in which to place the remains ; and so alarming were the rats—and such huge animals were they—that we had to watch during the night so that they should not touch her. She, the first to go of our little band (viz. the Roman Catholic sisters), had been full of life and energy the day before. We were all very sad, and we wondered who would be the next."

A burial-place was found for Sister Winifred on a piece of ground between two rocks, on the hills of Balaclava, where her remains could repose without fear of desecration. The funeral formed a contrast to that of the Protestant sister at Smyrna, but was equally impressive. We can picture the sad cavalcade, distinguished by the symbols of the Roman Catholic faith, wending its way up the hillside to the lonely spot in the rocks above the Black Sea. Two priests preceded the coffin, chanting the prayers, and the black-robed nuns came closely behind, while soldiers and military and medical officers followed.

Amongst the mourning band walked one tall, slight figure dressed simply in black whose presence arrested attention. It was Florence Nightingale, who had come to pay her tribute of love and honour to the sister who, if divided by faith, had been united with her in holy work and deeds of mercy.

A tribute was paid to the memory of Sister Winifred in a poem by a friend, from which we quote the following verses :—

They laid her in her lonely grave upon a foreign strand,
Far from her own dear island home, far from her native land.
They bore her to her long last home amid the clash of arms,
And the hymn they sang seemed sadly sweet amid war's fierce
    alarms.

They heeded not the cannon's roar, the rifle's deadly shot,
But onward still they sadly went to gain that lowly spot ;
And there, with many a fervent prayer and many a word of
    love,
They left her in her lowly grave with a simple cross above.

Yet far away from her convent grey, and far from her lowly
   cell,
And far from the soft and silvery tone of the sweet convent
   bell,
And far from the home she loved so well, and far from her
   native sky,
'Mid the cannon's roar on a hostile shore she laid her down
   to die.

*   *   *   *   *

She went not forth to gain applause, she sought not empty
   fame ;
E'en those she tended might not know her history or her
   name ;
No honours waited on her path, no flattering voice was nigh ;
For she only sought to toil and love, and 'mid her toil to
   die.

They raise no trophy to her name, they rear no stately bust,
To tell the stranger where she rests, co-mingling with the
   dust ;
They leave her in her lowly grave, beneath that foreign sky,
Where she had taught them how to live, and taught them how
   to die.

The grave of Sister Winifred was, unhappily, not
destined to remain solitary. In the early spring
of 1856—to anticipate the sequence of our
narrative a little—another funeral was seen wending
its way, to the chanting of priests, up the hills of
Balaclava. It was the body of Sister Mary Elizabeth,
who had died of fever, caught amongst the patients
of her ward. Our informant, Sister Mary Aloysius,
thus describes the death scene as it occurred amid a

storm which threatened to unroof the wooden hut where the dying sister lay: "It was a wild, wild night. The storm and wind penetrated the chinks so as to extinguish the lights, and evoked many a prayer that the death-bed might not be left roofless. It was awful beyond description to kneel beside her during these hours of her passage and to hear the solemn prayers for the dead and dying mingling with the howling of the winds and the creaking of the frail wooden hut. Oh, never, never can any of us forget that night : the storm disturbed all but her, that happy being for whom earth's joys and sorrows were at an end, and whose summons home had not cost her one pang or one regret."

They buried Sister Mary Elizabeth beside Sister Winifred, and the 89th Regiment requested the honour of carrying the coffin. Hundreds of soldiers lined the way in triple lines from the hospital to the hut where the body lay, and a procession of various nationalities and differing faiths followed the body to its lonely resting place on the rocky ledge of Balaclava heights.

Later, when the graves of the two sisters were visited, it was found that flowers and evergreens were growing in that lonely spot, planted by the hands of the soldiers they had tended. On the white cross of Sister Winifred's grave was found a paper, on which were written the following lines :—

Still green be the willow that grows on the mountain,
And weeps o'er the grave of the sister that's gone;

*   *   *   *   *

And most glorious its lot to point out to the stranger,
The hallowed remains of the sainted and blest;
For those angels of mercy that dared every danger
To bring to the soldier sweet comfort and rest.

It was discovered that these lines had been composed and placed there by one of Sister Winifred's orderlies.

CHAPTER XVII

SAILS FOR THE CRIMEA AND GOES UNDER FIRE

On Board the *Robert Lowe*—Story of a Sick Soldier—Visit to the
Camp Hospitals—Sees Sebastopol from the Trenches—Recognised and Cheered by the Soldiers—Adventurous Ride Back.

> The walls grew weak; and fast and hot
> Against them pour'd the ceaseless shot,
> With unabating fury sent,
> From battery to battlement;
> And thunder-like the pealing din
> Rose from each heated culverin:
> And here and there some crackling dome
> Was fired before th' exploding bomb."
>
> BYRON.

ON May 2nd, 1855, Florence Nightingale,
having completed six months' continuous
labour in establishing a system of good administration in the hospitals at Scutari, set out for Balaclava.
She was anxious to see how the sick and wounded
were faring at the actual seat of war, and it was
also her duty as Superintendent of the Nursing Staff
in the East to inspect the hospitals in the Crimea.

There were some sad good-byes to say before
she quitted the scene of her work at Scutari, for

LADY HERBERT OF LEA.

[*To face p.* 192.

death would have claimed many brave fellows ere she returned to her old post. Sorrowful eyes followed the gleam of the familiar lamp as she went her final rounds on the night before her departure, and heads were pathetically turned to catch a last look at her shadow as it passed on the whitened wall.

Rarely has any human being had such a retrospect of harrowing experience and of insuperable difficulties overcome as passed through Florence Nightingale's mind when she reviewed the past six months. The Barrack Hospital as she had found it, crowded with suffering humanity in the most appalling state of loathsome neglect, seemed like a hideous nightmare, scarcely to be realised in comparison with the order, comfort, and cleanliness which now prevailed.

It was with a heart of thankfulness to the Giver of all Good that she had been permitted to accomplish this great work that Florence Nightingale on a bright May morning stepped aboard the good ship *Robert Lowe* and set sail for the Crimea. She was accompanied by a staff of nurses and her friend Mr. Bracebridge, and by M. Soyer, the celebrated *chef*, who was going to reform culinary matters at the " front," and attended by her boy Thomas, a young drummer who had abandoned his " instruments and sticks," as he called them, to devote himself to the Lady-in-Chief. No general in the

13

field had a more devoted aide-de-camp than Florence
Nightingale had in Thomas.   He was a lad of
twelve, full of life, fun, and activity and of amusing
importance, but such was his devotion that he
would have been cut to bits ere harm came near his
beloved mistress.

The short voyage was made in lovely weather,
when the spring air was redolent with perfume
and freshness, and scarcely a ripple moved the blue
waters of the Bosphorus.   Miss Nightingale greatly
enjoyed being on deck as the vessel glided past
some of the most beautiful scenes in that Eastern
land.   There rose the mosques and minarets of
Constantinople, enveloped, as it seemed, in golden
vapour, then the Golden Horn was passed, and
the European and Asiatic shores opened out in a
scene of Oriental beauty.   The picturesque caiques
skimmed the waters like magic craft, and Miss
Nightingale was fortunate in seeing the gorgeous
flotilla of the Sultan, consisting of large caiques
brilliantly decorated with gilded and rich silken
hangings, and manned by gaily dressed oarsmen,
leave the marble staircase of the Dolmabatchke Palace
to convey the Sultan and his suite to the Mosque
of Sultan Mahomet, for it was Friday, the Turkish
Sunday.   Fifty guns proclaimed the departure of
the nautical procession.   Then Kullali was passed,
and the voyagers thought sadly of the young sister

who had recently died there at her post in the hospital. On went the vessel, past the Sweet Waters of Asia, where the Turks hold high festival, and the resorts of Therapia and Buyukdére, until at length the dazzling Oriental coast was almost lost to view as the ship entered the Black Sea.

However, Miss Nightingale's delight in the sights and scenes through which she was passing did not render her oblivious to her fellow-passengers. There were six hundred soldiers on board and many officers and Government officials. The second day of the voyage, being Sunday, Miss Nightingale, accompanied by the captain, visited the lower deck and talked with the soldiers, and having heard that there were some invalids on board, asked to see them. In passing from sufferer to sufferer, she at length came to a fever patient who had refused to take his medicine.

"Why will you not take the medicine?" asked Miss Nightingale.

"Because I took some once," the man replied, "and it made me sick; and I haven't liked physic ever since."

"But if I give it to you myself," said the Queen of Nurses with a pleasant smile, "you will take it, won't you?"

The poor fellow looked very hard at her and replied, "Well, sure enough, ma'am, it will make me sick just the same." However, he took the draught and forgot the anticipated consequence as Miss Nightingale chatted to him about the last engagement he was in.

The distant booming of the cannon in Sebastopol intimated to the travellers that they were nearing their destination, and on one of the high peaked mountains they could plainly see the Russian picket mounting guard. An hour later the vessel reached the harbour of Balaclava, which presented a wonderful sight with the numerous great ships lying at anchor. The news had spread that Miss Nightingale was expected to arrive that day, and the decks of the vessels in harbour were crowded with people anxious to get a glimpse of her. Immediately the *Robert Lowe* came to anchor, the chief medical officer of the Balaclava Hospital and other doctors and officials came on board to welcome Miss Nightingale, and for an hour she held what her fellow-voyager, M. Soyer, facetiously termed "a floating drawing-room." Later, Lord Raglan, Commander-in-Chief of the British forces, came to welcome the illustrious heroine, but only to find that she had already landed and begun her work of hospital inspection.

Next day, Miss Nightingale, accompanied by Mr. Bracebridge, M. Soyer, and an escort of other friends, set out for the camp to return Lord Raglan's visit. She "was attired simply in a genteel amazone, or riding-habit," relates M. Soyer, "and had quite a martial air. She was mounted upon a very pretty mare, of a golden colour, which, by its gambols and caracoling, seemed proud to carry its noble charge. The weather was very fine. Our cavalcade produced an extraordinary effect upon the motley crowd of all nations assembled at Balaclava, who were astonished at seeing a lady so well escorted."

The people did not, however, know how illustrious the lady was, for Miss Nightingale preserved an incognito on her way to the camp. At that time there were only four ladies in the Crimea, excepting the sisters of mercy, who were never seen out, so there was great curiosity as the cavalcade approached headquarters to know who the lady was, and Mr. Bracebridge had to give evasive replies to enquiring officers.

Florence Nightingale's ride to camp proved an adventurous one. The road was bad and not nearly wide enough for all the traffic. Crowds of many nationalities, together with a ceaseless stream of mules, horses, oxen, artillery waggons, cannon, infantry, and cavalry struggled over the uneven muddy road, drivers and officers shouting, horses kicking, sometimes a waggon overturned, and everybody in a state of turmoil. Miss Nightingale's horse kicked and pranced in company with the

horses of her escort, and but for a cool nerve and
steady hand she would certainly have come to
grief.   But the skill in horsemanship which she
had acquired as a girl amongst the hills and dales
of Derbyshire now served her in good stead, and
the ride was accomplished in safety.

The first halt was made at the hospital in a small
Greek church at the village of Kadikoi.   After a
little tour of inspection Miss Nightingale and her
party galloped up to the top of a high hill from
which was visible a panorama of the camp, with
its myriads of white tents dotted over the landscape.
Now, indeed, she was in touch with that great
bivouac of warfare which the wounded at the
Barrack Hospital in Scutari had raved about in their
fever wanderings.   Upon the air came the roar
of the cannon from Sebastopol, the sound of
trumpets, the beating of drums, and the general
din of military manœuvres.   Around the martial
plain rose the rugged heights of Balaclava with
that valley of death sacred to the " noble six
hundred " :—

> Stormed at with shot and shell,
> Boldly they rode and well,
> Into the jaws of Death,
> Into the mouth of Hell
>   Rode the six hundred.

Florence Nightingale sat long on her horse,

gazing afar at the stirring scene and then turned
sadly away. She knew that hundreds of poor
fellows away in yonder trenches were doomed to
swell the ranks of the dead and wounded ere the
siege of Sebastopol was ended.

Proceeding on her way to headquarters, Miss
Nightingale called to inspect several of the small
regimental hospitals. When at length the vicinity
of Lord Raglan's house was reached, Mr. Bracebridge, acting as advance guard, galloped forward,
to announce the approach of the Lady-in-Chief, only
to find, however, that the Commander-in-Chief,
who had not received intimation of her coming, was
away. Miss Nightingale having left a message of
thanks to Lord Raglan for his visit of the previous
day, now proceeded to the General Hospital before
Sebastopol.

This hospital contained some hundreds of sick
and wounded, and great was the joy of the poor
fellows at receiving a visit from the " good lady
of Scutari," as they called Miss Nightingale. When
she went out past the huts to the cooking en-
campment, some of the men who had been patients
at the Barrack Hospital recognise[1] Miss Nightingale
and gave her three hearty cheers, followed by three
times three. She was much affected by such an
unexpected demonstration, and being on horseback
could only bow to the men by way of thanks.

The shouts grew so vociferous that Miss Nightingale's horse turned restive, and one of her friends was obliged to dismount and lead it by the bridle until the men's enthusiasm had abated.

The party now proceeded through the French and English camps which surrounded Sebastopol. Miss Nightingale expressed a wish to have a peep into the besieged stronghold, and a column was formed to escort her to a convenient point. Some sharp firing was going on, and as the visitors approached a sentry in much trepidation begged them to dismount, pointing to the shot and shell lying around, and remarking that a group of people would attract the enemy to fire in their direction. Miss Nightingale laughingly consented to seek the shelter of a stone reboubt where she could view Sebastopol through a telescope. From this vantage ground she obtained an excellent sight of the doomed city, being able to discern the principal buildings and to see the duel of shot proceeding between the allied armies and the enemy.

Miss Nightingale was in an adventurous mood, and proposed to go still farther into the trenches up to the Three-Mortar Battery. Her friends Mr. Bracebridge, Dr. Anderson, and M. Soyer were favourable to her wish, but the sentry was in a great state of consternation.

"Madam," said he, "if anything happens I call

on these gentlemen to witness that I did not fail to warn you of the danger."

"My good young man," replied Miss Nightingale, "more dead and wounded have passed through my hands than I hope you will ever see in the battlefield during the whole of your military career; believe me, I have no fear of death."

The party proceeded and, arrived at the battery, obtained a near view of Sebastopol. M. Soyer was in his most volatile mood, and relates that the following incident occurred: "Before leaving the battery, I begged Miss Nightingale as a favour to give me her hand, which she did. I then requested her to ascend the stone rampart next the wooden gun carriage, and lastly to sit upon the centre mortar, to which requests she very gracefully and kindly acceded." Having thus unsuspectedly beguiled Miss Nightingale into this position, the irrepressible Frenchman boldly exclaimed:

"Gentlemen, behold this amiable lady sitting fearlessly upon that terrible instrument of war! Behold the heroic daughter of England—the soldier's friend!" All present shouted "Bravo! Hurrah! hurrah! Long live the daughter of England."

When later Lord Raglan was told of this incident, he remarked that the battery mortar ought to be called "the Nightingale mortar."

While in that elevated position the heroine was recognised by the 39th Regiment, and the men set up such ringing cheers as wakened echoes in the caves of Inkerman and startled the Russians in Sebastopol.

The sun was beginning to sink below the horizon and shadows to gather over the trenches and fortifications of the besieged city when Miss Nightingale started on the return journey. She and her party, proceeding at a sharp gallop through the camps, were overtaken by darkness when only half-way back to Balaclava, and losing their way, found themselves in a Zouave camp, where the men were drinking coffee and singing their favourite African song. They informed the travellers that brigands were roaming about, and that it was dangerous to take the road after nightfall. However, brigands or not, there was nothing for it but to push on down the deep ravine which now faced them. The road was so steep and slippery that one of the gentlemen dismounted to lead Miss Nightingale's horse by the bridle. When they halted to water the horses, this gentleman received a severe blow in the face by coming in sharp contact in the dark with the head of Miss Nightingale's steed. He concealed the injury, though his face was streaming with blood and his eyes blackened, until they reached Balaclava hospital, when the Queen of Nurses returned his kind attention by helping to dress his wounds. Proceeding to the harbour, she retired to her state cabin on the *Robert Lowe*, and so ended Florence Nightingale's adventurous visit to the camp hospitals before Sebastopol.

CHAPTER XVIII

STRICKEN BY FEVER

Continued Visitation of Hospitals—Sudden Illness—Conveyed to
Sanatorium—Visit of Lord Raglan—Convalescence—Accepts
Offer of Lord Ward's Yacht—Returns to Scutari—Memorial
to Fallen Heroes.

> Know how sublime a thing it is
> To suffer and be strong.
> LONGFELLOW.

NOTHING daunted by the fatiguing journey
to the camp hospitals at headquarters
related in the last chapter, Miss Nightingale,
although she was feeling indisposed, set out the
next morning to visit the General Hospital at
Balaclava and the Sanatorium. She was accompanied
by the ubiquitous M. Soyer, who was carrying
out his culinary campaign at the Crimean hospitals,
and attended by her faithful boy Thomas.

After spending several hours inspecting the wards
of the General Hospital, Miss Nightingale proceeded
to the Sanatorium, a collection of huts perched
on the Genoese heights nearly eight hundred feet

above the sea. She was escorted by Mr. Bracebridge, Dr. Sutherland, and a sergeant's guard. The weather was intensely hot, as is usual in the Crimea during the month of May, and the journey, following on the fatigue of the previous day, proved a trying one. Half-way up the heights, Miss Nightingale stopped to visit a sick officer in one of the doctor's huts, and afterwards proceeded to inspect the Sanatorium.

She returned to Balaclava, and next day went to install three nurses in the Sanatorium; and on her way up again visited the invalid officer in his lonely hut. During the succeeding days she continued her inspection of the hospitals in Balaclava, and also removed her quarters to the *London*, as the *Robert Lowe*, in which she sailed, was ordered home.

It was when on board the *London*, while she was transacting business with one of her nursing staff, that Miss Nightingale was suddenly seized with alarming illness. The doctors pronounced it to be the worst form of Crimean fever, and ordered that she should be immediately taken up to the Sanatorium. She was laid on a stretcher, and tenderly carried by sad-eyed soldiers through Balaclava and up the mountain side amid general consternation. Her own private nurse, Mrs. Roberts, attended her, a friend held a large white umbrella to protect her face from the glaring sun, and poor Thomas, the page-boy, who had proudly called himself " Miss Nightingale's man," followed his mistress, crying piteously. So great was the lamenting crowd that it took an hour to get the precious burden up to the heights. A hut was selected near a small stream, the banks of which were gay with spring flowers, and there for the next few days Florence Nightingale lay in a most critical condition, assiduously nursed by Mrs. Roberts and attended by Drs. Henderson and Hadley.

It seemed strange to every one that Miss Nightingale, after passing unscathed through her hard labours at Scutari, when she had been in daily contact with cholera and fever, should have succumbed to disease at Balaclava, but the fatigues of the past days, undertaken during excessive heat, accounted largely for the seizure, and some of her friends thought also that she had caught infection when visiting the sick officer on her way up to the Sanatorium.

Alarmist reports quickly spread, and at Balaclava it was currently reported that Florence Nightingale was dying. The sad tidings were told at the Barrack Hospital at Scutari amidst the most pathetic scenes. The sick men turned their faces to the wall and cried like children. The news in due time reached London, and the leading articles in the papers of the time show that the public regarded the possible death of our heroine as a great national calamity. Happily the suspense was brief, and following quickly on the mournful tidings came the glad news that the worst symptoms were passed, and that in all human probability the precious life would be spared.

Miss Nightingale, in a touching bit of auto-biography, attributes her first step towards convalescence to the joy caused on receiving a bunch of wild-flowers.

During the time that Miss Nightingale lay in her hut on the Genoese heights, some very sharp skirmishes were taking place between the allied troops and the enemy, and it was reported that the Russians were likely to attack Balaclava by the Kamara side. Miss Nightingale's hut being the nearest to that point, would, in the event of such a plan being carried out, have been the first to be attacked. Thomas, the page boy, constituted himself guard of his beloved mistress and was ready to die valiantly in her defence. It would, however, be an injustice to the Russian troops to imply that they would knowingly have harmed even a hair of Florence Nightingale's head. Her person was sacred to friend and foe alike.

Lord Raglan was deeply concerned at Miss Nightingale's illness, and as soon as he heard from the doctors in attendance that he might visit her, rode over from headquarters for the purpose. Mrs. Roberts, the nurse, thus related to M. Soyer the account of the Commander-in-Chief's unexpected call :—

" It was about five o'clock in the afternoon when he came. Miss Nightingale was dozing, after a very restless night. We had a storm that day, and it was very wet. I was in my room sewing when two men on horseback, wrapped in large gutta-percha cloaks and dripping wet, knocked at the door. I went out, and one inquired in which hut Miss Nightingale resided.

" He spoke so loud that I said, ' Hist ! Hist ! don't make such a horrible noise as that, my man,' at the same time making a sign with both hands for him to be quiet. He then repeated his question, but not in so loud a tone. I told him this was the hut.

" ' All right,' said he, jumping from his horse, and he was walking straight in when I pushed him back, asking what he meant and whom he wanted.

" ' Miss Nightingale,' said he.

" ' And pray who are you ? '

" ' Oh, only a soldier,' was the reply ; ' but I must see her—I have come a long way—my name is Raglan—she knows me very well.'

" Miss Nightingale overhearing him, called me

FLORENCE NIGHTINGALE AS A GIRL.

drawn o her sister Lad V

in, saying, 'Oh! Mrs. Roberts, it is Lord Raglan. Pray tell him I have a very bad fever, and it will be dangerous for him to come near me.'

"'I have no fear of fever or anything else,' said Lord Raglan.

"And before I had time to turn round, in came his lordship. He took up a stool, sat down at the foot of the bed, and kindly asked Miss Nightingale how she was, expressing his sorrow at her illness, and thanking and praising her for the good she had done for the troops. He wished her a speedy recovery, and hoped that she might be able to continue her charitable and invaluable exertions, so highly appreciated by every one, as well as by himself.

"He then bade Miss Nightingale good-bye, and went away. As he was going out, I said I wished 'to apologize.'

"'No! no! not at all, my dear lady,' said Lord Raglan; 'you did very right; for I perceive that Miss Nightingale has not yet received my letter, in which I announced my intention of paying her a visit to-day—having previously inquired of the doctor if she could be seen.'"

Miss Nightingale became convalescent about twelve days after her seizure, and the doctors were urgent that she should immediately sail for England. This our heroine steadfastly declined to do, feeling

14

that her mission was not accomplished, and that she could not desert her post.   Although in a state of extreme weakness and exhaustion, she felt that time would accomplish her recovery, and she decided to return in the meantime to Scutari, with the intention of coming back to the Crimea to complete her work.

A berth was arranged for her in the *Jura*, and Miss Nightingale was brought down from the Sanatorium upon a stretcher carried by eight soldiers and accompanied by Dr. Hadley, Mrs. Roberts (the nurse), several Sisters of Charity and other friends. When the procession reached the *Jura*, tackle was attached to the four corners of the stretcher, and the invalid was thus swung on deck by means of pulleys.   She was carefully carried to the chief cabin, and it was hoped that she would now accomplish the voyage in comfort.   Unfortunately, a disagreeable smell was discovered to pervade the *Jura*, caused by a number of horses which had recently been landed from it, and shortly after being brought aboard Miss Nightingale fainted.   The page Thomas was dispatched to recall Dr. Hadley, who, when he arrived, ordered that the illustrious patient should at once be conveyed to another vessel.

Miss Nightingale was temporarily taken to the *Baraguay d'Hilliers*, until an order could be procured from the admiral for another vessel.

Meantime Lord Ward, afterwards Earl of Dudley and father of the present Lord-Lieutenant of Ireland, who had been active in sending help to the sick and wounded, heard with great concern of the inconvenience, and indeed danger to life, which Miss Nightingale was suffering, and at once offered her the use of his yacht, the *New London*, to take her to Scutari. Lord Ward further arranged that the yacht should be at her entire disposal, and no one should be on board except his medical man and those whom she chose to take with her. Miss Nightingale was pleased to accept Lord Ward's offer, and she was accordingly conveyed to the yacht, and established in great ease and comfort. Besides her personal attendants Miss Nightingale was accompanied by Mr. Bracebridge and M. Soyer.

Before her departure Lord Raglan visited Miss Nightingale on board the *New London*, but little did she think that in a few short weeks the brave commander would have passed to the great majority. He had shown himself most sympathetic to her mission to the East, and had received her letters in regard to reforms in the hospitals with attention, while in his dispatches to the Government he had paid the highest tribute to the value of her work amongst the sick soldiers. During the period of Miss Nightingale's convalescence, he sent frequent inquiries after her health.

Meantime, Lord Raglan's difficulties as Commander-in-Chief of the British forces were daily increasing. On June 18th, 1855, the allied armies were to make the general assault on Sebastopol. Lord Raglan had proposed to preface the assault by a two hours' cannonade to silence the guns remounted by the enemy during the night, but Pélissier, the French commander, pressed for an immediate attack at daybreak, and Lord Raglan yielded rather than imperil the alliance. The result was disastrous, ending in the terrible assault and repulse of the British troops at the Redan. The Commander-in-Chief felt the failure deeply, and it was to announce this defeat that he wrote his last dispatch to the Government, June 26th. On the 28th he breathed his last, worn out and disheartened by the gigantic task with which he had been called to grapple.

Miss Nightingale, in her own weakened condition, was deeply affected by Lord Raglan's death. He was a man of charming and benevolent disposition, and thoroughly straightforward in all his dealings. Wellington described him as "a man who wouldn't tell a lie to save his life." He had served under that great commander during half his career, and was proud to the last, when he had to contend with much adverse criticism, that he had enjoyed the confidence of Wellington.

Lord Raglan was blamed for not visiting the camps during the earlier stages of the Crimean war and ascertaining the condition of his soldiers, whereby much of the sickness and misery might have been obviated, but his biographers say that this charge, though not groundless, was exaggerated. Lord Raglan was a rough and ready soldier, who disliked ostentation, and in this way many of his visits to the camp passed almost unnoticed. The impromptu call which he made at Miss Nightingale's hut, already related, was thoroughly characteristic of Lord Raglan's methods.

Miss Nightingale returned to Scutari a little more than a month after she had left for the Crimea, and was received on landing by Lord William Paulet, Commandant, Dr. Cumming, Inspector-General, and Dr. Macgregor, Deputy-Inspector. Lord Stratford de Redcliffe, the Ambassador, offered her the use of the British Palace at Pera, but Miss Nightingale preferred to use the house of the chaplain, the Rev. Mr. Sabin, and there she made a good recovery under the care of solicitous friends.

Often in these days of returning strength she would stroll beneath the trees of the cemetery of Scutari, where so many of our brave men lay. It is situated on a promontory high above the sea, with a fine outlook over the Bosphorus. Flowers planted by loving hands were decking

the graves of many of her friends who had
passed away during the winter, and the grasses
had begun to wave above the deep pits where the
soldiers lay in a nameless grave.   During these
walks Miss Nightingale gathered a few flowers here,
a bunch of grasses there, and pressed and dried
them, to keep in loving memory of the brave dead.
They eventually formed part of a collection of
Crimean mementoes which she arranged after her
return home to Lea Hurst.

This burying-ground was really a portion of
the ancient cemetery of Scutari, the most sacred
and celebrated in the Ottoman Empire.   Travellers
have described the weird effect of the dense masses
of cypress-trees, which bend and wave over three
miles of unnumbered tombs, increasing each year
in extent.   The Turks never disturb their dead,
and regard a burying-ground with great veneration,
hence the ancient and yet modern character of the
Scutari cemetery, and the great extent of the graves
over the wide solitude.   So thick are the cypress-
trees that even the Oriental sun does not penetrate
their shade.   Byron has described the scene as—

> The place of thousand tombs
> That shine beneath, while dark above
> The sad but living cypress glooms
> And withers not, though branch and leaf
> Are stamped by an eternal grief.

According to a poetic legend, myriads of strange birds hover over the tombs, or flit noiselessly from the Black Sea to the fairer one of Marmora, when they turn and retrace their flight. These birds have never been known to stop or feed, and never heard to sing. They have a dark plumage, in unison with the sombre cypress-trees over which they incessantly flit. When there is a storm on the Bosphorus, they send up sharp cries of agony. The Turks believe that the weird birds are condemned souls who have lived an evil life in this world, and are not permitted to rest in a tomb, and so in a spirit of unrest they wander over the tombs of others. One of the most beautiful monuments in the vast cemetery is the one which marks the grave of Sultan Mahmoud's favourite horse.

The Turkish Government gave a piece of ground adjacent to the sacred cemetery to serve as a burying-place for the British soldiers who fell in the Crimea. And it was at the instance of Miss Nightingale that a memorial was erected there to the fallen heroes. She started the scheme during her period of convalescence at Scutari, and it was completed after the conclusion of the war. Some four thousand British soldiers lie in the cemetery, and in the midst of the nameless graves rises a gleaming column of marble. The shaft is supported by four angels with drooping wings.   On each side of the base is inscribed in four different languages :—

" THIS MONUMENT WAS ERECTED BY

QUEEN VICTORIA

AND HER PEOPLE."

CHAPTER XIX

CLOSE OF THE WAR

Fall of Sebastopol—The Nightingale Hospital Fund—A Carriage
Accident—Last Months in the Crimea—"The Nightingale
Cross"—Presents from Queen Victoria and the Sultan—Sails
for Home.

> How many now are left of those whose serried ranks
> Were first to land on Eupatoria's hostile shore;
> Who rushed victoriously up the Alma's banks,
> And won the primal honours of that mighty war?
>
> Theirs were the fadeless laurels!—yet not theirs alone,
> Who bore the stern privations of that Eastern camp:—
> Scutari's coronet of glory is thine own,
> O Florence Nightingale, dear
> Lady with the Lamp.
> MAJOR A. ST. JOHN SEALLY.

THE autumn of 1855 brought the final act
in the great drama of the Crimean War.
On the morning of September 8th the allied armies
before Sebastopol were ready for the final assault.
The day dawned gloriously, and by five o'clock the
guards were on the march for the besieged city,
and troops from all quarters pressed silently in
the same direction. The supreme moment had

come; the long tension of the siege was broken, and each man braced him to the fight and looked for death or glory.

The elements seemed to voice the situation. A brilliant sky gave the promise of victory, then suddenly changed to storm-clouds which burst in a furious tempest as the batteries opened fire upon the doomed city. The earth groaned and shook with the noise of cannon and the air was filled with the rattle of musketry. An hour elapsed, and then came the first shouts of victory. The French allies had captured the Malakhoff and the British had taken the Redan, the fort which three months before had repulsed the attacking force with fearful carnage and brought Lord Raglan to a despairing death. The fight raged fiercely until nightfall and ere another day dawned the Russians had retreated, leaving Sebastopol in flames.

On the morning of September 9th the tidings spread far and wide that the mighty stronghold had fallen and the power of the enemy was broken. The news was received in London with a universal outburst of rejoicing. The Tower guns proclaimed the victory, every arsenal fired its salute, and the joy-bells rang from cathedral minster to the humblest village church as the tidings spread through the land. The long night of War was over, and white-robed Peace stood on the threshold.

With the plaudits that rang through the land in honour of the victorious armies, the name of Florence Nightingale was mingled on every hand. The nation was eager to give our heroine a right royal welcome home, but she sought no great ovation, no public demonstration, and her home-coming was not to be yet. The war had ended, but the victims still remained in hospital ward and lonely hut, and as long as the wounded needed her care Florence Nightingale would not leave her post.

Meanwhile, however, the Queen and all classes of her people were eager to give proof of the nation's gratitude to the noble woman who had come to the succour of the soldiers in their dire need. Mr. and Mrs. Sidney Herbert were approached on the matter by Mrs. S. C. Hall as to what form of testimonial would be most acceptable to Miss Nightingale, and Mrs. Herbert replied :—

"49, BELGRAVE SQUARE,
"*July*, 1855.

" MADAM,—

"There is but one testimonial which would be accepted by Miss Nightingale.

"The one wish of her heart has long been to found a hospital in London and to work it on her own system of unpaid nursing, and I have suggested to all who have asked for my advice in this matter to pay any sums that they may feel disposed to give, or that they may be able to collect, into Messrs. Coutts' Bank, where a subscription list for the purpose is about to be opened, to be called the 'Nightingale Hospital Fund,' the sum subscribed to be presented to her on her return home, which will enable her to carry out her object regarding the reform of the nursing system in England."

A Committee to inaugurate such a project was formed. It was presided over by His Royal Highness the late Duke of Cambridge, and included representatives of all classes. The Hon. Mr. Sidney Herbert and Mr. S. C. Hall acted as honorary secretaries, and the latter summarised the variety of interests represented when he described the Committee as having "three dukes, nine other noblemen, the Lord Mayor, two judges, five right honourables, foremost naval and military officers, physicians, lawyers, London aldermen, dignitaries of the Church, dignitaries of Nonconformist Churches, twenty members of Parliament, and several eminent men of letters." While no state party was omitted, none was unduly prominent. It was resolved by the Committee to devote the money subscribed to the Nightingale Fund to founding an institute for the training, sustenance, and protection of nurses and hospital attendants, to embrace the paid and the unpaid, for whom a home should be provided and a retreat for old age. A copy of the resolution was forwarded to Miss Nightingale at Scutari and she replied to Mrs. Herbert in the following letter :—

" Exposed as I am to be misinterpreted and misunderstood, in a field of action in which the work is new, complicated, and distant from many who sit in judgment on it, it is indeed an abiding support to have such sympathy and such appreciation brought home to me in the midst of labours and difficulties all but overpowering. I must add, however, that my present work is such I would never desert for any other, so long as I see room to believe that which I may do here is unfinished. May I then beg you to express to the Committee that I accept their proposals, provided I may do so on their understanding of this great uncertainty as to when it will be possible for me to carry it out ? "

The gift, indeed, gave Florence Nightingale a further task to perform on her return home, but as Mr. Sidney Herbert said : " Miss Nightingale looks to her reward from this country in having a fresh field for her labours, and means of extending the good that she has already begun. A compliment cannot be paid dearer to her heart than in giving her more work to do."

A public meeting was held at Willis's Rooms on November 29th, 1855, to inaugurate the scheme. It was presided over by the Duke of Cambridge and addressed by the venerable Lord Lansdowne, Sir John Pakington (Lord Hampton), Monckton-Milnes (Lord Houghton), Lord Stanley (Earl of Derby), the Lord Mayor, the Marquis of Ripon, Rev. Dr. Cumming, and Dr. Gleig, the Chaplain-General. All paid eloquent tributes to the work accomplished by Miss Nightingale, but the most touching incident of the meeting was when Mr. Sidney Herbert read a letter from a friend who said: "I have just heard a pretty account from a soldier describing the comfort it was even to see Florence pass. 'She would speak to one and another,' he said, 'and nod and smile to many more, but she could not do it to all, you know, for we lay there by hundreds; but we could kiss her shadow as it fell, and lay our heads on the pillow again content.'" That story brought £10,000 to the Nightingale Fund, and the soldier who had related it out of the fulness of his heart must have felt a proud man.

Public meetings in aid of the scheme were held during the ensuing months in all the principal cities and towns throughout the kingdom, and also in all parts of the Empire, including India and the colony in China. Never, I believe, has the work of any British subject been so honoured and recognised in every part of our vast dominions as that of Florence Nightingale.

Collections were made for the 'fund' in churches and chapels of varying creeds in all parts of the country, and concerts and sales of work were got up by enthusiastic ladies to help the subscriptions. As in the dark winter of 1854-5 everybody was doing their part to strengthen Miss Nightingale's hands by supplying her with comforts and necessaries for the soldiers, so in the joyous winter of 1855-6 people gave of their time and money to present the heroine with means for inaugurating a scheme which should revolutionise the nursing methods of the civil and military hospitals, and render impossible the suffering and misery among the sick soldiers which had characterised the late war.

There were no more enthusiastic and grateful supporters of the Nightingale Fund than the brave " boys " of the Services. The officers and men of nearly every regiment and many of the vessels contributed a day's pay.

Books were opened by the principal bankers throughout the kingdom, and a very handsome gift to the fund came from M. and Madame Goldschmidt (Jenny Lind), who gave a concert at Exeter Hall on March 11th, 1856, which realised nearly £2,000. M. and Madame Goldschmidt defrayed all the expenses of the concert, amounting to upwards of £500, and gave the gross receipts to the Committee. In recognition of their generosity a gift was made to M. and Madame Goldschmidt of a marble bust of Queen Victoria, the result of a private subscription.

In course of time the Nightingale fund reached £44,000, and in evidence of the widespread interest which it evoked the detailed statement of the honorary secretaries may be quoted :—

GENERAL ABSTRACT OF SUBSCRIPTIONS TO THE NIGHTINGALE FUND

	£	s.	d.
From Troops of all arms in various parts of the world, including the Militia	8,952	1	7
From the officers and men of sixty-one ships of Her Majesty's Navy	758	19	8
From the officers and men of the Coastguard service, thirty-nine stations	155	9	0
From the officers and men of Her Majesty's Dock-yards at Woolwich and Pembroke	29	6	4
From East and West Indies, Australia, North America, and other British possessions	4,495	15	6
From British residents in foreign countries, transmitted through their respective ambassadors, consuls, etc.	1,647	16	10
From provincial cities and towns, collected and forwarded by local committees	5,683	15	4
From church or parish collections in other towns and villages, transmitted by the clergy and ministers of various denominations	1,162	4	9
From merchants, bankers, etc., connected with the City of London	3,511	13	6
Carried forward	26,397	2	6

	£	s.	d.
Brought forward...	26,397	2	6
From other general subscriptions not included under the above heads, made up of separate sums from one penny to five hundred pounds	15,697	14	10
The contribution of M. and Madame Goldschmidt, being the gross proceeds of a concert given by them at Exeter Hall	1,872	6	0
Proceeds of sale of the "Nightingale Address" (a lithographic print and poem published at one shilling), received from Mrs. F. P. B. Martin ...	53	0	0
Proceeds of a series of "Twelve Photographic Views in the Interior of Sebastopol," by G. Shaw-Lefevre, Esq.	18	18	0
Total £44,039	1	4

There is little doubt that the fund would have reached the £50,000 which the Committee had set itself to obtain if Miss Nightingale, after her return home, had not herself brought the subscription list to a close in order that public benevolence might be diverted to the fund raised to help the victims of the devastating inundations in France in 1857. Miss Nightingale had seen with great admiration the self-sacrificing work of French ladies and sisters amongst the soldiers in the Crimea, and had been supported in her own efforts by the sympathy of commanding officers of the French troops, so that it gave her peculiar pleasure to promote a fund for helping our late allies when distress came upon their country.

Meantime, the heroine whose work had evoked

the great outburst of national gratitude of which
the Nightingale Fund was the expression, still
remained in the East, to complete her work, for
though the fall of Sebastopol had brought the war
to an end, the sick and wounded soldiers still
lay in the hospitals, and there was an army of
occupation in the Crimea pending the conclusion
of the peace negotiations. None knew better than
Miss Nightingale the evils which beset soldiers in
camp when the exigencies of active warfare no
longer occupy them, and she now divided her
attention between administering to the sick and providing recreation and instruction for the convalescents
and the soldiers in camp.

As soon as her health was sufficiently established
after the attack of fever, she again left Scutari for
the Crimea. Two new camp hospitals, known as the
" Left Wing " and the " Right Wing," consisting
of huts, had been put up on the heights above
Balaclava, not far from the Sanatorium, and Miss
Nightingale established a staff of nurses there, and
took the superintendence of the nursing department.
She lived in a hut consisting of three rooms with
a medical store attached, situated by the Sanatorium
and conveniently near the new camp hospitals.

Three of the Roman Catholic sisters who had
been working at Scutari accompanied Miss Nightingale to the Crimea, and writing from the hut en-

campment there to some of the sisters who remained at Scutari, she says : "I want my 'Cardinal' (a name bestowed on a valued sister) very much up here. The sisters are all quite well and cheerful, thank God for it! They have made their hut look quite tidy, and put up with the cold and inconveniences with the utmost self-abnegation. Everything, even the ink, freezes in our hut every night."

The sisters and their Chief had a rough experience on these Balaclava heights. One relates that their hut was far from weather-proof, and on awakening one morning they found themselves covered with snow, which had fallen heavily all night. They were consoled for those little discomforts by the arrival of a gentleman on horseback "bearing the princely present of some eggs, tied up in a handkerchief." The benefactor was the Protestant chaplain, and the sisters returned his kindness by washing his neckties. But alas! there was no flat iron available, and the sisters, not to be beaten, smoothed out the clerical lawn with a teapot filled with boiling water!

One of the sisters was stricken by fever, and Miss Nightingale insisted on nursing her herself. While watching over the sick bed one night, she saw a rat upon the rafters over the sister's head, and taking an umbrella, knocked it down and killed it without disturbing her patient.

Strict Protestant as Miss Nightingale was, she maintained the most cordial relations with the Roman Catholic nurses, and was deeply grateful for the loyal way in which they worked under her. When the Rev. Mother who had come out with the sisters to Scutari returned in ill-health to England, Miss Nightingale sent her a letter of farewell in which she said : " You know that I shall do everything I can for the sisters whom you have left me. I will care for them as if they were my own children. But it will not be like you. I do not presume to express praise or gratitude to you, Rev. Mother, because it would look as though I thought you had done this work, not unto God, but unto me. You were far above me in fitness for the general superintendency in worldly talent of administration, and far more in the spiritual qualifications which God values in a superior ; my being placed over you was a misfortune, not my fault. What you have done for the work no one can ever say. I do not presume to give you any other tribute but my tears. But I should be glad that the Bishop of Southwark should know, and Dr. Manning [afterwards Cardinal], that you were valued here as you deserve, and that the gratitude of the army is yours."

The roads over this mountain district where Miss Nightingale was located in the Crimea were very uneven and dangerous, and one day while driving to the hospitals she met with an accident. Her carriage was drawn by a mule, and being carelessly driven by the attendant over a large stone, was upset. Miss Nightingale suffered some injury, and one of the Sisters accompanying her was severely wounded.

To prevent the repetition of such an accident, Colonel Macmurdo presented Miss Nightingale with a specially constructed carriage for her use. It is described as " being composed of wood battens framed on the outside and basket-work. In the interior it is lined with a sort of waterproof canvas. It has a fixed head on the hind part and a canopy running the full length, with curtains at the side to enclose the interior. The front driving seat removes, and thus the whole forms a sort of small tilted waggon with a welted frame, suspended on the back part, on which to recline, and well padded round the sides. It is fitted with patent breaks to the hind wheels so as to let it go gently down the steep hills of the Turkish roads." This is the carriage which after many vicissitudes is now preserved at Lea Hurst.

The carriage was one of the most interesting exhibits in the Nursing Section of the Victorian Era Exhibition at Earl's Court. Its preservation and removal to this country are due to the excellent

M. Soyer, who on the eve of his departure from the Crimea rescued it from the hands of some Tartar Jews. Miss Nightingale had left it behind, doubtless thinking that it had served its purpose, and being too modest to imagine that it would be of special interest to her fellow-countrymen. M. Soyer, however, saw in that old battered vehicle a precious relic for future generations, and hearing that some Jews were going to purchase it next day, along with a lot of common carts and harness, he obtained permission from Colonel Evans of the Light Infantry to buy the carriage. He afterwards sent it to England by the *Argo*. The sketch reproduced was taken by Mr. Landells, the artist representing *The Illustrated London News* in the Crimea. The carriage was an object of great public interest when it arrived at Southampton on the *Argo*. The Mayor took charge of it until the arrival of M. Soyer, who had the extreme pleasure of restoring it to its famous owner.

After Miss Nightingale received the gift of this convenient vehicle, she redoubled her exertions on behalf of the soldiers still remaining in the Crimea. The winter was severe and snow lay thick on the ground, but it did not deter her from constantly visiting the camp hospitals, and she was known to stand for hours at the top of a bleak rocky mountain near the hospitals, giving her instructions while the snow was falling heavily. Then in the bleak dark night she would return down the perilous mountain road with no escort save the driver. Her friends remonstrated and begged her to avoid such risk and exposure, but she answered by a smile, which seemed to say, " You may be right, but I have faith." M. Soyer was so impressed by the danger that Miss Nightingale was incurring, that he addressed, as he relates, " a letter to a noble duchess, who I knew had much influence with her." I am afraid, however, that neither the solicitous M. Soyer nor the " noble duchess" deterred Miss Nightingale from following what she felt to be the path of duty.

During this period she was much engaged in promoting schemes for the education and recreation of the convalescent soldiers and those forming the army of occupation. She formed classes, established little libraries or " reading huts," which were supplied with books and periodicals sent by friends at home. Queen Victoria contributed literature and the Duchess of Kent sent Miss Nightingale a useful assortment of books for the men. All the reading huts were numerously and constantly attended, and Miss Nightingale remarked in her after report that the behaviour of the men was " uniformly quiet and well-bred."

Lectures and schoolrooms were established for

the men, both at Scutari and in the Crimea, by various officers and chaplains, and in these Miss Nightingale took a deep interest and was herself instrumental in establishing a café at Inkerman, to serve as a counter-attraction to the canteens where so much drunkenness prevailed. As she had ministered to the bodily needs of the men while sickness reigned, now she tried to promote their mental and moral good by providing them with rational means of occupation and amusement.

With solicitous womanly thought for the wives and mothers at home, Miss Nightingale had from the first encouraged the men to keep up communication with their families by supplying those in hospital with stationery, and stamps and writing materials were now at her instance supplied to the convalescent and other reading huts. In the first months of the war the men had been allowed to send any letters to Miss Nightingale's quarters in the Barrack Hospital to be stamped, and many a reckless lad who had run away and enlisted was by her gentle persuasions prevailed upon to write home and report himself.

Often she herself had the painful duty of writing to wives and mothers to tell of the death of their dear ones, and several of these letters were published by the recipients in journals of the time, and are full of that thoughtful practical help which

distinguished all the Lady-in-Chief's efforts. She
would send home little mementoes, the last book
perhaps which the dying man had read, and would
tell the bereaved women how to apply for their
widow's allowance, send papers for them to fill up,
and in cases of doubtful identity would sift matters
to the bottom to discover whether such or such a
man was among the slain.

Another matter of concern with Miss Nightingale
was to induce the men to send their pay home to
their families. For this purpose she formed at
Scutari an extempore money order office in which
she received, four afternoons in the month, the
money of any soldier who desired to send it home
to his family. Each month about £1,000 was sent
home in small sums of twenty or thirty shillings,
which were, by Post Office orders obtained in England,
sent to their respective recipients. "This money,"
as Miss Nightingale says, "was literally so much
rescued from the canteen and drunkenness."

Following her initiative, the Government during
the last months that the army remained in the
East established money order offices at Constantinople, Scutari, Balaclava and headquarters, Crimea,
and in the course of about six months, from
January 30th to July 26th, 1856, no less than
£71,000 was sent home by the men. "Who will
say after this," writes Miss Nightingale, "that the

soldier must needs be reckless, drunken, or disorderly?" But it may be added that Miss
Nightingale's presence in the Crimea during the
months which followed victory, when "Tommy"
was in an exulting state of mind and ready to
drink healths recklessly, and make each day an
anniversary of the fall of Sebastopol, had a great
moral effect on the men.

The Treaty of Peace was signed at Paris on
March 30th, 1856, and the final evacuation of
the Crimea took place on the following July 12th,
on which day General Codrington formally gave
up Sebastopol and Balaclava to the Russians. Not
until all the hospitals were closed, and the last
remnant of the British army was under sailing
orders for home, did Florence Nightingale quit
the scene of her labours. Just before leaving the
Crimea, she was amazed to find that some fifty
or sixty women, who had followed their husbands
to the Crimea without leave, but had been allowed
to remain because they were useful, were actually
left behind before Sebastopol when their husbands'
regiments had sailed. The poor women gathered
around Miss Nightingale's hut in great distress,
and she managed to induce the authorities to send
them home on a British ship.

Miss Nightingale's last act before leaving the
Crimea was to order, at her own expense, the

erection of a monument to the dead. It took the form of a monster white marble cross twenty feet high, and was placed on the peak of a mountain near the Sanatorium above Balaclava, and dedicated to the memory of the fallen brave, and to those sisters of her " Angel Band " who slept their last sleep in that far-away Eastern land. She caused it to be inscribed with the words,

Lord, have mercy upon us.
Gospodi pomilori nass.

The " Nightingale Cross," as the monument came to be called, strikes the eye of the mariner as he crosses the Black Sea, and to the British sailor it must ever be an object to stir a chivalrous feeling for the noble woman who thus honoured the brave dead.

On her way home from the Crimea, Miss Nightingale called at Scutari, that place of appalling memories, and saw the final closing of the hospitals. The Barrack Hospital had now been taken back by the Turkish authorities, but the suite of rooms which Miss Nightingale had occupied in the southern tower were preserved as she left them, and kept so for some years.

The Sultan had been an admiring witness of Miss Nightingale's labours, and presented her with a magnificent diamond bracelet as a farewell gift and a mark of his estimation of her devotion.

Before leaving the Crimea Miss Nightingale had received from Queen Victoria a beautiful jewel, for which the Prince Consort made the design. It consists of a St. George's Cross in red enamel, on a white field, representative of England. On the cross are the letters V.R., surmounted by a crown in diamonds. A band of black enamel, inscribed in gold letters with the words " Blessed are the merciful," surrounds the cross. Palm leaves, in green enamel, form a framework for the shield, and on the blue enamel ribbon which confines the palms is inscribed in letters of gold "Crimea." On the back of the jewel is an inscription written by Queen Victoria, recording that the gift was made in memory of services rendered to her " brave army " by Florence Nightingale. The following letter accompanied the gift.

"WINDSOR CASTLE,
"*January* 1856.

"DEAR MISS NIGHTINGALE,—You are I know, well aware of the high sense I entertain of the Christian devotion which you have displayed during this great and bloody war, and I need hardly repeat to you how warm my admiration is for your services, which are fully equal to those of my dear and brave soldiers, whose sufferings you have had the *privilege* of alleviating in so merciful a manner. I am, however, anxious of marking my feelings in a manner

which I trust will be agreeable to you, and therefore send you with this letter a brooch, the form
and emblems of which commemorate your great and
blessed work, and
which I hope you will
wear as a mark of the
high approbation of
your Sovereign !

THE NIGHTINGALE JEWEL.

" It will be a very
great satisfaction to
me when you return
at last to these shores,
to make the acquaint-
ance of one who has
set so bright an example
to our sex. And with
every prayer for the
preservation of your valuable health, believe me,
always, yours sincerely,   " VICTORIA R."

The Government did not forget to officially
acknowledge the work of the Lady-in-Chief, and
when the Treaty of Peace was under consideration
in the spring of 1856, Lord Ellesmere paid the
following eloquent tribute to her services :—

" My Lords, the agony of that time has become
a matter of history. The vegetation of two suc-
cessive springs has obscured the vestiges of Balaclava and of Inkerman. Strong voices now answer

to the roll-call, and sturdy forms now cluster round the colours. The ranks are full, the hospitals are empty. The angel of mercy still lingers to the last on the scene of her labours ; but her mission is all but accomplished. Those long arcades of Scutari, in which dying men sat up to catch the sound of her footstep or the flutter of her dress, and fell back on the pillow content to have seen her shadow as it passed, are now comparatively deserted. She may be thinking how to escape, as best she may, on her return, the demonstration of a nation's appreciation of the deeds and motives of Florence Nightingale."

Lord Ellesmere had correctly guessed Miss Nightingale's desire to escape a public demonstration. She declined the Government's offer of a British man-of-war to convey her home, and, embarking at Scutari on a French vessel, sailed for Marseilles. She passed through France at night, halted in Paris to visit her old friends, the Sisters of St. Vincent de Paul, and then, accompanied by her aunt, Mrs. Smith, and travelling incognito as " Miss Smith," proceeded to Boulogne and sailed for dear old England. What a life-time of memories had been crowded into those twenty-one months which had elapsed since she had left on her great mission !

CHAPTER XX

THE RETURN OF THE HEROINE

Arrives Secretly at Lea Hurst—The Object of Many·Congratulations—Presentations—Received by Queen Victoria at Balmoral—Prepares Statement of "Voluntary Gifts"—Tribute to Lord Raglan.

Then leave her to the quiet she has chosen; she demands
No greeting from our brazen throats and vulgar clapping hands.
Leave her to the still comfort the saints know that have striven.
What are our earthly honours? Her honours are in heaven.

Punch.

FLORENCE NIGHTINGALE, under a carefully preserved incognito, arrived quietly at Whatstandwell, the nearest station to her Derbyshire home, on August 8th, 1856, and succeeded in making her way unrecognised to Lea Hurst. According to local tradition she entered by the back door, and the identity of the closely veiled lady in black was first discovered by the old family butler. The word quickly circulated round Lea and the adjacent villages that " Miss Florence had come back from the wars," and dearly would the good people have liked to light a bonfire on Crich Stand or som other available height to testify their joy, but all demonstration was checked by the knowledge that Miss Florence wanted to remain quiet.

During the ensuing weeks hundreds of people from the surrounding towns of Derby, Nottingham, and Manchester, and from more distant parts, crowded the roads to Lea Hurst and stood in groups about the park, hoping to catch a glimpse of the heroine. "I remember the crowds as if it was yesterday," said an old lady living by the park gate, "it took me all my time to answer them. Folks came in carriages and on foot, and there was titled people among them, and a lot of soldiers, some of them without arms and legs, who had been nursed by Miss Florence in the hospital, and I remember one man who had been shot through both eyes coming and asking to see Miss Florence. But not ten out of the hundreds who came got a glimpse of her. If they wanted help about their pensions, they were told to put it down in writing and Miss Florence's maid came with an answer. Of course she was willing to help everybody, but it stood to reason she could not receive them all; why, the park wouldn't have held the folks that came, and besides, the old squire wouldn't have his daughter made a staring stock of."

London shared the disappointment of Derby-

THE CARRIAGE USED BY MISS NIGHTINGALE IN THE CRIMEA.

shire in not being permitted to give Florence
Nightingale a public welcome, but the situation
was realised by the genial Mr. *Punch* in the
sympathetic lines quoted at the heading of this
chapter.

Punch had had his joke when the "dear
Nightingales" first went to the succour of the
soldiers, but the day for raillery was past; a great
humanitarian work had been accomplished, which
the genial humorist was quick to acknowledge on
the return of the heroine in a cartoon showing
"Mr. *Punch's* design for a statue to Miss Nightingale." It represented her in nurse's dress, wearing
the badge "Scutari" across her breast, and holding a
wounded soldier by the hand. Below was a scene
portraying the good Samaritan.

The public interest in Miss Nightingale was
testified in many ways. Not only did platforms
all over the land resound with her praises, but
her portrait became a popular advertisement for
tradesmen. I have seen preserved in the Derby
Town Library paper bags used in the shops of
Henry Calvert, grocer, Hulme, the tobacconist, and
Bryer, provision merchant, Derby, decorated with
portraits of Florence Nightingale. Playbills displayed the heroine's name, beside Romeo and
Juliet, songs and musical compositions were dedicated to the "good angel of Derbyshire." There

was the " Nightingale Varsoviana " and " The Song of the Nightingale," published with a full-page picture of the heroine on the cover. Almanacks displayed her portrait and ballads innumerable told of her gentle deeds. Street minstrels found a Nightingale song the most remunerative piece in their repertoire, and people who had hitherto been guiltless of versifying were compelled to satisfy an importunate muse by writing verses on Florence Nightingale. Broadsheet ballads were sung and sold in the streets, and the following extract is from one emanating from Seven Dials :—

> When sympathy first in thy fair breast did enter,
>   The world must confess 'twas a noble idea,
> When through great danger you boldly did venture,
>   To soothe the afflicted in the dread Crimea.
> No female on earth sure could ever be bolder;
>   When death and disease did you closely surround,
> You administered comfort to the British soldier—
>   You soothed his sorrows and healed his wounds.

Before her return home Miss Nightingale's services had been recognised by an influential meeting at St. George's Hospital, presided over by the late Duke of Cambridge. It was moved by Viscount Chelsea that " Miss Nightingale should be elected an honorary Governor of St. George's Hospital in testimony of the respectful admiration felt by the supporters of this charity for her self.

denial and disinterestedness and her devoted heroism." The Duke of Cambridge spoke of what he had himself seen of Miss Nightingale's work amongst the sick and wounded soldiers during his stay at Scutari, and said that her name was revered alike by English, French, Turks, and Russians.

Letters of congratulation and expressions of esteem from all sorts and conditions of people poured in upon Miss Nightingale after it was known that she was settled in her Derbyshire home, and public associations and societies sent deputations. If Florence Nightingale could have been persuaded to hold a reception, it would have been attended by delegates from every representative body in the kingdom ; but while such a national appreciation of her labours was very gratifying to our heroine, her chief desire now was to escape publicity, and her enfeebled health made quietude a necessity.

She was specially pleased by an address sent by the workmen of Newcastle-on-Tyne, and replied in the following beautiful letter :—

"*August 23rd*, 1856.

" My Dear Friends,—

"I wish it were in my power to tell you what was in my heart when I received your letter.

" Your welcome home, your sympathy with what has been passing while I have been absent, have touched me more than I can tell in words. My dear friends, the things that are the deepest in our hearts are perhaps what it is most difficult for us to express.

" ' She hath done what she could.' These words I inscribed on the tomb of one of my best helpers when I left Scutari. It has been my endeavour, in the sight of God, to do as she has done.

" I will not speak of reward when permitted to do our country's work—it is what we live for ; but I may say to receive sympathy from affectionate hearts like yours is the greatest support, the greatest gratification, that it is possible for me to receive from man.

" I thank you all, the eighteen hundred, with grateful, tender affection. And I should have written before to do so, were not the business, which my return home has not ended, been almost more than I can manage. Pray believe me, my dear friends, yours faithfully and gratefully.

" FLORENCE NIGHTINGALE."

The working men of Sheffield subscribed a testimonial to Miss Nightingale and presented her with a case of cutlery. Each blade, instead of bearing the maker's name in the customary way, was stamped with the words " Presented to Florence Nightingale, 1857." The oak case containing the cutlery was bound in silver, and the top inlaid with a device representing the " Good Samaritan," and inscribed with the words " Inasmuch as ye have done it unto one of the least of these My brethren, ye have done it unto Me."

Another very interesting and tenderly prized gift was a writing-desk, inlaid with pearl, presented to Miss Nightingale by her friends in the neighbourhood of her Derbyshire home. On the front of the desk was a silver plate inscribed with the words " Presented to Florence Nightingale on her safe arrival at Lea Hurst from the Crimea, August 8th, 1856, as a token of esteem from the inhabitants of Lea, Holloway, and Crich." Miss Nightingale, on being told that her friends and neighbours wished to celebrate her home-coming by a presentation, requested that it might be done as privately as possible ; accordingly a small deputation waited on her at Lea Hurst a few weeks after her arrival and presented the desk.

Amongst other old friends whom Miss Nightingale received on her return home was the late Duke of Devonshire, who drove over from Chatsworth to Lea Hurst and presented his distinguished neighbour with a silver owl and some other tokens of his esteem. The duke caused a collection of press notices—there were no press cutting agencies in those days—to be made with regard to Miss Nightingale and her work and made into a scrap-book, which His Grace eventually presented to the Derby Town Library.

During these weeks, in which Miss Nightingale was recruiting her health at Lea Hurst, she entertained from time to time little parties of her humble friends and neighbours, who enjoyed the privilege of seeing the mementoes which she had brought from the Crimea.

There are still living a few old people in the neighbourhood of Lea Hurst who recall the awe and wonder with which they regarded cannon balls from Sebastopol, bullets taken from Balaclava heroes, and other martial objects in Miss Florence's collection, and the emotion they felt at sight of the flowers and grasses which she had gathered from the graves of the soldiers in the cemeteries of Scutari and Balaclava. Then there was " Miss Florence's Crimean dog," a large Russian hound which was the wonder of the countryside, second only in interest to the drummer boy Thomas, who attended his lady home from the war and was a very big person indeed as " Miss Nightingale's own man." For graphic and thrilling narrative of the fall of Sebastopol, Thomas could outvie the special correspondent of *The Times*, and if he was unavoidably absent from the Balaclava charge, he had the details of the engagement by heart.

Queen Victoria had taken from the first a deep interest in Miss Nightingale's work, and was wishful to receive and thank her in person, while the young Princesses were with natural girlish enthusiasm eager to see the heroine of the war. Accordingly, it was arranged that Miss Nightingale should proceed to Balmoral, where the Queen and Prince Consort were spending the autumn. She arrived in the middle of September, a month after her return from the Crimea, and was privately received by the Queen. The favourable impression made by Miss Nightingale on the royal circle is recorded in the Life of the Prince Consort. One can imagine, too, the emotions of the Crown Princess and Princess Alice, whose desire to help the suffering soldiers had been fired by the visitor's noble work. Both these young Princesses were destined to experience the anxiety of the soldier's wife whose husband is at the front, and both followed in the footsteps of Florence Nightingale in organising hospital work in the Prussian War of 1866 and in the Franco-German War of 1870, while tiny Princess Helena was to become in after years an accomplished nurse, and an active leader in the nursing movement of this country ; and, alas ! to yield her soldier son on the fatal field of South Africa.

Miss Nightingale spent several weeks in the Highlands as a guest at Birkhall, near Balmoral. She was present at a dance at the Castle, and sat with the Royal Family at one end of the hall, and is described as looking very graceful and pleasing. She wore a pretty lace cap to conceal her short hair, her abundant tresses having been cut off during her attack of Crimean fever. On Sundays Miss Nightingale worshipped at the old church of Crathie, and her sweet, pale face was affectionately regarded by the village congregation, for there were many brave sons of Scotland whose pains she had soothed and whose dying lips had blessed her.

After leaving the Highlands, Miss Nightingale joined her family for the customary stay at Embley Park, her Hampshire home, where she was received by the people with many expressions of congratulation. At Embley she was in the near vicinity of Wilton House, the home of her friends, the Hon. Mr. and Mrs. Sidney Herbert, with whom there was much to discuss regarding the founding of the training home for nurses to which the Nightingale Fund was to be devoted. The fund was the people's gift to Florence Nightingale, and continued to be enthusiastically supported by private contributions, from the pennies of the poor to the cheques of the rich, and by means of public entertainments throughout the winter which succeeded the return of the heroine from the Crimea.

During the months which succeeded her return, Miss Nightingale, with characteristic business promptitude, prepared a clear and comprehensive statement regarding the " free gifts " which had been sent to her for the sick and wounded, and in the latter months of the war for the convalescent soldiers. One can read between the lines of this report the general muddle which characterised the transit of goods from London to the seat of war, in consequence of which bales of things sent by benevolent people made wandering excursions everywhere but to the Scutari hospitals where they were so urgently wanted, and in some instances were actually brought back to their donors unopened. This was owing to the fact that from May, 1854, when our army first encamped at Scutari, until March, 1855, no office for the reception and delivery of goods had been established either at Scutari or Constantinople. In consequence packages arriving by merchant vessels not chartered by Government passed into the Turkish Custom House, from which they were never extracted without delay and confusion, and many were destroyed or lost. In cases of ships chartered by Government, masses of goods were delayed, as Miss Nightingale wittily remarks, by "an unnecessary trip to Balaclava and back" before they reached her at Scutari.

In face of such confusion the task of giving a detailed account of the "free gifts" would have hopelessly baffled a less clear head than Miss Nightingale's. "The Statement of the Voluntary Contributions" which she had received for the hospitals in the East was published in 1857, and in it Miss Nightingale took occasion to pay a tribute to the devotion and zeal of the medical officers in the hospitals, who had been so handicapped by the lack of proper medical supplies and comforts in the early part of the campaign. She also refers to the liberality of the British Government and the support which she had received from the War Office, and acknowledges the sympathy and help received from various general and commanding officers, both British and French, and pays the following tribute to her old friend Lord Raglan, the Commander-in-Chief: "Miss Nightingale cannot but here recall, with deep gratitude and respect, the letters of support and encouragement which she received from the late Lord Raglan, who invariably acknowledged all that was attempted for the good of his men with the deepest feeling, as well as with the high courtesy and true manliness of his character. No tinge of petty jealousy against those entrusted with any commission, public or private, connected with the army under his command, ever alloyed his generous benevolence."

At this period, though in weakened health, Miss Nightingale was under the impression that she was still " good for active service." When the Indian Mutiny broke out, she wrote to her friend Lady Canning, the wife of the Governor-General, offering to go out to organise a nursing staff for the troops in India. Lady Canning writes, November 14th, 1857 : " Miss Nightingale has written to me. She is out of health and at Malvern, but says she would come at twenty-four hours' notice if I think there is anything for her to do in her ' line of business.' " Lady Canning did not, however, encourage Miss Nightingale to undertake a task for which she had not the strength, neither did she at that time see the practicability of forming nursing establishments in the up-country stations of India. That Miss Nightingale made the offer is characteristic of her indomitable spirit.

CHAPTER XXI

THE SOLDIER'S FRIEND AT HOME

Ill Health—Unremitting Toil—Founds Nightingale Training School at St. Thomas's Hospital—Army Reform—Death of Lord Herbert of Lea—Palmerston and Gladstone pay Tributes to Miss Nightingale—Interesting Letters—Advises in American War and Franco-German War.

> Her heart it means good—for no bounty she'll take,
> She'd lay down her life for the poor soldier's sake,
> She prays for the dying, she gives peace to the brave,
> She feels that a soldier has a soul to be saved.
> The wounded they love her, as it has been seen,
> She's the soldiers' preserver, they call her their queen.
> May God give her strength and her heart never fail!
> One of Heaven's best gifts is Miss Nightingale.
>
> *Ballad of the Time.*

AFTER Miss Nightingale's return from the Crimea it was expected that she would become the active leader of the nursing movement which her brilliant example had initiated. " We intend to be merciless to Miss Nightingale in the future," said Mr. Sidney Herbert, " and see that her abilities are not allowed to slumber. The diamond has shown itself and must not be allowed to return to the mine. Miss Nightingale must be chained to the oar for the rest of her life. It is hers to raise the system of nursing to a pitch of efficiency never before known."

Gladly indeed would Miss Nightingale have started on the great work of nursing reform had her health permitted. The spirit was more than willing, it was eager to start, but the flesh was weak. It was hoped that a few months' rest would restore her health, and that she would herself be able to organise an institute for the training of hospital nurses, to which purpose she proposed to devote the Nightingale Fund. Unfortunately, as time passed it became apparent that the malady from which she suffered was increasing, and that she would never again be able to lead her old active life.

It was indeed a hard cross to bear for a woman comparatively young and with a mind full of humanitarian projects, and as the first years of waiting passed Florence Nightingale drank deep of the cup of life's disappointments. But she faced the situation with noble resignation. All through the land were brave fellows who had returned from the war maimed or shattered in health, and the soldier's nurse showed the soldier's heroism in the service of her country.

But though compelled to be a recluse, not a day of Miss Nightingale's time was passed unoccupied.

Work, work, ever work, was her great panacea.
She spent a good deal of her time in London, for
she liked to be in the "hum" of things and
within easy communication of kindred spirits in the
great city. .

Her sick-room might have passed for an adjunct
of the War Office, so filled was it with schemes
for army hospital reform and communications from
all sorts and conditions of soldiers. Whenever
"Tommy" had a grievance, he wrote to Miss
Nightingale. She was still his Lady-in-Chief, and
invested in his mind with unlimited power and
influence, and to some extent he was not mistaken.
The War Office authorities had such a profound
belief in Miss Nightingale's judgment and discrimination that any recommendation made by her
received attention. She was able to render help
to deserving men with regard to their pensions,
and in procuring civil occupation for the maimed
and disabled, while she was an ever-helpful friend
to the widows and orphans, and by her influence
obtained grants from the Patriotic Fund for many
destitute soldiers' families. The amount of work
of this kind which Miss Nightingale did in the year
succeeding the war is incalculable.

When in 1854 her name had first come before
the public, nothing was known of Miss Nightingale,
but now that it was understood that she was the

daughter of a rich and influential gentleman, she was overwhelmed with begging letters. These increased to such an extent that she was forced to make a public protest in *The Times* and state her inability to reply to the letters which poured in upon her. However, let it be stated to the honour of the army that not a single begging letter for money was ever sent to Miss Nightingale by a British soldier.

During the first years of her illness Miss Nightingale still hoped against hope that she might be sufficiently restored to health as to be able to take active steps for the formation of an institute for nurses, and in 1859 it was still thought by the Committee that she would eventually be able to administer the Nightingale Fund, and it agreed to hold the scheme in abeyance. At this time the sum subscribed and the accumulated interest amounted to £48,000. After another year had passed and her health showed no signs of improvement, Miss Nightingale entered into an arrangement by which she placed the money in the hands of trustees for the training of hospital nurses. The net income of the fund amounted to £1,426 and a Council was named to administer it. Miss Nightingale, to whom the fund had been a personal gift from the nation, only reserved to herself the power to give advice. The **Hon.**

Sidney Herbert, shortly to become Lord Herbert of Lea, was the guiding spirit of the Council.

It was arranged with Miss Nightingale's approval to devote two-thirds of the income to the maintenance and instruction of nurses at St. Thomas's Hospital, the probationers engaging to take service in public hospitals and infirmaries. The remaining third was to be spent at King's College Hospital for the maintenance and instruction of midwifery nurses, the want of whom was at that time much felt in the villages of England.

The movement thus begun by Florence Nightingale for the systematic training of lay hospital nurses was first established at old St. Thomas's Hospital, near London Bridge, in 1860. This hospital was one of the oldest foundations in the country, having been first established in 1213 as an "almery" or hospital in connection with the Priory of Bermondsey. It was later assigned for the use of the poor. At the dissolution of the monasteries St. Thomas's was surrendered to Henry VIII. It had then forty beds for poor people, a master, six brethren, and three lay sisters. Later it was enlarged and opened as a hospital for the sick poor under the patronage of the young King Edward VI. During the period of the Restoration it was used as a military hospital, and is mentioned in this connection by Pepys in his Diary. In 1732 it was rebuilt and the grand entrance made from Wellington Street, Southwark. It is interesting to find that at this period each ward of the hospital was under the care of a sister and two or three nurses.

In selecting St. Thomas's for the home and training school of her pioneer nurses, Miss Nightingale was carrying on the traditions of the hospital, as nursing sisters had been associated with it from early times. It also specially commended itself to her sympathies as being one of the oldest institutions in the kingdom where the sick poor could be relieved. Later, the hospital was rebuilt in palatial style on its present site on the Thames Embankment, and the Nightingale Training Home became a part of the new hospital.

Meantime, an upper floor in a new wing of old St. Thomas's was arranged as the quarters for the Nightingale nurses. There was a separate bedroom for each probationer, a common sitting-room, and two rooms for the sister-in-charge.

In May, 1860, candidates were advertised for, and on June 15th the first fifteen probationers were admitted. They were under the authority of the matron and subject to the rules of the hospital. They were provided with board and lodging, received a salary of £10 during the first year of their probation, and were to serve as assistant nurses

in the wards and receive instruction from the sisters
and medical officers.   At the end of a year those
who passed examination were certified as nurses
and entered into hospital work.   The first superintendent of the Nightingale Training School was
Mrs. Wardroper.

During the first year of the experiment four
probationers were dismissed and others received
in their places.   Out of those who were placed on
the register as certified nurses, six received appointments in St. Thomas's, and two entered workhouse
infirmaries.

It was an anxious year for Miss Nightingale,
and many heart-felt prayers went up from her sick-
room that the work might be successful, while she
encouraged the young probationers by friendly chats
and advice.   The Council considered the result
of the first year satisfactory, and the scheme
continued to steadily work.

It is clear, however, that the girls of England
were not then all " mad to be nurses." The
profession had not become fashionable.   Mrs.
Grundy still shook her head over " young females "
nursing in hospitals and feared wholesale elopements
with medical students.   Parents were afraid of infection ; the fastidious thought attendance upon
the sick poor incompatible with the feelings of a
lady, and there was the conventional idea that

it was derogatory to the position of a gentlewoman to enter a wage-earning profession.

Miss Nightingale fought steadily and patiently against criticism and prejudice, and now and again from her sick-room came stirring appeals to the young womanhood of England that they would regard the nursing of the sick as the noblest work to which they could devote themselves. " We hear so much of idle hands and unsatisfied hearts," she wrote, " and nowhere more than in England. All England is ringing with the cry for ' Woman's Work' and 'Woman's Mission.' Why are there so few to do the work ? . . . The remunerative employment is there, and in plenty. The want is the women fit to take it."

Miss Nightingale then goes on to explain the kind of training given to her nurses at St. Thomas's, and although this was written in the first stage of the work, when she was asking for recruits, it remains the basis upon which the Nightingale Training School in the present palatial St. Thomas's Hospital is conducted.

" We require," she writes, " that a woman be sober, honest, truthful, without which there is no foundation on which to build.

" We train her in habits of punctuality, quietness, trustworthiness, personal neatness. We teach her how to manage the concerns of a large ward or establishment. We train her in dressing wounds and other injuries, and in performing all those minor operations which nurses are called upon day and night to undertake.

" We teach her how to manage helpless patients in regard to moving, changing, feeding, temperature, and the prevention of bed sores.

" She has to make and apply bandages, line splints and the like. She must know how to make beds with as little disturbance as possible to their inmates. She is instructed how to wait at operations, and as to the kind of aid the surgeon requires at her hands. She is taught cooking for the sick ; the principle on which sick wards ought to be cleansed, aired, and warmed ; the management of convalescents, and how to observe sick and maimed patients, so as to give an intelligent and truthful account to the physician or surgeon in regard to the progress of cases in the intervals between visits—a much more difficult thing than is generally supposed.

" We do not seek to make ' medical women,' but simply nurses acquainted with the *principle* which they are required constantly to apply at the bedside.

" For the future superintendent is added a course of instruction in the administration of a hospital, including, of course, the linen arrangements and what else is necessary for a matron to be conversant with.

"There are those who think that all this is intuitive in women, that they are born so, or, at least, that it comes to them without training. To such we say, by all means send us as many such geniuses as you can, for we are sorely in want of them."

While Miss Nightingale was thus piloting nursing reform in the country and endeavouring to enlist recruits, she was also actively engaged in assisting the Hon. Sidney Herbert in carrying out his important schemes for the improvement of the condition of the soldier, a work to which Mr. Herbert devoted himself most strenuously in the last years of his life.

Up to the period of the Crimean War the sanitary condition of the soldier was utterly neglected. He was as a general rule left to his chance. At home in barracks he was ill-lodged and ill-fed, and during active service was practically uncared for. He was a constant victim to preventable disease by reason of unhealthy camps and ill-managed and defective hospitals. Fever and dysentery slew their tens of thousands. The mortality returns showed a deplorable death rate. Seventeen out of every thousand soldiers died annually at home as against eight in every thousand of civilians. It was calculated at this period that of every two soldiers who died, one died from causes which a proper attention to his surroundings would have removed.

Miss Nightingale had probably the best first-hand knowledge of any person in the country of the ills to which the soldiers in camp and hospital were subjected during active warfare, and the wealth of her experience and knowledge were given to Mr. Sidney Herbert when he started on his campaign of reform.

We have already seen the marvellous change which Miss Nightingale had been instrumental in bringing about in the military hospitals in the East, and the useful work she had accomplished during the last months in the Crimea by providing useful occupation and recreation for the convalescent soldiers and the men in camp, and by furthering reforms in the cooking and diet of the soldiers. The war was ended, the army was home again, and it now remained to see that the men who took up arms for their country should have their lives protected by the ordinary rules of health and sanitation, and that they should be educated, encouraged to live like self-respecting citizens of the Empire for which they fought, and that their wives and children should be cared for. Our heroine was not actuated by mere passing emotions easily roused and as readily quieted. Florence Nightingale had sacrificed her own health to cure the ills arising from the soldiers' neglected condition and now turned her attention to prevention.

The horrors of the Crimean War impelled Sidney Herbert to concentrate his attention on army reform, a matter upon which he had been engaged before the outbreak of hostilities. Now he returned to it with redoubled vigour. Barracks as well as hospitals must be reorganised, the soldier preserved in health as well as tended in sickness. There must be good sanitary regulations, improved military cookery, and the soldier must have some enjoyment in life.

Mr. Sydney Herbert had to endure his share of blame with the other members of Lord Aberdeen's Government for the terrible sufferings of the troops during the Crimean War, but for which in the light of history no one seemed less to blame than he, if blame there was, and he atoned for it now by a long penance of work for the good of the soldier. For every man who had perished in those bitter trenches before Sebastopol, died in the ill-fed camps of hunger or disease, or groaned his life away in the crowded and pestilential hospitals, Sidney Herbert saved at least the life of one British soldier by his labours.

He was the mainspring of the Royal Commission which, after the return of the troops from the

Crimea, was appointed to inquire into the sanitary
condition of the army, and on his suggestion and
with his assistance four supplementary Commissions
were issued on the subjects of Hospitals and Barracks,
Army Medical Department, Army Medical Statistics,
and on a Medical School at Chatham, and he drafted
the code of regulations for the Army Medical
Department which appeared in October, 1859.

With the return of Lord Palmerston to power
in the summer of that year, Sidney Herbert again
took office as Secretary for War. He now laboured
more assiduously than ever in army reform, and
in the furthering of those schemes which he had
been compelled to abandon on the outbreak of
hostilities. To his efforts were due the constitution of the militia, the reconstruction of the
artillery system, the amalgamation of the Indian
and the general forces, and the consolidation of
what were then the " new " volunteers. At Alder-
shot he established instruction in barrack and hospital
cookery, and in place of that peculiar method which
required that the soldier should fit his foot to the
boot, had the machinery of the boot-factory constructed to secure a variety of sizes to suit different
feet, thereby adding to the comfort and marching
power of the troops.

Sidney Herbert began the overwhelming task of
reorganising the War Office, but the strain of work

unfortunately compelled him to retire from active official position, and in 1859 he accepted a peerage and entered the House of Lords as Baron Herbert of Lea.

Lord Herbert still continued his efforts on behalf of bettering the condition of the soldier morally and physically, but his beneficent career was soon to be cut short. To the deep regret of all classes in the country Lord Herbert of Lea died on August 2nd, 1861, at Wilton House, Salisbury. Just before his death he had reformed the Hospital Corps, and the very day on which he died saw the opening of the General Hospital at Woolwich, which had been planned under his auspices as a model of what a military hospital should be. It was ultimately transformed into the present magnificent building, on which Queen Victoria fittingly bestowed the name of the Herbert Hospital.

Next to his devoted widow and children there was no one who felt more keenly the loss of Lord Herbert of Lea than Florence Nightingale. To his inspiration and support she owed in great measure the success of her mission to the Eastern hospitals, and since her return she had laboured with him to promote the betterment of the soldier's condition. How much the nation really owes to Miss Nightingale for her labours in the sanitary and educational reform of the army during the years 1857-60 in which, though a prisoner in her sick-room, she toiled with Lord Herbert, will not be known until the private records of that period are published. At the request of the War Office she drew up an exhaustive and confidential report on the working of the Army Medical Department in the Crimea, which materially assisted in the re-organisation of the medical branch of the service then taking place.

In writing on " The Sanitary Condition of the Army " in *The Westminster Review* for January, 1859, Lord Herbert frequently quotes the opinions of Miss Nightingale, based on her experiences of the defects of the military hospitals' nursing system, and mentions her recommendations for reform.

Her services and advice were not only highly valued by Lord Herbert, but were acknowledged by the first statesmen of the day. In the tributes paid to the memory of Lord Herbert at the time of his death, the name of Florence Nightingale was coupled with his in the work of army reform.

At a meeting held in Willis's Rooms on November 28th, 1861, to consider the erection of a memorial in London to Lord Herbert of Lea, Lord Palmerston, then Prime Minister, speaking of the work in army reform accomplished by Lord Herbert, with the assistance of the Duke of Cambridge, Commander-in-Chief, said : " There were not only two ; there was a third engaged in these honourable exertions, and Miss Nightingale, though a volunteer in the service, acted with all the zeal of a volunteer and was greatly assistant."

Mr. Gladstone, then Chancellor of the Exchequer, followed with a similar appreciation. Referring to the above remarks of Lord Palmerston, he said : " My noble friend who moved the first resolution directed attention to one name in particular that ought never to be mentioned with any elaborate attempt at eulogy ; for the name of Miss Nightingale by its own unaided power becomes a talisman to all her fellow-countrymen."

Mr. Gladstone then proceeded to summarise the work of Lord Herbert in which our heroine had so signally helped. " To him we owe the Commission for Inquiry into Barracks and Hospitals, to him we are indebted for the reorganisation of the Medical Department of the Army. To him we owe the Commission of Inquiry into and remodelling the medical education of the army. And lastly we owe him the Commission for presenting to the public the vital statistics of the army in such a form, from time to time, that the great and living facts of the subjects are brought to view."

Such was the perfect knight, the gallant gentleman, and the high-souled reformer whose loss Florence Nightingale now deplored. From her sick-room she followed with interest the schemes to honour his memory. It was proposed to erect his statue outside the War Office in Pall Mall, and to endow an exhibition of gold medals in connection with the Army Medical School at Chatham, which had been founded under his auspices. At Salisbury, the city where the names of Lord and Lady Herbert were household words as benefactors to the sick and distressed, a public meeting was held to promote a fund for erecting a bronze statue to Lord Herbert and for the support of a Convalescent Hospital at Charmouth as a branch of the Salisbury Hospital, to which he had been such a liberal benefactor.

Miss Nightingale had also the satisfaction of knowing that the reforms at which she had laboured with him were already bearing fruit. This was being demonstrated in China at this time (1860–64) where General Gordon was waging war against the Taiping Rebellion. While, during the first seven months of the Crimean War, the mortality amongst the soldiers had been at the alarming rate of sixty-one in every hundred per annum, exclusive of those killed in action, in the Chinese campaign, when the army had been sent half across the globe to an unhealthy country, the death-rate, including the wounded, was little more than three men in every hundred per annum, while the loss of those killed in action amounted to less than six men in every hundred per annum.

But now her chief was gone, cut off in the prime of his manhood, and at the pinnacle of public estimation and usefulness, and Miss Nightingale's usually hopeful spirit grew despondent. The following letter, written fourteen months after Lord Herbert's death, reveals how sorely she was suffering in body and in spirit. She writes :—

"*October 22nd,* 1861.

" DEAR SIR,—

". . . In answer to your kind inquiry, I have passed the last four years between four walls, only varied to other four walls once a year ; and I believe there is no prospect but of my health becoming ever worse and worse till the hour of my release. But I have never ceased, during one waking hour since my return to England five years ago, labouring for the welfare of the army at home, as I did abroad, and no hour have I given to friendship or amusement during that time but all to work. To that work the death of my dear chief, Sidney Herbert, has been a fatal blow. I assure you it is always a support-giving strength to me to find a national sympathy with the army and our efforts for it—such a sympathy as you express.

" Believe me, dear sir,
" Sincerely yours,
" FLORENCE NIGHTINGALE."

Happily the succeeding years brought some improvement in health, and the gloomy forebodings of this letter were not realised. After her recovery from the shock occasioned by Lord Herbert's death, Miss Nightingale continued to give her experience and advice in matters of army and hospital reform both at home and abroad. She had correspondents in all parts of the globe, and the builders of hospitals and pioneers in nursing and sanitary reforms all drew from the fount of her practical knowledge.

She took a deep and sympathetic interest in the Italian War for Liberty, for she had herself been born on Italian soil, and felt something of the patriot's spirit as she followed the progress of the Italian arms both in the struggle for independence and in the Austro-Prussian War of 1866.

In response to a request in 1866 from Cavaliere Sebastiano Fenzi, one of the committee for organising a system of volunteer assistance to the hospital department of the Italian army, that she would come to Florence to give advice and personal superintendence, Miss Nightingale replied giving a lengthy series of recommendations. We quote the conclusion of the letter for its personal interest :—

" Thus far," writes Miss Nightingale, " I have given dry advice as drily as I could. But you must permit me to say that if there is anything I could do for you at any time, and you would command me, I should esteem it the greatest honour and pleasure. I am a hopeless invalid, entirely a prisoner to my room, and overwhelmed with business. Otherwise how gladly would I answer to your call and come and do my little best for you in the dear city where I was born. If the giving my miserable. life could hasten your success but by half an hour, how gladly would I give it. But you will not want for success or for martyrs, or for volunteers or for soldiers.

" Our old General, Lord Clyde (he is dead now), was standing at the port of Balaclava when, eleven years ago, the Italian Bersagliere were landing ; and he turned round and said to his companion (a man high in office), 'I wish to hide my face— I blush for ourselves when I see the perfect way in which those glorious troops are brought up to their work.' And what have not the Italians done since, in those eleven years ?—the work of almost eleven centuries !

" I, too, remember the Italian (Sardinian) hospitals on the heights of Balaclava, and their admirable government ; and since then what has not the progress been ? I wish you God-speed with my whole heart, and by that you will believe me, sir, your ever faithful servant,

" FLORENCE NIGHTINGALE."

" *Cavaliere Sebastiano Fenzi, Florence.*"

Miss Nightingale would certainly have been cheered in her sick-room if she could have seen the enthusiasm and emotion excited in her native city when her letter was read to the people.

The United States, which has to-day such an efficient organisation for the succour of the sick and wounded soldiers, owes the inception of the movement to Florence Nightingale. When the American Civil War broke out in 1860, her name had become a talisman not only to her fellow-countrymen, but to English-speaking people all over the world, and to her example the women of the United States looked when their land became devastated by war. Soon after the outbreak of hostilities, women in the leading cities of the States formed themselves into working parties to provide lint and bandages and suitable clothing for the suffering soldiery. But as the colossal needs of the regiments being formed all over the States became apparent, a special Sanitary Commission was, at the instance of various Medical and Relief Associations, founded by the Secretary of War to deal with the sick and wounded in hospital and camp. Hundreds of women volunteered as nurses, and in time a most efficient organisation was built up.

The observations and advice of Miss Nightingale were continually laid before this Commission, and

MISS NIGHTINGALE AFTER HER RETURN FROM THE CRIMEA
(Photo by Keene, Derby.)

[*To face p* 272.

her name became almost as much a household word in the States as at home. She was regarded as the great friend of the American soldiers and the beneficent genius of their hospitals. Had Miss Nightingale been in a more robust state of health, there is little doubt that she would have visited America during this great crisis, to give personal help in the initial work of the establishment of army nursing.

About this period, also, the seed of her example bore fruit in the establishment of the Red Cross Society, the branches of which to-day cover the civilised world. The honour of the inception belongs to M. Henri Dunant, a citizen of Geneva, who, appalled by the fearful carnage and disease among the soldiery in the Italian campaign, succeeded in drawing together an International Congress at the city of Geneva on October 26th, 1863, to consider how a neutral body might be formed for the relief of the wounded in battle. The result of Henri Dunant's grand scheme was the extension of the work begun by Florence Nightingale in the Crimea over the entire Continent of Europe by means of the Red Cross Societies, which act in close relationship with their respective Governments and in conjunction with the army.

The work thus begun spread rapidly when that most sanguinary struggle of modern times, the

Franco-German War, broke out in 1870. During that period Miss Nightingale's advice was repeatedly sought and she was specially appealed to by the German authorities when organising their medical and nursing corps.

CHAPTER XXII

WISDOM FROM THE QUEEN OF NURSES

Literary Activity—*Notes on Hospitals*—*Notes on Nursing*—Hints for the Amateur Nurse—Interest in the Army in India—Writings on Indian Reforms.

> This noble ensample to his sheep he gaf,
> That first he wroughte and afterward he taught.
> CHAUCER.

IN the years succeeding her return from the Crimea Miss Nightingale, in addition to the important labours recorded in the foregoing chapter, was actively engaged with her pen. Her writings dealt with the subjects so near her heart of hospital reform, sick nursing and household sanitation. If the soldier needed hygienic reforms in barracks and camps, so did the great mass of the people in their own homes. Miss Nightingale's interest in army reform did not absorb her attention to the neglect of civil matters.

Her writings are distinguished not only by expert and technical knowledge, but by much homely practical wisdom. There is nothing of the blue-stocking about Florence Nightingale. She puts aside formulas, and with tender human feeling, enlivened by witty epigram and racy humour, goes right to the heart of her subject, particularly in regard to the needs and management of the sick.

Her first published work after her return home was a statistical account of her distribution of the "Voluntary Contributions," placed at her disposal for the sick soldiers, which has already been dealt with. In the following year (1858) she issued her *Notes on Matters affecting the Health, Efficiency, and Hospital Administration of the British Army,* which was of great value to the Commission on the War, then sitting, and led to the institution of many reforms.

In 1859 Miss Nightingale published her *Notes on Hospitals,* the basis of which was a paper she prepared for the Social Science Association. " It may seem a strange principle," she writes with grim humour, " to enunciate as the very first requirement in a hospital that it should do the sick no harm. It is quite necessary, nevertheless, to lay down such a principle, because the actual mortality *in* hospitals, especially in those of large crowded cities, is very much higher than any calculation founded on the mortality of the same class of diseases among patients treated *out of* hospital would lead us to expect."

It was the knowledge of this unsatisfactory fact

which led Miss Nightingale to thoroughly in-
vestigate the influence which hospital construction
exercised on the death-rate of patients received into
the wards. The result was her *Notes on Hospitals*,
which in the enlarged edition, published in 1863,
became a standard work on the subject. It is
technical in character, and, in addition to recommendations on the conduct and arrangements of
hospitals, gives plans for hospital construction. It
covers the whole field from floors and walls to
hospital furniture.

In the following year of 1860 came that ever
popular book, *Notes on Nursing : What it Is, and
What it is Not*, of which more than one hundred
thousand copies have been sold. In it Miss Nightingale gives such homely advice as can be put into
practice by every girl and woman in the land. The
subject is always topical, and I cannot do better than
cull some of the words of wisdom from the Queen
of Nurses.

The *Notes*, she explains, are not intended as a
manual for nurses but simply to give hints for
thought to women who have personal charge of
the health of others, and almost every woman in
England has some time or other the charge of the
health of another. " Every woman is a nurse."
Then she proceeds with piquant saying and homely
illustration to give simple rules for the amateur

nurse. "No need to discuss," she says, "whether the top of Mont Blanc will ever be inhabited —it will be thousands of years before we have reached the bottom of Mont Blanc in making the earth healthy. Nursing has been limited to signify little more than the administration of medicines and the application of poultices. It ought to signify the proper use of fresh air, light, warmth, quiet, and proper selection and administration of diet."

She goes on to refer to the "coxcombries" of education, by which the elements of astronomy are taught to every schoolgirl while the future wives and mothers are not instructed in those laws which God has assigned to the relations of our bodies with the world in which He has put them. It is no use to blame the climate, which we cannot control, for sickness. "What can we do with the east wind?" people ask.

"Who is it who knows when the wind is in the east?" returns Miss Nightingale. "Not the Highland drover, certainly exposed to the east wind, but the young lady who is worn out with the want of exposure to fresh air, to sunlight. Put the latter under as good sanitary condition as the former, and she too will not know when the wind is in the east."

Miss Nightingale groups young ladies and soldiers

together as the most frequent victims of consumption, owing to foul air and exposure to chills. "Young ladies, like soldiers, go out in all weathers, the one to parties, the other to sentry duty ; both enter foul air, the one in ball-rooms, the other in guard-rooms ; both go home in damp night air after skin and lungs are oppressed in their functions by overcrowding." She implores young ladies to open their windows and bedcurtains at night, and not be afraid of spoiling their complexions. This was written, it must be remembered, more than forty years ago, when girls were more afraid of fresh air than they are to-day, now that cycling, hockey, and golf have inured them even to east winds.

After dealing with household hygiene in chapters on "Ventilating and Warming," and "Health of Houses," she proceeds to consider the bad results of "Petty Management," under which heading the want of relays of nurses is dealt with both in institutions and in private homes. A tired, jaded nurse is almost worse than no nurse at all. The nurse must have needed rest ; still, the patient should not be left alone. "I once heard a neglectful official rebuked," says Miss Nightingale, "in the words, 'Patients, sir, will not stop dying while we are in church.'"

The subject of "Noise" gives Miss Nightingale the occasion to speak plainly on the dress of the amateur nurse. She wrote in the days of crinolines, but her strictures would equally apply to the woman who in modern times gets her long skirts entangled in the furniture, and creates as much noise and upset in the sick chamber as did the nurse of the olden days with her crinoline. Miss Nightingale endorses Lord Melbourne's sentiments when he said : "I would rather have men about me when I am ill. I think it requires very strong health to put up with women." It was "the fidget of silk and crinoline, the crackling of starched petticoats, the creaking of stays and shoes," which led Lord Melbourne to make this ungallant observation.

Miss Nightingale advises the private woman called upon to nurse in her own family to copy the neat, trim style of dressing adopted by the professional nurse. Her manner should be as motionless as possible. "Never gesticulate when speaking to the sick," cultivate conciseness and calmness, and avoid an irresolute manner.

The chapter on "Variety" deals in a beautiful and sympathetic spirit with the effect of colour and variety of objects on the sick person. "The effect in sickness," she writes, "of beautiful objects, of variety of objects, and especially of brilliancy of colour, is hardly at all appreciated. Such cravings are not fancies. . . . Variety of form and brilliancy of colour in the objects presented to patients are actual means of recovery," and she recalls her own case, already quoted, when a nosegay of wild-flowers brought to her hut on the heights of Balaclava, where she lay with fever, seemed to put new life into her. "Form and colour," she says, "will free your patient from his painful ideas better than any argument." People say it is the effect on the patient's mind. It is no such thing ; the effect is on the body too. While variety in objects is necessary, "it must be a *slow* variety ; don't show a patient ten or twelve engravings successively." One fresh picture a day hung on his wall or brought to his bedside will be more appreciated.

The Queen of Nurses combats the frequently accepted idea that cut flowers and growing plants are unhealthy in a sick-room, even at night. "The carbonic acid they give off at nights," she writes, "would not poison a fly. Nay, in overcrowded rooms they actually absorb carbonic acid and give off oxygen. Cut flowers also decompose water and produce oxygen gas." The nurse should observe what colours are most pleasing to her patient. "Some sick persons feel stimulus from looking at scarlet flowers, others exhaustion from looking at deep blue."

This reminds me of an incident which occurred while the present writer was going over Netley

Hospital when it was filled with wounded from the battlefields of South Africa. The convalescent soldiers were doing fancy woolwork, and a sister came into a ward bearing a parcel of wool sent by a benevolent lady. When opened, the wool was found to be all in khaki colour. The men turned their heads in disgust. " Didn't we see enough of khaki in South Africa, sister ? " they exclaimed. " Why don't these kind ladies send us bright colours which will drive the thought of khaki out of our minds." A moment's intelligent reflection on the colours most likely to please the brave fellows at Netley would have prevented such a foolish mistake. Miss Nightingale's words of wisdom, written forty years ago, are not obsolete yet.

The subject of " Taking Food " is next dealt with, and Miss Nightingale vigorously attacks the accepted traditions. It is a common error " that beef tea is the most nutritious of all articles. Now just try and boil down a pound of beef into beef tea, evaporate your beef tea, and see what is left of your beef—barely a tablespoonful of solid nourishment to half a pint of water in beef tea." Still, Miss Nightingale admits that there is a certain reparative quality in beef tea, as in ordinary tea. She denounces that favourite article with the friends of the sick, jelly, which usually contains no nourishment at all.

Miss Nightingale is constantly called the " soldier's friend " and one may add that she is above all the patient's friend. "Attend," she writes, "to the intelligent cravings of the sick. Patients crave for things laid down in no sick dietary. It often happens that the patient's stomach is right and the book wrong. You can't diet a patient from a book."

How many weary invalids will thank the Queen of Nurses for granting them the too often condemned cup of tea. " A great deal too much against tea is said by wise people," she writes. " When you see the natural and almost universal craving in English sick for their 'tea,' you cannot but feel that Nature knows what she is about. I should be very glad if any of the abusers of tea would point out what to give to an English patient after a sleepless night, instead of tea. It is the almost universal testimony of English men and women who have undergone great fatigue, such as riding long journeys without stopping, or sitting up for several nights in succession, that they could do it best upon an occasional cup of tea—and nothing else. Let experience, not theory, decide upon this as upon all other things." Cocoa increases fat, but has no restorative power, and it is " pure mockery to offer it as a substitute for tea—you might," adds Miss Nightingale, " as well offer patients chestnuts instead of tea." She gives the warning, however, that too much tea is given to the sick by foolish people, and that as a rule neither tea nor coffee should be given to invalids after five o'clock.

The remarks on "Beds and Bedding" are not as relevant now as when they were written in the days of the much be-curtained four-post bedstead and luxurious feather beds. Most people now acknowledge the superiority of the iron bedstead with spring mattress. The bed coverings should be light as well as warm and "a true nurse," says Miss Nightingale, "always makes her patient's bed and does not leave it to the housemaid." She recommends that the bed should always be in the lightest place in the room, and the patient able to see out of window. "A fashionable physician," she writes, "has been saying that he turns his patients' faces from the light. Yes, but Nature is stronger than fashionable physicians, and depend upon it, she turns the faces back and *towards* such light aa she can get." Observation of the sick shows that patients do not turn their faces to the wall.

Miss Nightingale, in illustration of the craving of the sick to see out of window, relates a beautiful story of a nurse's self-sacrifice. A poor man in one of the hospitals was suffering from spinal accident and expressed an intense longing just to nave one look out of the window. The nurse, moved with compassion for the poor fellow's craving, raised him on her back so that he might take his coveted look at the outside world once again. His joy was great, but the effort cost the nurse a long and serious illness.

Under the heading of " Chattering Hopes and Advices," Miss Nightingale evidently speaks out of the fulness of her own experience. " 'Chattering Hopes,' " she says, " may seem an odd heading. But I really believe there is scarcely a greater worry which invalids have to endure than the incurable hopes of their friends. There is no one practice against which I can speak more strongly from actual experience, wide and long, of its effects during sickness, observed both upon others and upon myself. I would appeal most seriously to all friends, visitors, and attendants of the sick to leave off this practice of attempting to ' cheer ' the sick by making light of their danger and by exaggerating their probabilities of recovery. . . . The fact is that the patient is not ' cheered ' at all by these well-meaning, most tiresome friends." The advice or opinion of the experienced does not of course come under the head of " Chattering Hopes," but it is the advice of " inexperience to bitter experience " which Miss Nightingale condemns, and which amounts to nothing more than this, " that you think

I shall recover from consumption, because somebody knows somebody, somewhere, who has recovered from fever." Nurses should protect their patients from visitors of the class indicated.

The "Observation of the Sick" is a quality which needs cultivation. "The most important practical lesson that can be given to nurses is to teach them what to observe," writes Miss Nightingale, also "how to observe," and to accurately state the result of observation. It is a more difficult thing to speak the truth than people commonly imagine. "Courts of justice seem to think that anybody can speak 'the whole truth and nothing but the truth,' if he does but intend it." It requires many faculties combined of observation and memory to do that. She quotes a little incident to illustrate the point. "I know I fibs dreadful; but believe me, miss, I never finds out I have fibbed until they tells me so," was a remark once made to her, which is, as she says, "one of more extended application than most people have the least idea of."

Needless to say, unintentional "fibbing," or in other words lack of observation, which leads a nurse to wrongly inform the doctor regarding the patient, often leads to disastrous results. "I knew," says Miss Nightingale, "a very clever physician of large dispensary and hospital practice, who invariably began his examination of a patient with 'Put your finger where you *be* bad.' That man would never waste his time with collecting inaccurate information from nurse or patient." Nothing leads to inaccurate information more than putting "leading questions" to sick people. "How do you sleep?" "How is your appetite?" A tactful and observant nurse will be better able to answer such questions than the patient himself.

Miss Nightingale thinks that Englishwomen are not naturally good observers, though capable of attaining to it by training. The French or Irish woman is much quicker. She records a homely little example of want of observation. "I remember when a child," she writes, "hearing the story of an accident related by some one who sent two nieces to fetch a 'bottle of sal-volatile from her room.' 'Mary could not stir,' she said; 'Fanny ran and fetched a bottle that was not sal-volatile, and that was not in my room.' If Fanny had observed the bottle of sal-volatile in the aunt's room every day she was there, she would have found it when it was suddenly wanted. This habit of inattention generally pursues a person through life, a woman is asked to fetch a large new-bound red book lying on the table by the window, and she fetches five small old boarded brown books lying on the shelf by the fire."

In contrast to this type of careless person, Miss

Nightingale instances the trained observations of a famous actress. "I was once taken," she writes, "to see a great actress in Lady Macbeth. To me it appeared the mere transference upon the stage of a death-bed, such as I had often witnessed. So, just before death, have I seen a patient get out of bed and feebly re-enact some scene of long ago, exactly as if walking in sleep." The actress played her part so well because she had actually observed life.

"The very alphabet of a nurse," says Miss Nightingale, "is to observe so well that she is able to interpret every change which comes over a patient's countenance, without causing him the exertion of saying what he feels. . . . A patient is not merely a piece of furniture, to be kept clean and arranged against the wall, and saved from injury or breakage—though to judge from what many a nurse does and does not do, you would say he was." Then comes a caution that all sick people dislike being watched, and the nurse must observe without appearing to do so. Miss Nightingale relates that the best observer she ever knew was a distinguished doctor for lunacy. "He leans back in his chair, with half-shut eyes," she relates, "and, meanwhile, he sees everything, observes everything, and you feel he knows you better than many who have lived with you twenty years. I

believe it is this singular capacity of observation and of understanding what observed appearances imply which gives him his singular influence over lunatics."

In a concluding chapter, Miss Nightingale refers to the dangers of "reckless physicking by amateur females," and tells of the lady who, having procured a prescription for a blue pill which suited her during one indisposition, proceeded to dose not only herself but her family too, "for all complaints upon all occasions." Then there are the women who have no ideas beyond calomel and aperients, and the Lady Bountifuls who dose their poorer neighbours with a favourite prescription when it would be doing more good if they persuaded the people to "remove the dung-hill from before the door, to put in a window which opens, or an Arnott's ventilator, or to cleanse and lime-wash their cottages."

She has some last words to say on nursing as a profession, and gives a humorous little thrust at "the commonly received idea among men, and even among women themselves, that it requires nothing but a disappointment in love, the want of an object, a general disgust, or incapacity for other things, to turn a woman into a good nurse." "This reminds one of the parish where a stupid old man was set to be school-master because he was 'past keeping the pigs.'"

19

Miss Nightingale sums up the matter with some condensed wisdom on the question as to whether women are fitted for the medical and other professions. She urges them to keep clear of "the jargon" which impels a woman on the one hand to do things simply to imitate men, and on the other to refrain from doing what she has the power to accomplish simply because it has hitherto been considered man's work. "Surely woman," she writes, "should bring the best she has, *whatever* that is, to the work of God's world, without attending to either of these cries. For what are they, but listening to the 'what people will say' opinion, to the voices from without? No one has ever done anything great or useful by listening to the voices from without. You want to do the thing that is good, whether people call it 'suitable for a woman' or not. Oh, leave these jargons, and go your way straight to God's work, in simplicity and singleness of heart."

A year after the publication of *Notes on Nursing*, Miss Nightingale issued (1861) a modified edition of the work, under the title of *Notes on Nursing for the Labouring Classes*, adding a chapter on "Minding Baby," which is specially addressed to young girls in working families, who have a great deal to do with minding mother's baby. It is delightfully written and reveals how conversant the author was with the homes of the poor. It would do more good than many tracts if distributed by the district visitor, and would be a useful addition to the text-books of our elementary schools. With her usual quick insight the Queen of Nurses recognises the importance of the working-girl nurse. "One-half of all the nurses in service," she writes, "are girls of from five to twenty years old. You see you are very important little people. Then there are all the girls who are nursing mother's baby at home ; and in all these cases it seems pretty nearly to come to this, that baby's health for its whole life depends upon you, girls, more than upon anything else." Simple rules such as a girl of six coulu understand are given for the feeding, washing, dressing, nursing, and even amusement of that important person, " baby."

" The healthiest, happiest, liveliest, most beautiful baby I ever saw was the only child of a busy laundress," writes Miss Nightingale ; " she washed all day in a room with the door open upon a larger room, where she put the child. It sat or crawled upon the floor all day with no other play-fellow than a kitten, which it used to hug. Its mother kept it beautifully clean, and fed it with perfect regularity. The child was never frightened at anything. The room where it sat was the house-place ; and it always gave notice to its mother when anybody came in, not by a cry, but by a crow. I lived for many months within hearing of that child, and never heard it cry day or night. I think there is a great deal too much of amusing children now ; and not enough of letting them amuse themselves."

The versatility of Miss Nightingale's pen is shown by her next publication, *The Sanitary State of the Army in India*, which came out in 1863. The hand which could write with such tender womanly concern about baby could deal vigorous blows at the insanitary condition of the soldiers in India. She had been keenly interested in Lord Herbert's scheme for uniting the Indian with the Home army, and followed it up by a thorough investigation of the causes affecting the health of the army in India. An elaborate series of written evidence procured from all the principal stations of India by the Royal Commission appointed for the purpose, was laid before Miss Nightingale in 1861, and at the request of the Commission she wrote a valuable paper of comments on the reports. Lord Stanley succeeded Lord Herbert as President of the Commission, and to him Miss Nightingale addressed her observations, which form a book of some hundred pages. She points out in her usual concise style the evils arising from the defective sanitation of the camps, the bad water, lack of drainage, and the imperfections of the hospitals, and deals with the preventable causes which lead to drunkenness and a low tone of morality amongst the Indian troops.

The state of the army in India continued to be a matter of great concern to Miss Nightingale, and at the request of the National Social Science Congress she prepared a paper on the subject, to which she gave the arresting title "How People may Live and not Die in India." This was read at the Edinburgh meeting in 1863, and published in pamphlet form the following year. In a prefatory note Miss Nightingale refers with pleasure to the improvement in the condition of the soldiers which had taken place in many respects. The introduction of soldiers' gardens, trades, and workshops enabled the men to realise that it was better to work than to sleep and to drink, even during hot weather.

She gives an interesting instance of how these reforms had worked. "One regiment marching into a station," she writes, "where cholera had been raging for two years, were ' chaffed ' by the regiments marching out, and told they would never come out of it alive.

"The men of the entering battalion answered, They would see ; we *won't* have cholera. And they made gardens with such good effect that they had the pleasure not only of eating their own vegetables, but of being paid for them too by the commissariat. And this in a soil which no regiment had been able to cultivate before. And not a man had cholera. These good soldiers fought against disease, too, by workshops and gymnasia, and at a few hill stations the men have covered the whole hill-sides with their gardens."

She goes on to tell of the good results taking place from the introduction of gymnastics for the men and cricket and other outdoor sports. " In short," she adds in a pithy sentence, " work and all kinds of exercise cause sickly men to flourish." Soldiers' libraries were being established by Government, better cook-houses built, and the soldiers taught to cook. And so far she is glad to record that the soldiers' habits had improved. "But the main causes of diseases in India—want of drainage, want of water supply for stations and towns—remain as before," she ironically remarks, "in all their primitive perfection." The death-rate of troops serving in India was the alarming one of sixty-nine per thousand per annum. " It takes something more than climate to account for this," she writes. " All that the climate requires is that men shall adapt their social habits and customs to it, as, indeed, they must do to the requirements of every other climate under heaven. There is not a shadow of proof that India was created to be the grave of the British race."

Miss Nightingale then enumerates the simple rules for dress, diet, and exercise to be observed by soldiers serving in India. But though a man can regulate his personal habits, "he cannot," she adds, "drain and sewer his own city, nor lay a water supply on to his own station, nor build his own barracks," and she proceeds to urge that sanitary reform in India is still one of the most pressing questions for the Government. By wise measures the enormous death-rate of sixty-nine per thousand might be reduced to ten per thousand. "What a work, what a noble task for a Government—no ' inglorious period of our dominion ' that," she writes, " but a most glorious one ! "

Ten years later Miss Nightingale again returned to the "charge" and prepared a paper on " Life or Death in India," which was read at the meeting of the National Association for the promotion of Social Science at Norwich in 1873, and afterwards published as a pamphlet with an appendix on "Life or Death by Irrigation."

In this paper Miss Nightingale pointed out the cheering fact that during the past ten years in which sanitary reforms had been progressing the death-rate of the army in India had been reduced from sixty-nine per thousand to eighteen per thousand—

that is, eighteen men died where sixty-nine had died before. Still, she considered that this only sufficed to show the work that yet remained to be done, especially with regard to the drainage, water supply, and the irrigation of the country for commercial purposes, on account not only of the soldier, but to promote the health of the teeming millions of our fellow-subjects in India and their general prosperity.

Miss Nightingale disposes of the "caste" difficulty with an amusing incident. When the Government's new water supply "was first introduced into Calcutta, the high-caste Hindoos still desired their water-carriers to bring them their *sacred* water from the *river*; but these functionaries, finding it much easier to take the water from the new taps, just rubbed in a little (vulgar not sacred) mud, and presented it as Ganges water.

"When at last the filthy fraud was discovered, public opinion, founded on experience, had already gone too far to return to dirty water. And the new water supply was, at public meetings, adjudged to be *theologically* as well as physically safe."

Miss Nightingale urges that irrigation schemes should be set on foot by the Government as a preventive against the ever-recurring famines which afflict our fellow Indian subjects so severely. "Is not the Government of India," she asks, "too much like a dispensary, which does all that man can do to cure when too late to do anything to prevent ? "

While Miss Nightingale's pen was pleading so eloquently and practically during this period for the good of the great Empire in the East, she was not unmindful of the people at home. Her writings and work in connection with the sick poor must form the subject of a separate chapter.

CHAPTER XXIII

THE NURSING OF THE SICK POOR

Origin of the Liverpool Home and Training School—Interest in
the Sick Paupers—"Una and the Lion" a Tribute to Sister
Agnes Jones—Letter to Miss Florence Lees—Plea for a Home
for Nurses—On the Question of Paid Nurses—Queen Victoria's
Jubilee Nursing Institute—Rules for Probationers.

Nursing is an Art; and if it is to be made an art, requires as exclusive
a devotion, as hard a preparation, as any painter's or sculptor's work;
for what is the having to do with dead canvas, or cold marble, compared
with having to do with the living body—the temple of God's spirit. . . . It
is one of the Fine Arts; I had almost said, the finest of the Fine Arts.—
FLORENCE NIGHTINGALE.

THERE is no branch of sick nursing which
appeals more strongly to Miss Nightingale
than the care of the sick poor. It was as a visitor
in the homes of her poorer neighbours at Lea Hurst
and Embley that she began her philanthropic work,
and though the outbreak of the Crimean War drew
her into the public arena and concentrated her
attention on the army, she had not ceased to feel the
importance of attending to the needs of the sick
poor, and repeatedly drew attention to the fact that

England was behind other nations in providing for the sick poor at home, and in infirmaries.

She recognised also that for this work a special training was needed. A nurse who had received a course of instruction in a hospital was not necessarily competent to nurse the poor in their own homes. Special knowledge and special experience were needed before a woman, however skilled in the technical side of nursing, could become a good district nurse.

About the same period that Miss Nightingale was establishing and organising her Training School for Nurses at St. Thomas's Hospital, she was also working in conjunction with Mr. William Rathbone, M.P., and other philanthropic people to found a special training school for nurses for the poor. It was at her suggestion that this branch of pioneer work was started in connection with the Liverpool Infirmary, which had already made some provision on similar lines. The prospectus for the Liverpool Training Home for Nurses was made public in 1861-2, and a commodious building was subsequently erected in the grounds of the infirmary.

In 1865 Miss Nightingale wrote an introduction to a work describing the " Origin and Organisation of the Liverpool School and Home for Nurses." " It is the old story, often told ! " she writes, " but this book opens a new chapter of it. It gives us hope for a better state of things. An institution for training nurses in connection with the infirmary has been built and organised. This is a matter of necessity, because all who wish to nurse efficiently must learn how to nurse *in a hospital.*

" Nursing, especially that most important of all its branches—nursing of the sick poor at home—is no amateur work. To do it as it ought to be done requires knowledge, practice, self-abnegation, and as is so well said here, direct obedience to and activity under the highest of all Masters and from the highest of all motives. It is an essential part of the daily service of the Christian Church. It has never been otherwise. It has proved itself superior to all religious divisions, and is destined, by God's blessing, to supply an opening the great value of which, in our densely peopled towns, has been unaccountably overlooked until within these few years."

With such noble words did Florence Nightingale usher in a movement which has now spread to all parts of the kingdom. There is not now a workhouse infirmary which has not its trained nurses in place of the rough-handed and unskilled inmate, nor any town and few villages which have not some provision for nursing the sick poor in their own homes, and our beloved Queen Victoria found it the worthiest object to which she could devote the people's offering in commemoration of her Jubilee.

The main objects of the pioneer Training Home at Liverpool were :—

1. To provide thoroughly educated professional nurses for the poor.

2. To provide district nurses for the poor.

3. To provide sick nurses for private families.

Miss Nightingale watched the progress of the home with keen interest and gave her advice from time to time. She was also actively engaged in promoting workhouse reform. A sick pauper was to her a human being, not a "chattel" to be handed over to the tender mercies of the Mr. Bumbles and Mrs. Corneys. It afforded her great satisfaction that two out of the first lot of nurses which left her St. Thomas's Training School went as matrons to workhouse infirmaries. A reform in workhouse hospitals had been brought about by Mr. Gathorne-Hardy's Metropolitan Poor Act of 1867. But the introduction of trained nurses on the Nightingale system grew directly out of the experience and information which followed the founding of the Liverpool Training Home.

Hitherto the workhouse nurses were the pauper women, untrustworthy and unskilled. At Brownlow Hill, Liverpool, Infirmary Mr. Rathbone relates that there were twelve hundred beds occupied by people in all stages of every kind of disease, and the only assistants of the two women officers who superintended the nursing were pauper women who were as untrustworthy as they were unskilful. This was a fair example of workhouse infirmaries all over the country.

The Select Vestry of Liverpool, having received an anonymous offer to defray the cost of the experiment for three years, consented to try Miss Nightingale's plan. With her assistance, Miss Agnes Jones, a lady who had been trained at Kaiserswerth like Miss Nightingale, and also at the Nightingale School at St. Thomas's, was appointed Lady Superintendent, and she brought with her a staff of twelve nurses from St. Thomas's. At first Miss Jones tried to get extra help by training the able-bodied pauper women as nurses, but out of fifty-six not one proved able to pass the necessary examination and, worse still, the greater number used their first salary to get drunk. The painful fact was established that not a single respectable and trustworthy nurse could be found amongst the workhouse inmates, and the infirmary nursing had to be taken entirely out of their hands.

After a two years' trial Miss Jones's experiment with her trained and educated nurses proved so satisfactory that the guardians determined never to return to the old system, and to charge the rates with the permanent establishment of the new one.

To the deep regret of every one, however, Miss Agnes Jones sank under the labours which she had undertaken, and died in February, 1868.

Miss Nightingale contributed a beautiful tribute to the memory of her friend and fellow worker in *Good Words* for June, 1868, under the title " Una and the Lion," which subsequently formed the " Introduction" to *The Memorials of Agnes Elizabeth Jones*, by her sister.

" One woman has died," writes Miss Nightingale, " a woman, attractive and rich, and young and witty ; yet a veiled and silent woman, distinguished by no other genius but the divine genius—working hard to train herself in order to train others to walk in the footsteps of Him who went about doing good. . . . She died, as she had lived, at her post in one of the largest workhouse infirmaries in this kingdom—the first in which trained nursing has been introduced. . . . When her whole life and image rise before me, so far from thinking the story of Una and her lion a myth, I say here is Una in real flesh and blood—Una and her paupers far more untamable than lions. In less than three years she had reduced one of the most disorderly hospital populations in the world to something like Christian discipline, and had converted a vestry to the conviction of the economy as well as humanity of nursing pauper sick by trained nurses."

We must refrain from quoting more of this singularly fine tribute of the Chief to one of her ablest generals in the army of nursing reform, with the exception of the beautiful closing words : " Let us add living flowers to her grave, 'lilies with full hands,' not fleeting primroses, not dying flowers. Let us bring the work of our hands and our heads and our hearts to finish her work which God has so blessed.   Let us not merely rest in peace, but let hers be the life which stirs up to fight the good fight against vice and sin and misery and wretchedness, as she did—the call to arms which she was ever obeying :—

> The Son of God goes forth to war,
> Who follows in His train ?

Oh, daughters of God, are there so few to answer ? "

One cannot leave the subject without a reference to the influence which Miss Nightingale's own early example had had on the gifted woman whose memory she extolled.   On the eve of going into training at St. Thomas's Miss Agnes Jones wrote: " It is well that I shall, at my first outset in hospital work, bear the name of ' Nightingale Probationer,' for that honoured name is associated with my first thought of hospital life.   In the winter of '54, when I had those first earnest longings for work,

Dec 26 1870

MRS. DACRE CRAVEN (NÉE FLORENCE LEES).

(From a drawing by the Crown Princess of Germany (the late Empress Frederick), when
* had charge of the Crown Princess's Lazaretto at Homburg during the*
[*To face p.* 304.

nd had for months so little to satisfy them, how I wished I were competent to join the Nightingale band when they started for the Crimea ! I listened to the animadversions of many, but I almost worshipped her who braved all, and I felt she must succeed."

The system inaugurated by Miss Agnes Jones at Liverpool Infirmary spread over the country, and Miss Nightingale had the satisfaction of seeing in a comparatively short time a great improvement in the nursing and treatment of the sick in work-houses. Gaols had long been visited and reformed, lunatic asylums opened to inspection, and it seemed unaccountable that the misery of sick workhouse paupers should have been so long overlooked.*

The success of the introduction of trained nurses into workhouses gave an impulse to sick poor nursing generally, and in 1868 the East London Nursing Society was founded by the Hon. Mrs. Stuart Wortley and Mr. Robert Wigram. In 1874 the movement received a further important impulse from the formation of the National Nursing Association, to provide skilled nurses for the sick poor in their own homes, to establish district or-ganisations in London and in the country, and to establish a training school for district nurses in connection with one of the London hospitals.

* Miss Louisa Twining in 1854 began her pioneer efforts in workhouse reform, which resulted in 1874 in the establishment of the Workhouse Nursing Association.

This work appealed most strongly to Miss Nightingale, and she expressed her sympathy in the following letter to that devoted pioneer of district nursing, Miss Florence Lees,* now Mrs. Dacre Craven, who was the indefatigable honorary secretary of the newly founded National Nursing Association.

"As to your success," writes Miss Nightingale, - "what is not your success? To raise the homes of your patients so that they never fall back again to dirt and disorder : such is your nurses' influence. To pull through life and death cases—cases which it would be an honour to pull through with all the appurtenances of hospitals, or of the richest in the land, and this without any sick-room appurtenances at all. To keep whole families out of pauperism by preventing the home from being broken up, and nursing the bread-winner back to health."

The next point in Miss Nightingale's letter was one which was at the root of the movement and which she invariably emphasised : "To drag the noble art of nursing out of the sink of relief doles." It was believed that nothing would so effectually stop the pauperising of the people by indiscriminate charity as the trained nurse in the homes of the sick poor, who would teach her patients how best to help

* Miss Lees was described by Kinglake as "the gifted and radiant pupil" of Florence Nightingale. She was a probationer at the St. Thomas's Training School when it was temporarily located in the old Surrey Gardens.

themselves. "To carry out," continues Miss Nightingale, " the practical principles of preventing disease by stopping its causes and the causes of infections which spread disease. Last but not least, to show a common life able to sustain the workers in this saving but hardest work under a working head, who will personally keep the training and nursing at its highest point. Is not this a great success?

" District nursing, so solitary, so without the cheer and the stimulus of a big corps of fellow-workers in the bustle of a public hospital, but also without many of its cares and strains, requires what it has with you, the constant supervision and inspiration of a genius of nursing and a common home. May it spread with such a standard over the whole of London and the whole of the land."

Two years later (1876) Miss Nightingale made an eloquent plea in a long letter to *The Times* for the establishment of a Home for Nurses in connection with the National Society for Providing Trained Nurses for the Poor. This letter was later reprinted as a pamphlet on *Trained Nursing for the Sick Poor*. In specially pleading for a Central Home for Nurses, she wrote, "If you give nurses a bad home, or no home at all, you will have only nurses who live in a bad home, or no home at all," and she emphasises the necessity for the district nurse to have a knowledge of how " to nurse the

home as well as the patient," and for that reason
she should live in a place of comfort herself free
from the discomforts of private lodgings.

Miss Nightingale's plea bore fruit in the establishment of the Central Home for Nurses, 23,
Bloomsbury Square, under the able management
of Miss Florence Lees. Nothing pleased Miss
Nightingale better than to get reports of the experience of the district nurses amongst the poor, and
to hear how the people received their visits and what
impression they were able to make on the habits of
the people. She was specially delighted with the
story of a puny slum boy who vigorously rebelled
against a tubbing which Miss Lees was administering.

"Willie don't like to be bathed," he roared ;
" oo may bath de debil, if oo like ! " The implica-
tion that Miss Lees was capable of washing the
devil white Miss Nightingale pronounced the finest
compliment ever paid to a district nurse.

She has always impressed upon district nurses
the need not only of knowing how to give advice,
but how to carry it out. The nurse must be able
to show how to clean up a home, and Miss Nightingale used frequently to quote the case of a bishop
who cleansed the pigsties of the normal training
school, of which he was master, as an example—
" one of the most episcopal acts ever done," was
her comment.

At first the district nurses were recruited almost entirely from the class known as "gentlewomen," as it was thought both by Miss Nightingale and Miss Lees that it required women of special refinement and education to exercise influence over the poor in their own homes. Also, one of the objects of the National Association was to raise the standard of nursing in the eyes of the public. It was soon proved that the lady nurses did not shirk any of the disagreeable and menial offices which fall to the lot of the district nurse. Broadly speaking, it is only the educated women with a vocation for nursing who will undertake such duties; the woman who merely wants to earn an income will choose hospital or private nursing. In the earlier stages of the movement the district nurses received high remuneration, and on this question of fees the Queen of Nurses may be quoted :—

"I have seen somewhere in print that nursing is a profession to be followed by the 'lower middle-class.' Shall we say that painting or sculpture is a profession to be followed by the 'lower middle-class'? Why limit the class at all? Or shall we say that God is only to be served in His sick by the 'lower middle-class'?

"It appears to be the most futile of all distinctions to classify as between 'paid' and unpaid art, so between 'paid' and unpaid nursing—to make into a test a circumstance as adventitious as whether the hair is black or brown, viz., whether people have private means or not, whether they are obliged or not to work at their art or their nursing for a livelihood. Probably no person ever did that well which he did only for money. Certainly no person ever did that well which he did not work at as hard as if he did it solely for money. If by amateur in art or in nursing are meant those who take it up for play, it is not art at all, it is not nursing at all. You never yet made an artist by paying him well ; but an artist ought to be well paid."

A most important outcome of the introduction of a system of trained nurses for the sick poor was the establishment of the Queen's Jubilee Nurses. Queen Victoria, moved by the great benefit which the National Nursing Association had conferred, decided, on the representations of the Committee of the Women's Jubilee Fund, furthered by Princess Christian, to devote the £70,000 subscribed, to the extension of this work.* The interest of the fund, amounting to £2,000 per annum, was applied to founding an institution for the education and maintenance of nurses for tending the sick poor

* Mrs. Dacre Craven had in 1877 proposed, in a letter laid before Queen Victoria, that a part of the fund of St. Katharine's Royal Hospital should be devoted to founding a Training Institute for District Nurses of gentle birth, to be called " Queen's Nurses."

in their own homes, with branch centres all over the kingdom. The charter for the new foundation was executed on September 20th, 1890.

The central institute was at first connected with St. Katharine's Royal Hospital, Regent's Park, an institution which had always been under the patronage of the Queens of England since it was founded by Queen Matilda, the wife of Stephen, at St. Katharine's Wharf, near the Tower of London. Subsequently the headquarters of the Queen Victoria's Jubilee Nursing Institute was removed to Victoria Street. Central homes have also been established at Edinburgh, Dublin, and Cardiff, and district homes all over the kingdom are affiliated to the Institute.

The National Association for Providing Trained Nurses for the Sick Poor, in which Miss Nightingale had so deeply interested herself, was affiliated to the Queen Victoria's Jubilee Institute, but it still has its original headquarters at the Nurses' Home, 23, Bloomsbury Square, so ably managed by the present Lady Superintendent, Miss Hadden. The Chairman of the Executive Committee is Henry Bonham Carter, Esq., an old friend and fellow worker of Miss Nightingale, while the Hon. Secretary is the Rev. Dacre Craven, Rector of St. Andrew's, Holborn, whose wife was Miss Florence Lees, the first Superintendent-General of the home and branches, and one of Miss Nightingale's devoted friends. Her Royal Highness Princess Christian is President of the Association.

There is probably no movement which has spread over the country so rapidly, and which appeals to the goodwill of all classes, as the nursing of the sick poor in their own homes, and its success has been one of the chief satisfactions of Miss Nightingale's life. She is always eager to hear of fresh recruits being added to the nursing army of the sick poor, and it may prove of interest to quote the regulations issued by the National Association :—

REGULATIONS FOR THE TRAINING OF NURSES FOR THE SICK POOR,

AND THEIR SUBSEQUENT ENGAGEMENT

1. A Nurse desiring to be trained in District Nursing must have previously received at least two years' training in a large general Hospital, approved by the Committee, and bring satisfactory testimonials as to capacity and conduct.

2. If considered by the Superintendent likely to prove suitable for District Nursing, she will be received on trial for one month. If at the end of that time she is considered suitable, she will continue her course of training, with technical class instruction for five months longer.

3. The Nurse will, at the end of her month of trial, be required to sign an agreement with the Queen Victoria's Jubilee Institute that she will, for one year from the date of the completion of her District training, continue to work as a District Nurse wherever the District Council of the Queen's Institute may require her services.

4. While under training, the Nurse will be subject to the authority of the Superintendent of the Training Home, and she must conform to the rules and regulations of the Home. She will be further subject, as to her work, to the inspection of the Inspector of the Queen's Institute.

5. If, during the time of her training, the Nurse be found inefficient, or otherwise unsuitable, her engagement may, with the consent of the Inspector of the Queen's Institute, be terminated by the Superintendent of the Training Home, at a week's notice. In the case of misconduct or neglect of duty she will be liable to immediate dismissal by the Superintendent of the Training Home, with the concurrence of the Inspector of the Queen's Institute.

6. During her six months' training she will receive a payment of £12 10s., payable, one-half at the end of three months from admission, and the remainder at the end of six months; but should her engagement be terminated from any cause before the end of her training, she will not, without the consent of the Queen's Institute, be entitled to any part payment. She will be provided with a full board, laundry, a separate furnished bedroom or cubicle, with a sitting room in common, as well as a uniform dress, which she will be required to wear at all times when on duty. The uniform must be considered the property of the Institute.

7. On the satisfactory completion of her training, the Nurse will be recommended for engagement as a District Nurse, under some Association affiliated to the Queen's Institute, the salary usually commencing at £30 per annum.

CHAPTER XXIV

LATER YEARS

The Nightingale Home—Rules for Probationers—Deaths of Mr. and Mrs. Nightingale—Death of Lady Verney—Continues to Visit Claydon—Health Crusade—Rural Hygiene—A Letter to Mothers—Introduces Village Missioners—Village Sanitation in India—The Diamond Jubilee—Balaclava Dinner.

When a noble life has prepared old age, it is not the decline that it reveals, but the first days of immortality.—MADAME DE STAEL.

MISS NIGHTINGALE'S work for the profession which her name and example had lifted into such high repute continued with unbated energy. The year 1871 brought what must have seemed like the crowning glory of her initial work when the Nightingale Home and Training School was opened as an integral portion of the new St. Thomas's Hospital, the finest institution of its kind in Europe. This circumstance added greatly to the popularity of nursing as a profession for educated women.

Queen Victoria had laid the foundation-stone of the new hospital on May 13th, 1868, on the fine site skirting the Thames Embankment opposite the Houses of Parliament. It was erected on the block system, which Miss Nightingale has always recommended, and she took a keen interest in all the model appliances and arrangements introduced into this truly palatial institution for the sick.

The hospital extends from the foot of Westminster Bridge along the river to Lambeth Palace, and has a frontage of 1,700 ft. It is built in eight separate blocks or pavilions. The six centre blocks are for patients, the one at the north end next Westminster Bridge is for the official staff, and the one at the south end is used for lecture rooms and a school of medicine. Each block is 125 ft. from the other, but coupled by a double corridor. The corridor fronting the river forms a delightful terrace promenade. Each block has three tiers of wards above the ground floor. The operating theatre is capable of containing six hundred students. A special wing in one of the northern blocks was set apart for the Nightingale Home and Training School for Nurses. All the arrangements of this wing were carried out in accordance with Miss Nightingale's wishes.

The hospital contains in all one thousand distinct apartments, and the building cost half a million of money. It was opened by Queen Victoria on June 21st, 1871, and *The Times* in its account of the proceedings is lost in admiration of "the lady nurses, in their cheerful dresses of light grey [blue is the colour of the Sisters' dresses], ladies, bright, active, and different altogether from the old type of hospital nurse whom Dickens made us shudder to read of and Miss Nightingale is helping us to abolish." The new building gave increased accommodation and provided for forty probationers. The rules for admission remained practically the same as when the Training School was first started at the old St. Thomas's.

At a dinner to inaugurate the opening of the new hospital, the Chairman, Sir Francis Hicks, related that Miss Nightingale had told him that she thought it "the noblest building yet erected for the good of our kind."

But our interest centres in the Nightingale wing. The dining hall is a pleasant apartment which contains several mementoes of the lady whose name it bears. One is a unique piece of statuary enclosed in a glass case and standing on a pedestal. To the uninitiated, it might stand for a representation of a vestal virgin, but we know it to have a nobler prototype than the ideal of womanly perfection sacred to the Romans. That statuette is not the blameless priestess of Vesta, "the world forgetting, by the world forgot," but our heroine, whom the sculptor has modelled in the character of "The Lady with the Lamp." She stands, a tall, slim figure, in simple nurse's dress, holding in one hand a small lamp—such as she used when going her nightly rounds at Scutari hospital—which she is shading with the other hand. There is also a bust of Miss Nightingale in the hall, a portrait of her brother-in-law, the late Sir Harry Verney, for many years the Chairman of the Council of the Nightingale Fund, and a portrait of Mrs. Wardroper, the first head of the Nightingale Home when originally founded. There is also a clock presented by the Grand Duchess of Baden, sister of the late Emperor Frederick of Germany, who was a great admirer of Miss Nightingale's work and herself an active organiser of relief for the sick soldiers during the Franco-German War.

The dining-hall leads into the nurses' sitting-room. Each nurse has her own private room.

The number of probationers slightly varies from year to year, but is usually fifty-two, and there are always more applicants than can be entertained. They are divided into *Special* probationers, who are gentlewomen by birth and education, daughters of professional men, clergymen, officers, merchants, and others of the upper and middle classes, age from twenty-four to thirty, and *Ordinary* probationers.

The *Special* probationers are required to be trained to be future heads of hospitals, or of departments of hospitals. They learn every detail of a nurse's work, and also the duties to fit them for responsible posts as matrons, etc. The *Ordinary* probationers are trained to be efficient nurses, and after some years' service may obtain superior appointments.

All nurses who have passed through St. Thomas's are united by a special tie to Miss Nightingale, who rejoices in their successes, and likes to hear from time to time of the progress of their work in the various hospitals and institutions of which they have become heads.

Mr. Bonham Carter, her old and valued friend, remains the secretary of the Nightingale Fund, and Miss Hamilton is the matron of the hospital, and has control of the Nightingale Home.

In the same year (1871) that the new Nightingale Home and Training School was opened, Miss Nightingale published a valuable work on *Lying-in Hospitals*, and two years later she made a new literary departure by the publication in *Fraser's Magazine* of two articles under the heading "Notes of Interrogation," in which she dealt with religious doubts and problems. Miss Nightingale from her youth up has shown a deeply religious nature, and her attempt to grapple with some of the deep questions of faith, as she had thought them out in the solitude of her sick-room, merit thoughtful consideration.

Miss Nightingale has lived so entirely for the

public good that her private family life is almost lost sight of. But her affections never ceased to twine themselves around the homes of her youth. After busy months in London occupied in literary work and the furthering of various schemes, came holidays spent at Lea Hurst and Embley with her parents, when she resumed her interest in all the old people, and ministered to the wants of the sick poor. Though no longer able to lead an active life and visit amongst the people, she had a system of inquiry by which she kept herself informed of the wants and needs of her poorer friends. She was particularly interested in the young girls of the district, and liked to have them come to Lea Hurst for an afternoon's enjoyment as in the days gone by. It was soon known in the vicinity of her Derbyshire or Hampshire home when " Miss Florence " had arrived.

In January, 1874, Miss Nightingale sustained the first break in her old home life by the death of her father. He passed peacefully away at Embley in his eightieth year and was buried in East Willows Churchyard. His tomb bears the inscription :—

WILLIAM EDWARD NIGHTINGALE,

OF EMBLEY IN THIS COUNTY, AND OF LEA HURST, DERBYSHIRE.

Died January 5th, 1874, in his eightieth year.

" And in Thy Light shall we see Light."—*Ps.* xxxvi. 9.

After her father's death, Miss Nightingale spent much of her time with her widowed mother at Embley and Lea Hurst, between which residences the winter and summer were divided as in the old days. It was well known that " Miss Florence's " preference was for Lea Hurst, and she would linger there some seasons until the last golden leaves had fallen from the beeches in her favourite " walk " in Lea Woods.

Some of the old folks had passed away and the young ones had settled in homes of their own, but no change in the family history of the people escaped Miss Florence. She ministered through her private almoner to the wants of the sick, and bestowed her name and blessing on many of the cottage babes. By her thoughtful provision a supply of fresh, pure milk from the dairy of Lea Hurst was daily sent to those who were in special need of it. People on the estate recall that before she left in the autumn " Miss Florence " always gave directions that a load of holly and evergreens should be cut from Lea Woods and sent to the Nurses' Home at St. Thomas's, the District Nurses' Home in Bloomsbury Square, and the Harley Street Home, for Christmas decoration.

On February 1st, 1880, Miss Nightingale suffered another loss in the death of her beloved mother, whose last years she had so faithfully tended as far

CLAYDON HOUSE, THE SEAT OF SIR EDMUND VERNEY, WHERE THE "FLORENCE NIGHTINGALE" ROOMS ARE PRESERVED.

(*Photo by Payne, Aylesbury.*)

[*To face p.* 320

as her strength would allow. Mrs. Nightingale, to whose beautiful character and example her famous daughter owes so much, passed away at Embley and was buried beside her husband in East Willows Churchyard. Her tomb bears the inscription :—

Devoted to the Memory of our Mother,

FRANCES NIGHTINGALE,

WIFE OF WILLIAM EDWARD NIGHTINGALE, ESQ.

Died February 1st, 1880.

"God is Love."—1 *John* iv. 16.

"Bless the Lord, O my soul, and forget not all His benefits."—*Ps.* ciii. 2.

BY F. PARTHENOPE VERNEY AND FLORENCE NIGHTINGALE

After the death of her mother, Miss Nightingale still occasionally stayed at Lea Hurst and Embley, which had passed to her kinsman, Mr. William Shore Nightingale, and continued her old interest in the people of the district. In 1887 the members of a working men's club in Derbyshire presented Miss Nightingale with a painting of Lea Hurst, a gift which she received with peculiar pleasure. It was about this time that she paid her last visit to the loved home of her childhood.

Miss Nightingale's time was now passed between her London house, 10, South Street, Park Lane, and Claydon, the beautiful home near Winslow, Buckinghamshire, of her sister, who had in 1859 become the second wife of Sir Harry Verney. Sir Harry was the son of Sir Harry Calvert, Governor of Chelsea Hospital and Adjutant-General of the Forces. He had been a Major in the army, and in 1827 assumed the name of Verney. The family of Verney had been settled in Buckinghamshire since the fifteenth century. Sir Harry was at various times member of Parliament for Bedford and also Buckingham. He was deeply interested in all matters of army reform and in active sympathy with the schemes of his distinguished sister-in-law, and acted as Chairman of the Nightingale Fund.

At Claydon Miss Nightingale found a beautiful and congenial holiday retreat with Sir Harry Verney and her beloved sister, who was well known in literary and political circles; her books on social questions had the distinction of being quoted in the House of Commons. In the second year of her marriage (1861) Lady Verney had laid the foundation stone of the new Buckinghamshire Infirmary at Aylesbury, the construction of which Miss Nightingale watched with great interest during her visits to Claydon. Her bust adorns the entrance hall of the infirmary. During her summer visits to Claydon, Miss Nightingale frequently gave garden parties for the Sisters from St. Thomas's Hospital.

Lady Verney died, after a long and painful illness,

in 1890, sadly enough on May 12th, her sister's birthday. Sir Harry Verney survived his wife barely four years, and at his death Claydon passed to Sir Edmund Hope Verney, the son of his first marriage with the daughter of Admiral Sir George Johnstone Hope.

Sir Edmund was a gallant sailor, who as a young lieutenant had served in the Crimean War and received a Crimean medal, Sebastopol clasp. He had again distinguished himself in the Indian Mutiny, was mentioned in dispatches, and received an Indian medal, Lucknow clasp. He was Liberal M.P. for North Bucks 1885-6 and 1889-91, and represented Brixton on the first London County Council. Sir Edmund married the eldest daughter of Sir John Hay-Williams and Lady Sarah, daughter of the first Earl Amherst, a lady who has taken an active part in the movement for higher education in Wales, and served for seven years on a Welsh School Board. She is a member of the Executive Committee of the Welsh University. Sir Edmund has estates in Anglesey. Lady Verney is a member of the County Education Committee for Buckinghamshire. She is continuing her mother-in-law's work of editing the "Verney Memoirs." Sir Edmund takes great interest in education and rural questions. He is a member of the Bucks County Council and the Dairy Farmers' Association, and has published articles on Agricultural Education and kindred subjects.

After her sister's death Miss Nightingale continued to pass some of her time at Claydon until, in 1895, increasing infirmity made the journey impracticable, and she has continued to interest herself in the rural affairs of the district. The suite of apartments which Miss Nightingale occupied at Claydon are preserved by Sir Edmund and Lady Verney as when she occupied them, and are now styled " The Florence Nightingale Rooms." They consist of a large, charmingly furnished sitting-room with a domed ceiling, situated at a corner of the mansion and so commanding a double view over the grounds, and a bedroom and ante-room. Miss Nightingale's invalid couch still stands in her favourite corner of the sitting-room, and beside it is a large china bowl which loving hands once daily replenished with fresh flowers, such as our heroine loved to have about her when she occupied the room. In the adjoining apartment stands Miss Nightingale's half-tester bedstead and old-fashioned carved wardrobe and chest of drawers. A large settee is at the foot of the bed, and was a favourite lounge with Miss Nightingale during the day. Pictures and family portraits hang on the various walls, and to these have been added by Sir Edmund Verney a series of interesting pictures culled from various sources to illustrate events in Miss Nightingale's work in the East. The rooms will doubtless in time form an historic museum in Claydon House.

After her beloved sister's death Miss Nightingale was sad and despondent, and one detects the note of weariness in a letter which she addressed in 1890 to the Manchester Police Court Mission for Lads. She was anxious that more should be done to reclaim first offenders and save them from the contaminating influences of prison life. "I have no power of following up this subject," she wrote, "though it has interested me all my life. For the last (nearly) forty years I have been immersed in two objects, and undertaken what might well occupy twenty vigorous young people, and I am an old and overworked invalid."

Happily Miss Nightingale's work was not done yet. Two years later (1892) found her at the age of seventy-two starting a vigorous health crusade in Buckinghamshire in particular, and in the rural districts generally. The 1890 Act for the Better Housing of the Working Classes specially roused her attention in a subject in which she had always been interested. She had little faith in Acts of Parliament reforming the habits of the people. "On paper," she writes, "there could not be a more perfect Health Directory [than the Act] for making our *sanitary* authorities and districts worthy of the name they bear. We have powers and definitions. Everything is provided except the two most necessary : the money to pay for and the will to carry out the reforms." If the new Act were enforced, Miss Nightingale was of opinion that three-fourths of the rural districts in England would be depopulated and " we should have hundreds and thousands of poor upon our hands, owing to the large proportion of houses unfit for habitation in the rural districts."

In 1892 Miss Nightingale addressed a stirring letter to the Buckinghamshire County Council on the advisability of appointing a Sanitary Committee to deal with the health questions of the district. " We must create a public opinion which will drive the Government," she wrote, " instead of the Government having to drive us—an enlightened public opinion, wise in principles, wise in details. We hail the County Council as being or becoming one of the strongest engines in our favour, at once fathering and obeying the great impulse for national health against national and local disease. For we have learned that we have national health in our hands—local sanitation, national health. But we have to contend against centuries of superstition and generations of indifference. Let the County Council take the lead."

Miss Nightingale believed that the best method

for promoting sanitary reform among the people was to influence the women—the wives and mothers who had control of the domestic management of the homes. Her next step was, with the aid of the County Council Technical Instruction Committee, to arrange for a missioner to teach in the rural districts of Buckinghamshire. She selected three specially trained and educated women, who were not only to give addresses in village schoolrooms on such matters as disinfection, personal cleanliness, ventilation, drainage, whitewashing, but were to visit the homes of the poor and give friendly instruction and advice to the women.

She knew, and respected the feeling, that an Englishman regards his home, however humble, as a castle into which no one may enter uninvited. Miss Nightingale had no sympathy with the class of " visiting ladies " who lift the latch of a poor person's cottage and walk in without knocking. In launching her scheme of visitation she did the courteous thing by writing a circular letter to the village mothers, asking them to receive the missioners. The letter runs :—

" DEAR HARD-WORKING FRIENDS,

" I am a hard-working woman too. May I speak to you ? And will you excuse me, though not a mother ?

" You feel with me that every mother who brings a child into the world has the duty laid upon her of bringing up the child in such health as will enable him to do the work of his life.

" But though you toil all day for your children, and are so devoted to them, this is not at all an easy task.

" We should not attempt to practise dress-making or any other trade without any training for it ; but it is generally impossible for a woman to get any teaching about the management of health ; yet health is to be learnt. . . .

" Boys and girls must grow up healthy, with clean minds, clean bodies, and clean skins. And for this to be possible, the air, the earth, and the water that they grow up in and have around them must be clean. Fresh air, not bad air ; clean earth, not foul earth ; pure water, not dirty water ; and the first teachings and impressions that they have at home must all be pure, and gentle, and firm. It is *home* that teaches the child, after all, more than any other schooling. A child learns before it is three whether it shall obey its mother or not; and before it is seven, wise men tell us that its character is formed.

" There is, too, another thing—orderliness. We know your daily toil and love. May not the busiest and hardest life be somewhat lightened, the day mapped out, so that each duty has the same hours? It is worth while to try to keep the family in health, to prevent the sorrow, the anxiety, the trouble of illness in the house, of which so much can be prevented.

" When a child has lost its health, how often the mother says, 'Oh, if I had only known ! but there was no one to tell me.' And, after all, it is health and not sickness that is our natural state— the state that God intends for us. There are more people to pick us up when we fall than to enable us to stand upon our feet. God did not intend all mothers to be accompanied by doctors, but He meant all children to be cared for by mothers. God bless your work and labour of love.

" FLORENCE NIGHTINGALE."

Still following up the subject of rural sanitation, Miss Nightingale prepared a paper on " Rural Hygiene : Health Teachings in Towns and Villages," which was read at the Conference of Women Workers at Leeds in November, 1893. It was written in her usual clear and incisive manner, going straight to the root of the matter and illustrating her points with humorous illustrations. " What can be done for the health of the *home*," she asks, " without the women of the home ? . . . Let not England lag behind. It is a truism to say that the women who teach in India must know the languages, the religions, superstitions, and customs of the women to be taught in India. It ought to be a truism to say the very same for England." Referring to the village mothers, she says, " We must not talk *to* them, or *at* them, but *with* them."

As an instance of the happy-go-lucky style in which sick cottagers are occasionally treated, Miss Nightingale relates the following amusing stories :—

" A cottage mother, not so very poor, fell into the fire in a fit while she was preparing breakfast, and was badly burnt. We sent for the nearest doctor, who came at once, bringing his medicaments in his gig. The husband ran for the horse-doctor, who did not come, but sent an ointment for a horse. The wise woman of the village came of her own accord, and gave another ointment.

" ' Well, Mrs. Y.,' said the lady who sent for the doctor, ' and what did you do ? '

" ' Well, you know, miss, I studied a bit, and then I mixed all three together, because then, you know, I was sure I got the right one.'

" The consequences to the poor woman may be imagined !

" Another poor woman, in a different county, took something which had been sent to her husband for a bad leg, believing herself to have fever. ' Well, miss,' she said, ' it did me a sight of good,

and look at me, baint I quite peart?' The ' peartness '
ended in fever."

The manners of the women to their children in
many cases are greatly in need of reform, and Miss
Nightingale quotes the injunction of an affectionate
mother to her child about going to school, " I'll
bang your brains out if you don't do it *voluntally*."

Miss Nightingale deals in her paper with the
need for drastic measures to promote rural sanitation
such as drainage, proper water supply, scavenging,
removal of dust and manure heaps from close
proximity to the houses, and the inspection of
dairies and cowsheds. In regard to the latter she
writes, " No inspection exists worthy of the name."
This was in 1893, and the alarming facts about the
non-inspection of rural milk supplies exposed in
The Daily Chronicle in 1904 show that matters are
little improved since Miss Nightingale laid an
unerring finger on the defect eleven years ago.

In addition to an independent medical officer
and sanitary inspector under him, " we want,"
said Miss Nightingale, " a fully trained nurse for
every district and a health missioner," and she
defines her idea of the duties of a missioner. These
women must of course be highly qualified for their
work. They should visit the homes of the people
to advocate rules of health. Persuade the careful
housewife, who is afraid of dirt falling on to her

clean grate, to remove the sack stuffed up the unused chimney, teach the cottagers to open their windows in the most effective way for free ventilation. "It is far more difficult to get people to avoid poisoned air than poisoned water," says Miss Nightingale, "for. they drink in poisoned air all night in their bedrooms." The mothers should be taught the value of a daily bath, the way to select nourishing food for their families, what to do till the doctor comes and after he has left.

However, the first great step for the missioner is to get the trust and friendship of the women. And this "is not made by lecturing upon bedrooms, sculleries, sties, and wells in general, but by examination of particular rooms, etc." The missioner, above all, must not appear to "pry" into the homes, or to talk down to the women, neither should she give alms. The whole object of the recommendations was to teach people how to avoid sickness and poverty.

Miss Nightingale's efforts to promote sanitary reforms were not confined to our own land, but extended to far-away India, a country in which she has, as we have already seen, taken a great interest. She had watched the success of some of the sanitary schemes carried out by the municipalities of large towns of India with satisfaction, but there yet remained the vast rural population for which little was done, a very serious matter indeed when we consider that ninety per cent. of the two hundred and forty millions of India dwell in small rural villages. Miss Nightingale prepared one of her " searchlight " papers on " Village Sanitation in India," which was read before the Tropical Section of the eighth International Congress of Hygiene and Demography, held at Buda Pesth in September, 1894.

In this she considers the condition of the rural provinces of India from facts obtained by correspondence with people of authority on the spot, and deals with the defective sewage, water supply, and the difficulties arising from the insanitary habits of the people and their attachment to old customs. " Still," she pleads, " with a gentle and affectionate people like the Hindoos much may be accomplished by personal influence. I can give a striking instance within my own knowledge. In the Bombay Presidency there was a village which had for long years been decimated by cholera. The Government had in vain been trying to 'move' the village. ' No,' they said, 'they would not go ; they had been there since the time of the Mahrattas : it was a sacred spot, and they would not move now.'

" At last, not long ago, a sanitary commissioner —dead now alas !—who by wise sympathy, practical knowledge and skill had conquered the confidence of the people, went to the Pancháyat, explained to them the case, and urged them to move to a spot which he pointed out to them as safe and accessible. By the very next morning it had all been settled as he advised.

" The Government of India is very powerful, and great things may be accomplished by official authority, but in such delicate matters affecting the homes and customs of a very conservative people almost more may be done by personal influence exercised with kindly sympathy and respect for the prejudices of others."

The celebration of Queen Victoria's Diamond Jubilee in 1897 was an occasion of great interest to Miss Nightingale, and in her sick-room she followed all the events of that joyous time with keen appreciation. She was delighted at the idea of making a special feature of " Nursing " in the Women's Section of the Victorian Era Exhibition, and sent her Crimean carriage as an exhibit. All visitors to Earl's Court will recall the throngs of sight-seers who stood all day long peering into the recesses of the old vehicle as eagerly as though they expected to still find some remnant of the wounded. There was no more popular exhibit on view, while the smiling nurses in their becoming uniforms who flitted about the Nursing Section

were a living testimony to the revolution in the
art of nursing which Florence Nightingale had
effected. Lady George Hamilton, who had charge
of this section, was in frequent consultation with
Miss Nightingale while preparations were going
forward.

One of the most interesting celebrations of the
Diamond Jubilee year was the dinner of the
Balaclava Society on the anniversary of the famous

RECENT SPECIMEN OF MISS NIGHTINGALE'S HANDWRITING.

"Charge," October 25th. After the loyal toasts,
the health of Miss Nightingale was proposed by
Mr. F. H. Roberts, who amid ringing cheers said,
"Her name will live in the annals of England's
regiments as long as England lasts." The company
numbered one hundred and twenty, of whom sixty
were survivors of the Charge.

Miss Nightingale has continued to take an interest in the Hospital for Invalid Gentlewomen at

Harley Street, where she worked so assiduously before going to the Crimea.

This most useful institution continues its efforts for the relief of sick ladies with unabated vigour, under the able Lady Superintendent, Miss Tidy, who has laboured at her post now for fourteen years. The home looks so bright and cheerful that it must have a very beneficial effect on the minds of those suffering women who seek its shelter. In the pretty reception-room stands the old-fashioned mahogany escritoire which Miss Nightingale used more than fifty years ago, when she voluntarily performed the drudgery of super-intending the home. It was at this house in Harley Street that she stayed while organising her nursing band for the Crimea, and from it she set forth for her journey to the East.

In April, 1902, Margaret, Lady Verney laid the foundation stone of a new public library and village hall at Steeple Claydon. The cost of £1,500 was defrayed by Sir Edmund Verney. Miss Nightingale was much interested in the project and sent the following message to Sir Edmund and Lady Verney :—

" So glad the foundation stone is being laid of the Steeple Claydon Public Library. I do with all my heart wish it success, and think a public

library is good for body and soul. That God's blessing may rest upon it is the fervent wish of

"FLORENCE NIGHTINGALE."

Miss Nightingale also sent £50 for the purchase of books for the library.

The institution of the Royal Pension Fund for Nurses, in which Queen Alexandra has taken such an active interest, was a subject of satisfaction to Miss Nightingale, as helping to improve the position of the sisterhood which she has so much at heart. She was deeply interested in hearing accounts of the garden-parties given by the Queen, as Princess of Wales, to the nurses in the grounds of Marlborough House, and also of the reception of the nurses by the Queen after the King's accession.

CHAPTER XXV

AT EVENTIDE

Miss Nightingale to-day—Her Interest in Passing Events—Recent Letter to Derbyshire Nurses—Celebrates Eighty-fourth Birthday —King confers Dignity of a Lady of Grace—Appointed by King Edward VII. to the Order of Merit—Letter from the German Emperor—Elected to the Honorary Freedom of the City of London—Summary of her Noble Life.

> The golden evening brightens in the west;
> Soon, soon to faithful warriors comes their rest.
> DR. WALSHAM HOW.

THE shadows of evening have fallen about the life of our revered heroine. Miss Nightingale has not left her London house for many years, and remains principally in bed. Her mind is still unclouded, and she follows with something of the old eager spirit the events of the day, more particularly those which relate to the nursing world. She is no longer able to deal personally with her correspondence, all of which passes through the hands of her secretary. Nothing gives her greater pleasure than to chat over past days with her old friends and fellow-workers, and she occasionally receives by invitation members of the nursing profession who are heads of institutions with which her name is connected.

She followed with intense interest the elaborate preparations made for dealing with the sick and wounded in the South African War, bringing home to her as it so vividly did the difficulties of the pioneer work at the time of the Crimean campaign. It gave her peculiar pleasure to receive and bid God-speed to some of the nurses before their departure for South Africa.

Even at her great age Miss Nightingale retains the distinction of manner and speech which gave her such influence in the past, and now and again a flash of the old shrewd wit breaks out when views with which she is not in agreement are advanced. Her friends marvel most at the almost youthful roundness and placidity of her face. Time has scarcely printed a line on her brow, or a wrinkle on her cheeks, or clouded the clearness of her penetrating eyes, which is the more remarkable when it is remembered that she has been a suffering and over-worked invalid ever since her return from the Crimea. The dainty lace cap falling over the silver hair in long lapels gives a charming frame to Miss Nightingale's face which is singularly beautiful in old age. When receiving a visitor, she seems, as one phrased it, " to talk with her hands," which retain their beautiful shape, and which she has a habit of moving over the coverlet, as from a sitting posture she inclines towards her friends in the course of conversation.

A delightful trait in Miss Nightingale's character is the honour which she pays to the women of a younger generation, who are now bearing the heat and burden of the day. "Will you give me your blessing?" said the Superintendent of a benevolent institution to her recently, when taking her leave. "And you must give me *your* blessing," replied Miss Nightingale, as she took her hand. On another occasion she said to the same lady, after listening to an account of good work going successfully forward, "Why, you have put new life into me."

No subject interests Miss Nightingale more to-day than that of district nursing. She inquires minutely into the experiences of those engaged amongst the sick poor. "Are the people improving in their habits?" is a question she often asks, or again, "Tell me about these model dwellings, which they are putting up everywhere. Have they had a good effect on the personal habits of the people?" If a Sister chances to mention some new invalid appliance, the old keen interest comes to the surface and Miss Nightingale will have it all explained to her, even to the place where the apparatus was procured.

MISS NIGHTINGALE.
(From a memory sketch)

[*To face p.* 340.

The popularity of nursing as a profession is another topic of great interest to Miss Nightingale, and when she hears of more applications to enter the Training Home at St. Thomas's than the Council can entertain, she recalls the very different state of things when she used in the early days to issue her urgent call for recruits. While she is particularly anxious that a high standard of character and efficiency should be maintained amongst nurses, she keeps strictly to her original attitude that "a nurse should be a nurse and not a medical woman." Miss Nightingale feels that ability to pass a technical examination does not necessarily prove that a woman will make a good nurse. It is a profession in which natural aptitude and personal character count for a great deal; to use a familiar axiom, a nurse is "born, not made."

Often Miss Nightingale's mind travels back to her old Derbyshire home. Embley has passed out of the family, but Lea Hurst is occupied by a relative, Mrs. William Shore Nightingale, and Miss Nightingale keeps up her interest in the old people of the place. In August, 1903, the late Hon. Frederick Strutt, the Mayor of Derby and a distant cousin of Miss Nightingale's, entertained the nurses of the borough at Lea Hurst, which was specially lent for the occasion, and Miss Nightingale, hearing of what was about to take place, wrote the following letter to Mr. Strutt : " Will you," she said, "express to each and to all of them my very warmest wishes for their very highest success, in the best meaning of the word, in the life's work which they have chosen. We hear a great deal nowadays about nursing as a profession, but the question for each nurse is, ' Am I living up to my profession ? ' The nurse's life is above all a moral and practical life—a life not of show, but of practical action. I wish the nurses God-speed in their work, and may each one strive with the best that is in her to act up to her profession, and to rise continually to a higher level of thought and practice, character and dutifulness."

The reading of this letter from Miss Nightingale to the nurses assembled in the garden of her old home was an occasion of impressive interest. Fifty years ago she would not have predicted that Derby would ever possess such a large body of nurses, and still less that the members of the profession in Great Britain should have reached such a large total.

> Oh, small beginnings, ye are great and strong,
>   Based on a faithful heart and weariless brain !
> Ye build the future fair, ye conquer wrong,
>   Ye earn the crown, and wear it not in vain.

So far as her own personality is concerned, the founder of this sisterhood of ministry is " a veiled and silent woman," shunning publicity. Her name has circled the globe, her deeds are known in every clime, and people cite her noble heroism without even knowing that she still lives, at such pains has Miss Nightingale been to keep herself in strict seclusion. The power of her fame, the brilliance of her example, and the wisdom of her counsels are a national heritage. Women who now wear the garb of a nurse with honour and dignity owe it to the lofty tradition which has come down with the first of the gracious dynasty.

On May 12th, 1904, Miss Nightingale was the recipient of many congratulations from her friends on the attainment of her eighty-fourth birthday, and the King paid a graceful compliment to the lady who is without doubt the most illustrious heroine in His Majesty's Empire, by conferring upon her the dignity of a Lady of Grace of the Order of St. John of Jerusalem. Miss Nightingale received the Red Cross from Queen Victoria.

A more unique honour was however yet in store for the heroine of the Crimea and the founder of the modern nursing movement. In November 1907, King Edward VII. appointed Miss Nightingale to the Order of Merit, which was founded by His Majesty in 1902 and first announced in the Coronation Honours List. The King is Sovereign of the Order, which originally consisted of twelve men distinguished in war, science, letters, and art. Other names have since been added, but Florence Nightingale is the only woman placed amongst these Immortals. The conferring of the Order was not accompanied by any ceremony, as Miss Nightingale was unable, through failing health, to receive Sir Douglas Dawson, the representative appointed by the King, and the insignia was simply handed to Miss Nightingale's nephew. The badge of the Order is a cross of red and blue enamel of eight points, bearing the legend " For Merit " in gold letters within a laurel wreath. The reverse side shows the King's royal and imperial cipher in gold. Members of the Order rank after the Order of the Bath, and use the letters O.M. The appointment of Miss Nightingale to the Order was received with great enthusiasm throughout the country.

The German Emperor, who was visiting our shores at the time, took occasion to pay Miss Nightingale a very graceful compliment, by sending her a bouquet of flowers, accompanied by the following letter from the German Ambassador :

" DEAR MISS NIGHTINGALE,—His Majesty the Emperor, having just brought to a close a most enjoyable stay in the beautiful neighbourhood of your old home [Embley Park] near Romsey, has commanded me to present you with some flowers as a token of his esteem for the lady who, after receiving her education in nursing by the Sisters of Mercy at

Kaiserswerth, on the Rhine, rendered such invaluable services to the cause of humanity during the Crimean War, and subsequently founded a house for the training of nurses in England, which is justly considered to be a model institution of European fame.

"His Majesty sends you his best wishes, and I have the honour to remain,—Yours sincerely,

"P. METTERNICH,

"German Ambassador."

The following letter was sent in reply :

"YOUR EXCELLENCY,—I have the honour to acknowledge, on behalf of Miss Nightingale, the receipt of your letter of to-day, and of the very beautiful flowers, which she greatly appreciated.

"Miss Nightingale desires me to request you to be good enough to convey to His Majesty the Emperor how much she values his Majesty's gracious expressions of esteem and good wishes. She has always thought most highly of the nursing of the Sisters of Mercy at Kaiserswerth.

"She also recalls with deep gratitude the friendship and sympathy with which his Majesty's august mother, the late Empress, was pleased to honour her. Miss Nightingale would write personally but that failing health and eyesight prevent her.—I have the honour, etc.

"K. SHORE NIGHTINGALE."

The City of London might most fittingly have bestowed its honourable freedom upon Miss Nightingale when she returned from the Crimea in 1856, but the heroine's retiring disposition and the conservatism of an ancient corporation stood in the way of that honour being bestowed. The late Baroness Burdett-Coutts was the first woman presented with the freedom of the City, and she has had no successor until, in February 1908, the Corporation, with the Lord Mayor presiding, passed with great enthusiasm the following resolution moved by Mr. Deputy Wallace:

" That the honourable freedom of this City, in a gold box of the value of one hundred guineas, be presented to Miss Florence Nightingale, in testimony of this Court's appreciation of her philanthropic and successful efforts for the improvement of hospital nursing and management, whereby invaluable results have been attained for the alleviation of human suffering."

Mr. Deputy Wallace in moving the resolution said that, " never in the history of the freedom of the City, including on its roll of fame the names of monarchs, statesmen, soldiers, and famous men of all kinds and of all callings, had it enrolled among the recipients of its honorary freedom a nobler name than that of Florence Nightingale."

In accepting the honour of the Freedom of the City, thus offered, Miss Nightingale requested that the sum of one hundred guineas, which it was proposed to spend on the gold box for containing the scroll, should be given as a donation to the Queen Victoria Jubilee Institute for Nurses and the Hospital for Invalid Gentlewomen, Harley Street, of which Miss Nightingale was the first Superintendent.

The Court of Common Council acceded to Miss · Nightingale's request and arranged for an oak box to be used instead of the traditional gold casket.

Miss Nightingale was unable to make the journey to the Guildhall to receive the Freedom, and it was arranged that the presentation should be made, on her behalf, to her nearest relative.

The ceremony took place March 16th, 1908, in the Council Chamber at the Guildhall, the Right Hon. the Lord Mayor, Sir John Bell, Kt., presiding. There was a large attendance, invitations having been issued to leading medical and hospital authorities and to other representative people. There was a goodly gathering of nurses.

The City Chamberlain (Sir Joseph Dimsdale) asked Mr. L. H. Shore Nightingale, who represented Miss Nightingale, to accept the casket containing the Freedom, and made a most felicitous speech. A cheque for 106 guineas, to be devoted to any charities which Miss Nightingale was pleased to name, was given with the casket.

Mr. Shore Nightingale replied, regretting that

Miss Nightingale was unable to be present, and accepting the honour on her behalf.

Mr. Henry Bonham Carter, for many years secretary of the Nightingale Fund, gave an interesting account of his early recollections of Miss Nightingale, and related that on one occasion when they were young people she had given him first aid after an accident. In conclusion he spoke of the high qualities of heart, mind, and character which had enabled Miss Nightingale to achieve such great and signal success in the work to which she devoted her life.

We honour the soldier and applaud the valiant hero, but it required a more indomitable spirit, a higher courage, to purge the pestilential hospital of Scutari ; to walk hour after hour its miles of fetid corridors crowded with suffering, even agonised, humanity, than in the heat of battle to go " down into the jaws of death," as did the noble " Six Hundred." A grateful nation laid its offering at the feet of the heroine of the Crimea, poets wafted her fame abroad, and the poor and suffering loved her. In barracks, in hospital, and in camp the soldier has cause to bless her name for the comfort he enjoys, the sufferers in our hospital wards have trained nurses through her initiative, the sick poor are cared for in their own homes, and the paupers humanely tended in the workhouse, as a direct result of reforms which her example or counsel prompted. No honour or title can ennoble the name of Florence Nightingale ; it is peerless by virtue of her heroic deeds.

𝔍𝔫 𝔐𝔢𝔪𝔬𝔯𝔦𝔞𝔪

The death of Miss Nightingale occurred somewhat suddenly on the afternoon of August 13th, 1910, at her residence 10, South Street, Park Lane. The cause of death was heart failure. She sank peacefully to rest in the presence of two of her relatives. Until the day before her death she was in her usual health and bright spirits. In the previous May she celebrated her ninetieth birthday, spending the day quietly with her household. On that occasion she was the recipient of many congratulations from her friends, and her room was gay with spring flowers. The King, in the midst of his own bereavement, in the recent death of his father, was not unmindful of the heroine of the Crimea, and sent her the following message :

"To Miss Florence Nightingale, O.M.

" On the occasion of your Ninetieth Birthday, I offer you my heartfelt congratulations and trust that you are in good health.

" (Signed) George R. & I."

On receiving the tidings of Miss Nightingale's death, the King sent the following telegram from Balmoral to her relatives :—

" The Queen and I have received with deep regret the sad news of the death of Miss Florence Nightingale, whose untiring and devoted services to the British soldiers in the Crimea will never be forgotten, and to whose striking example we practically owe our present splendid organisation of trained nurses. Please accept the expression of our sincere sympathy.

" George R.I."

Amongst the soldier heroes in St. Paul's, or with the great ones in Westminster Abbey, would have been the fitting burial place for our greatest national heroine, whose deeds will live for ever in the records of our country. But she ever shunned publicity, and in deference to her wishes her funeral was not of a public character. The offer of the Dean and Chapter of Westminster of a burial place in the Abbey was declined by her executors. She was quietly laid to rest on Saturday, August 20th, in the little churchyard of East Wellow, Hampshire, near to her old home of Embley Park, and within sight of the hills where, as a child, she found her first patient in the old shepherd's dog.

An impressive Memorial Service for those wishing to pay a tribute of love and honour to the heroine of the Crimea was held on the day of the funeral, in St. Paul's Cathedral.

"On England's annals, through the long
Hereafter of her speech and song,
A light its rays shall cast
From portals of the past.

"A lady with a lamp shall stand
In the great history of the land,
A noble type of good,
Heroic womanhood."

PRINTED BY CASSELL AND CO., LTD., LA BELLE SAUVAGE, LONDON, E.C.

Lightning Source UK Ltd.
Milton Keynes UK
UKHW020511080219

336897UK00013B/1178/P